SMART COOKING

SMART COOKING

Quick and Tasty Recipes for Healthy Living

ANNE LINDSAY

Published in cooperation with the Canadian Cancer Society

Macmillan of Canada
A Division of Canada Publishing Corporation
Toronto, Ontario, Canada

Canadian Cataloguing in Publication Data
Lindsay, Anne, date.
  Smart cooking

"Published in cooperation with the Canadian Cancer Society."
Bibliography: p.
Includes index.
ISBN 0-7715-9703-7

1. Cookery. 2. Cancer—Nutritional aspects.
I. Canadian Cancer Society.   II. Title.

TX715.L56 1986   641.5'63   C86-093098-X

     13 14 15 16   BP 95 94 93 92 91

Photo on cover: Pasta Salad with Sweet Peppers and Dill (page 80)

Designed by Word & Image
Photo of Orange-Ginger Chicken by Mark Bird
All other photos by Fred Bird

Illustrations by Penelope Moir

Macmillan of Canada
A Division of Canada Publishing Corporation

Printed in Canada

CONTENTS

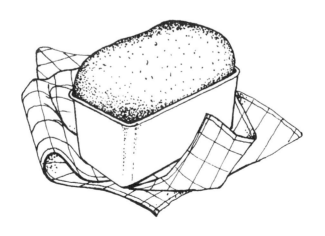

Author's Acknowledgements

This book exists because of Karen Hanley, Special Project Coordinator of the Ontario Division of the Canadian Cancer Society. It was her idea, and she made it possible. She wanted a cookbook to help make the public aware of the Canadian Cancer Society Dietary Guidelines, which may reduce the risk of cancer, and to raise funds for the society. I wish to thank Karen for asking me to write the book, for her encouragement, and for the countless hours she has spent in meetings with the society on this project and its promotion.

Thanks to Cheryl Moyer, Director of Public Education for the Canadian Cancer Society, for giving me the research and background information and for having the book reviewed by a panel of experts. My thanks to these experts: Dr. A. B. Miller, Director, National Cancer Institute of Canada, Epidemiology Unit, Faculty of Medicine, University of Toronto; Dr. Meera Jain, Nutritionist, Department of Preventive Medicine and Biostatistics, University of Toronto; Dr. Peter Scholefield, Executive Director, National Cancer Institute of Canada.

Thanks to the Ontario Division of the Canadian Cancer Society for their grant which made possible the color photographs and nutrient analysis of the recipes. I am grateful to the talented photographer Fred Bird for the creative but nerve-wracking week in his studio when Lynn Patterson and I prepared the food, Anna Carr organized the props and Fred took the pictures for this book. My admiration and thanks to Jennifer Kennedy for providing the nutrient analysis. She spent hours with the computer at the University of Toronto using the CANDAT system based on the Canadian Nutrient File. I am grateful for the assistance and information I received from Pam Verdier, Bureau of Nutritional Sciences, Food Directorate, Health Protection Branch, Health and Welfare Canada.

A huge thanks to home economist and dietitian Shannon Graham for her help in testing recipes and making sure I met my deadlines.

Thanks to Carol Ferguson and Marg Fraser, food editors at *Canadian Living* magazine, and again to Karen Hanley, editor of *City Woman* magazine. Some of the recipes first appeared in articles I wrote for these magazines, then were adapted to meet the low-fat requirements in this book.

Thanks also to Elizabeth Baird, Monda Rosenberg, Kay Spicer, Marsha Rosen, Teresa Tyrrell, Kathy Vanderlinden, Albina Santos, Arlene Lappin, Cathleen Hoskins, Stevie Cameron, and Louise Cantin.

Most of all, thanks to my family, my parents Hugh and Marion Elliott, and my husband Bob and children Jeff, John and Susie, for being my best critics and putting up with me while my life revolved around writing this book.

Anne Lindsay
December 1985

INTRODUCTION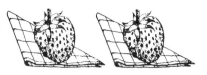

Food—that basic necessity and sublime pleasure—has become scary stuff. For years the media have rushed to bring us the latest horror story: cholesterol clogs our arteries, salt gives us hypertension, sugar is death, and—the clincher—*everything* causes cancer. Small wonder that, faced with this barrage of alarm, many of us give up, throw our fate to the gods, and dig into the barbecued ribs and chocolate cream pie.

But recently researchers have come out with exciting and encouraging new information. A solid body of scientific evidence suggests that, by making some not too arduous changes in our eating habits, by choosing foods consistent with healthy eating from every point of view, we may not only do good things for our general health, hearts and waistlines, but reduce our cancer risk as well.

Scientists estimate that as much as 80 percent of cancers in the world are caused by environmental and lifestyle factors and are therefore—theoretically—preventable. One of the most important of these is diet, which is thought to account for at least 35 percent of all cancers, except those of the skin—which means it may play an even greater role in cancer rates than does smoking (estimated at 30 percent).

Research findings to support importance of diet in cancer prevention

Causes of cancer cases in Canada associated with
- Diet: 27%
- Sunlight: 17%
- Tobacco: 16%
- Family History: 10%
- Occupation: 6%

Causes of cancer deaths associated with
- Diet: 32%
- Tobacco: 26%
- Occupation: 9%
- Family History: 8%

And we're not talking here about polysyllabic chemicals in the mayonnaise and insecticide residues on the raspberries. These are, relatively speaking, fringe concerns in the fight against cancer. We're talking about the mayonnaise and the raspberries.

Researchers have thought for decades that diet had something to do with cancer, but only in the last few years have they zeroed in on this area in an effort to uncover the exact relationship. And the results of their work to date seem to show that some things we eat—such as fat—may increase cancer risk especially of the breast and colon, while others—such as fiber—may have a protective effect, especially for cancers of the stomach and colon.

This doesn't mean that the perfect, 100-percent cancer-preventing diet for everyone can now be prescribed; that may never be possible. The research is still so new, and both cancer and nutrition are so complex, that it may be years before anything can be said with greater certainty about the cancer/diet connection.

Much research still needs to be done and many questions need to be answered. Cancer research is now at the point with diet that it was with smoking thirty years ago. The Canadian and American Cancer Societies decided then that the evidence against smoking, though limited, was sufficient to justify warning the public about the potential dangers. They have similarly concluded now that the data linking diet and cancer is convincing enough to justify issuing some general dietary guidelines. Health and Welfare Canada and the Canadian Heart Foundation have made similar recommendations, and the Canadian Dietetic Association has confirmed that the guidelines are consistent with a healthy lifestyle.

The recipes in this book are based on the following guidelines.

Canadian Cancer Society Diet Guidelines

1. Reduce your total daily fat intake to no more than 30 percent of total calories.

2. Eat more fiber-containing foods.

3. Have several servings of vegetables and fruits each day.

4. Keep your weight close to ideal.

5. If you drink alcohol, have two or fewer drinks per day.

6. Reduce your consumption of smoked, nitrate-cured and salted foods.

Before the guidelines are explained, a little background:

The research leading to these recommendations was carried out using three basic methods of investigation:

1. Descriptive epidemiology is the study of the occurrence of disease in populations. This method records the average diet and the incidence of different cancers in large groups (such as countries or communities), and compares these statistics with those of other groups.

2. Analytic epidemiology consists of clinical studies that compare the diets of groups of cancer cases with the diets of control groups (noncancer patients), or the incidence of cancer in groups following a specified diet with that in groups on free diets.

3. Biochemical studies in laboratories involve two kinds of research: experiments with animals, and experiments that test the effects of chemicals on bacteria or other cells or organisms. Chemicals that cause genetic changes (mutations) are immediately suspect, since it is known that mutagenic substances tend also to be carcinogenic (cancer-causing).

Much of the weight of evidence comes from epidemiological research, which consistently demonstrates a strong link between diets in modern, affluent countries and several cancers, especially those of the colon and the breast, and also the endometrium (lining of the uterus) and the prostate. (Other so-called Western diseases include coronary heart disease, diabetes, obesity, appendicitis, hiatus hernia and diverticulosis.) Our diet, though it has virtually eliminated many deficiency diseases, such as scurvy, rickets and pellagra, appears to encourage the development of others. For example, a survey of the international incidence of colerectal cancer (cancers of the colon and rectum) shows striking differences between Western and developing countries: in Canada, the disease is about eight times more common than in the African communities studied, where it accounts for only about 2 percent of cancer cases. In Canada it is the second-highest cause of cancer deaths in men and women.

Top Four Cancer Killers in Canada in 1985

Men	Women
Lung	Breast
Colorectal	Colorectal
Prostate	Lung
Stomach	Ovary

Additional evidence has come from the study of migration patterns. Groups of people who move from an area with a low incidence of a certain cancer to one with a high incidence (or vice versa) eventually develop the cancer rate of the new country (depending on how long it takes them to adopt the new lifestyle and diet). Japanese immigrants to Hawaii, for example, are developing a Western cancer pattern: high for colon and breast cancer, low for stomach cancer, the reverse of the Japanese pattern. The same is true of East European immigrants to North America and southern Europeans to Australia. If migrants retain their original eating habits in the new country, their cancer pattern tends to follow that of the home country.

Although it is easy enough to demonstrate a statistical association between some kinds of diet and some cancers, it is much more difficult to prove a causal relationship and to nail down which components of diet, if any, are the villains and which the white knights. Nevertheless, both epidemiological and experimental research have pointed to certain dietary factors as most likely to play a role in cancer.

First, the bad news

Fat

Of all dietary elements studied so far, high total fat intake seems to be the most important in increasing cancer risk. The research data strongly implicates high fat consumption, especially in cancers of the colon, breast and prostate—which are among the most common cancers in the country.

In one Canadian study of colorectal cancer, for example, the highest risk factor found was fat intake, with risk increasing with greater consumption. Men eating more than 100 grams of fat per day were at 70 percent higher risk than those who ate less than 100 grams of fat per day. Women eating more than 70 grams (about 36 percent of total daily calories) were at twice as high a risk as women who ate less than 70 grams of total fat a day. Breast cancer is also strongly associated with high fat consumption. Breast cancer rates are low in countries where fat intake is also low (Thailand, Japan, Mexico), and high where intake is high (Canada, United States, Denmark, New Zealand). And laboratory studies show that rats fed a high-fat diet have a high rate of mammary tumors.

Scientists think fat may have a promoting effect on some cancer development, and perhaps an initiating effect on other cancers. (In cancer, some agents appear to act as initiators, causing genetic changes in cells. Others act as promoters, furthering the malignant development of changes already initiated.) How fat works in these ways is not clear, though theories have been suggested. For instance, fat seems to affect hormone levels, and since cancers of the reproductive system are influenced by hormones, it is possible that fats and hormonal regulation may act together in the development of cancers of the breast, uterus, ovary and prostate. According to another theory, the role of fat in bowel cancer may relate to the fact that fat stimulates the secretion of bile acids and bile steroids in the digestive system and also increases the proportion of certain bacteria in the bowel. The bile acids and bacteria may then interact to form carcinogens.

Research results don't identify one particular kind of fat—saturated or unsaturated—as the promoting agent; all kinds seem to be implicated. Although saturated fats and cholesterol may be factors in coronary heart disease, it seems that total fat consumption is the important factor in cancer.

Obesity

Cancer research indicates that the significantly overweight (those 40 percent or more above ideal weight) have a higher cancer risk—as much as 50 percent in some studies. Whether it is the weight itself or the foods eaten that is responsible for the increased risk is not clear. A 12-year study conducted by the American Cancer Society indicated that marked obesity was associated with a much higher death rate from cancers of the gallbladder, kidney, stomach, colon, breast and endometrium than that found in people of normal weight. Other studies have confirmed that being overweight increases the incidence of endometrial and breast cancer in women after menopause. Earlier lab studies had shown that maintaining animals at normal weight both reduced their cancer rates and lengthened their lives.

Alcohol

Heavy drinkers have an unusually high risk of cancers of the mouth, esophagus and throat. If they also smoke, the risk increases dramatically. Epidemiological studies in the Western world consistently link high alcohol consumption especially with cancer of the mouth, larynx and esophagus, and some studies have shown heavy beer drinking to be linked to an increased risk of rectal cancer. In addition, excessive alcohol causes liver damage which may lead to liver cancer.

Nitrite, nitrate, salt and smoke

Nitrite, which is added to cured meats (bacon, sausages, cold cuts) to prevent botulism, can enhance the formation in the digestive system of nitrosamines, which have caused stomach and esophageal cancer in lab animals. In countries where people eat a lot of salt-cured and pickled foods, such as Japan and China, or where nitrate and nitrite are common in food and water, such as Colombia, incidence of stomach and esophageal cancers is high.

Nitrates, which are converted to nitrite in the body, are found naturally in many foods, but nitrate-containing foods (such as spinach and beets) are not thought to present a problem when eaten in sensible amounts. Some nitrate-containing foods also contain vitamin C, which blocks the conversion of nitrite into nitrosamines. It may be that nitrite poses a problem only when the diet is low in vitamin C. But whatever the full story turns out to be, cured meats are high in fat and salt, so it seems prudent to limit intake of these foods (high salt intake may be related to stomach cancer).

Smoke, whether inhaled from cigarettes or ingested from smoked hams, sausages, fish and other meats, contains tars or other substances that are potentially carcinogenic. Barbecuing may present similar dangers. When fat drips onto a wood or charcoal fire, potent carcinogens, such as benzopyrene, form and may be deposited on the food by the smoke or flames.

Now, the good news

Fiber

Among the dietary elements that seem to protect against cancer, fiber* is one of the most important. Fiber is the part of cereals, fruit and vegetables that is not digested, or is only partially digested. It is the "bulk" that cereal commercials laud for its ability to "aid irregularity." It certainly helps prevent constipation, but it also seems to play a part in preventing more serious bowel disorders.

International epidemiological studies support an association between high-fiber diets and low incidence of colorectal cancer and other diseases of the colon. One of the characteristics of diets in Western countries, where risk of colorectal cancer is high, is low fiber, whereas the opposite is true in Third World countries.

The Seventh-Day Adventists in California present an interesting opportunity for researchers, since they share with other Americans the same environment and economic affluence but have much lower rates of colorectal and lung cancer. Many Seventh-Day Adventists follow an ovolactovegetarian diet (no meat, but including eggs and milk products) which emphasizes high-fiber fruits, vegetables and whole-grain cereals. Seventh-Day Adventists discourage smoking and alcohol use. They also have a lower than average incidence of other Western diseases.

Several theories have been put forward to explain how fiber might protect against colorectal cancer. One is that fiber, particularly cereal fiber, by absorbing water, increases the bulk of waste products, thereby diluting the concentration of carcinogens in the bowel. Another is that by speeding up elimination, fiber reduces the time carcinogens are in contact with the bowel. Fiber may bind bile acids or alter the proportion of bacteria in the colon, thus preventing bacteria from metabolizing the acids into cancer-promoting end products.

There are six kinds of fiber, and some studies suggest that only one of these may be the active element; the evidence so far is inconclusive. Scientists also aren't certain whether it is the fiber itself which is protective, or the presence of the fiber interacting with other components in foods which could be the protective factor. However, fiber supplements in themselves are not enough. In any case, fiber aids elimination and serves as a wholesome substitute for fatty foods.

Vitamins A and C

Several studies of large groups all over the world have shown that vitamin A-containing foods may lower the risk of cancers of the larynx, esophagus, lung and bladder. In some of these studies, people recorded the food they ate, and the vitamin A content was calculated; other studies measured vitamin levels in the blood. Cancer rates of the low- and high-level groups were then compared. Laboratory studies also show that vitamin A reduces the incidence of certain cancers in animals. Scientists believe that vitamin A may be an agent that can reduce the tendency for malignant cells to multiply.

There are two forms of vitamin A in foods: preformed retinol (the vitamin itself), found in such foods as liver and milk, and beta-carotene, a compound that converts to vitamin A in the body, found in dark green and deep yellow-orange vegetables and fruits. Most of the research to date has involved foods containing carotene. Scientists are not sure whether it is the carotene or some other component in the foods that is the active element.

Epidemiological studies have indicated that vitamin C-containing foods appear to

*Fiber values given in *Smart Cooking* are as of August 1985.

protect against gastric and esophageal cancers. The studies here have been similar to those involving vitamin A: the subjects' intake of the vitamin was calculated from the foods they ate rather than from measured quantities of the vitamin. Again it is not certain whether it is the vitamin itself or some other component of vitamin C-containing fruits and vegetables that is protective. However, biochemical experiments with animals and with cells have shown that vitamin C inhibits the conversion of nitrites into carcinogenic nitrosamines, which indicates that vitamin C may be effective in dealing with that potential cancer threat.

Cancer researchers strongly discourage people from attempting to meet their needs for vitamins A and C by taking supplements. Pills are not a good substitute for foods, which are very complex mixtures of fiber and essential nutrients, some of which may also be important in cancer prevention. Vitamin pills can also be dangerous, since high doses of some vitamins, such as vitamin A, are toxic.

Brassica vegetables

One of the surprises in diet/cancer research has been the lowly cabbage: it and its relatives appear to help protect against some cancers of the gastrointestinal tract. Both epidemiological and laboratory studies show that brassica vegetables (such as broccoli, cabbage, Brussels sprouts, cauliflower and turnip) may reduce the incidence of cancers of the colon, stomach and esophagus. In animal experiments, they seem highly effective in inhibiting the effect of carcinogenic chemicals.

Brassica vegetables are part of the cruciferous family, a term also often used to identify this group of vegetables. As a bonus, most are a good source of fiber and certain vitamins.

Additives and other areas of investigation

Despite media cries of alarm, the importance of food additives in cancer is thought to be insignificant. One common preservative, BHA, for example, not only has shown no evidence of promoting cancer, but in some studies seemed to inhibit cancer growth under certain conditions. At present there is no clear evidence one way or the other.

Many other substances are being investigated to determine their role, if any, in cancer. Some of these—selenium, calcium, vitamin E—have shown some promise as possible protectors, but results so far are inconclusive.

Using the Diet Guidelines

In the following pages, there are dozens of suggestions and hundreds of recipes to help you plan a healthier style of eating. The underlying message is: Eat a variety of foods in moderation. Cut down on fat and eat more fiber.

1. Reduce your fat intake to no more than 30 percent of total calories.

Most Canadians have been living a little too literally off the fat of the land: about 40 percent of the calories we consume are from fat. The Canadian Cancer Society's recommended reduction is thought to be low enough to reduce cancer risk while moderate enough to be realistic.

Cutting down on fat has other benefits. You might lower your blood cholesterol level and consequently your risk of heart disease. Dieters who reduce fat intake and don't make up the calories with other food will lose weight.

We're talking here about cutting down on fat—not cutting out fat. We still need some fat to add flavor and richness to foods. All body tissues contain fat; it is needed for the constant manufacture of new cells. Fatty deposits serve as reserves of energy and protect our vital organs. Fats are also carriers of the fat-soluble vitamins A,D and E.

You can measure fat in terms of both weight (e.g. grams) and energy (e.g. calories). One gram of fat supplies nine calories (one gram of protein or of carbohydrate supplies four calories).

It's not easy to change the habits of a lifetime, but reducing fat intake to 30 percent of your total calories needn't be an exercise in penance. If you normally eat about 2,000 calories a day, for example, 40 percent of which is fat (800 calories ÷ 9 = 88 g), the reduction to 30 percent (600 calories ÷ 9 = 66 g) would mean cutting out only 200 calories, or 22 grams of fat. That amounts to one tablespoon (15 mL) of butter and one tablespoon (15 mL) of mayonnaise. To find out how many grams of fat you should cut in a day, refer to Appendix, page 228.

Since saturated or animal fats are associated with increased risk of heart disease, it makes sense to start there. If you don't have time for complicated calculations, the three easiest ways to reduce fat are:
- Trim fat off meats.
- Use less butter, margarine and oil.
- Eat fewer rich desserts (pastries, whipped cream).

Adjusting your cooking methods is another way to reduce fat intake: steam, poach, oven-broil and bake instead of frying.

And don't underestimate the fat hidden in foods such as baked goods, meat dishes, sauces and desserts. (See Tables C, D and E on pages 230–4 for the fat content of several common foods.)

Much of the fat we eat could be reduced without sacrificing taste. The following are fat-containing foods you might eat in a typical day, with some leaner substitutions. You don't have to make them all every day: just aim to reduce your fat intake.

Cut the Fat

Instead of	Choose	Grams fat saved
Fried egg (9)*	Boiled or poached egg (6)*	3
2 pats butter on toast (8)	1 pat butter (4)	4
Cream in coffee (3)	2% milk in coffee (0)	3
Hamburger (20)	Tuna sandwich (11)	9
Salad with French dressing (6)	Salad with diet dressing (2)	4
Ice cream (8)	Low-fat yogurt (2)	6
8 oz/250g round steak (30)	4 oz/125g round steak (15)	15
Asparagus with Hollandaise sauce (18)	Asparagus with grated mozzarella cheese (6)	12
15 French-fries (12)	Baked potato with 1 pat butter (4)	8
Apple pie (18)	Apple crisp (8)	10
Tea with cream (3)	Tea with 2% milk (0)	3
2 oz/60g potato chips (1 small bag) (24)	3 cups/750 mL unbuttered popcorn (2)	22
Almond Danish pastry (15)	Bran muffin (4)	11
	Total grams fat saved	110

*grams fat

2. Eat more fiber-containing foods.

Canadian diets tend to be woefully low in fiber,* so this one may take some work. It's not enough to switch to whole-wheat bread, though this is a good start. Nutritionists say that for general health we should have 20 to 30 grams of fiber per day. Even rich sources of fiber have only about six grams per serving, so that means eating several servings a day. It's wise to work up to the desired level gradually: digestive systems not used to much fiber may object to a sudden influx of it.

The following table lists excellent and good sources of fiber. Aim for three to five servings from the Excellent list or seven from the Good list (you can mix and match, of course). The ratings assume you eat the edible skins of fruits and vegetables.

CHOOSE SEVERAL FIBER-CONTAINING FOODS EACH DAY†

Excellent Sources (4.5 g or more/serving)	Good Sources (2 to 4.4g/serving)
BREAD AND CEREALS	
All-Bran (75 mL)	Muffets (1 or 2 biscuits)
100% Bran (75 mL)	Cracklin' Bran (75 mL)
Bran Buds (75 mL)	Corn Bran (75 mL)
Grape-Nuts (125 mL)	Grape-Nuts (75 mL)
	Bran Flakes (125 mL)
	Shreddies (125 mL)
	Shredded Wheat (1 or 2 biscuits)
VEGETABLES	
Beans, baked, canned (125 mL)	Corn, kernels (from 2 ears)
Beans, soaked and boiled (125 mL)	Peas, green (125 mL)
Lima beans, boiled, drained (125 mL)	Spinach (125 mL)
	Sweet potato (1)
	Lentils, boiled (125 mL)
	Potato, baked (1)
	Parsnips (125 mL)
	Brussels sprouts (8)
	Beans, green or yellow (125 mL)
FRUITS	
Prunes, dried, raw (6)	Avocado ($\frac{1}{2}$)
Apricots, dried halves (6)	Blueberries (125 mL)
Figs, dried (2)	Dates (10)
	Raspberries (125 mL)
	Raisins (125 mL)
	Apple, raw, with skin (1)
	Orange (1)
	Pear, raw, with skin (1)

*Health and Welfare Canada's Report of the Expert Advisory Committee on Dietary Fibre recommends that the average adult Canadian at least double his or her intake of dietary fiber. Fiber supplements are not the answer. Use only if your doctor has prescribed them.

† 125 mL is $\frac{1}{2}$ cup; 75 mL is $\frac{1}{3}$ cup.

Excellent Sources	Good Sources
NUTS Almonds (125 mL) Brazil nuts (125 mL) Peanuts (125 mL)	Walnuts (125 mL)

Note: Nuts and avocados have a high fat content, so shouldn't be used very often as a source of fibre.

Some people worry that they will be uncomfortable or have gas if they increase their fiber intake. Such problems can be easily overcome by changing your diet gradually, over the course of a week or so, and ensuring that you drink enough liquids every day—8 to 12 cups/2 to 3 liters of water, milk, juices, tea, coffee and other beverages are recommended.

Source: Health and Welfare, Canada

Some foods that seem to be likely candidates for high-fiber status are in fact poor sources: brown rice, corn-flake cereals, lettuce, green peppers and grapes are some examples.
Add extra fiber to your diet with:
- bran in meat loaf
- raisin-bran muffins
- oatmeal toppings on fruit crisps
- lentils or legumes in soups
- legumes in salads (chick-peas, kidney beans)
- wheat germ in muffins, on cereals
- fresh fruit for breakfast instead of juice

3. Have several servings of vegetables and fruits each day.

Your mother was right when she told you to eat your vegetables: they are among the few foods that can be unreservedly recommended. Fruits are another. With their enormous variety, fruits and vegetables can offer not only fiber and vitamins A and C, but almost every other essential nutrient, and most of them are fat and calorie bargains, too. You should have four or five servings of fruits and vegetables each day, at least two of them vegetables. Dark green and deep yellow vegetables and fruits are rich sources of vitamin A (in the form of carotene), so choose them often.

Eat Your Greens—and Yellows

Excellent sources of carotene	Good sources of carotene
broccoli	apricots
cantaloupe	beet greens
carrots	nectarines
spinach	peaches
squash	plums
sweet potatoes	tomatoes
	watermelon

See also lists of excellent vitamins A and C recipes, pages 238, 239.

The vitamin C group is another category of fruits and vegetables that seems to play a role in cancer prevention. Everyone knows that citrus fruits (oranges, grapefruit, lemons, limes) are high in vitamin C, but remember, when you select fruit juices such as apple, grape or pineapple, or fruit drinks, to look for the statement "vitamin C added." Several vegetables are also rich sources of vitamin C. Because vitamin C isn't stored in the body, it's important to include vitamin C-rich foods in your daily menu.

Vitamin C—More Than Just Citrus

Excellent sources	*Good sources*
apple juice (vitaminized)	cabbage
broccoli	cauliflower
Brussels sprouts	potatoes (baked or steamed)
citrus fruits and juices	rutabagas
green and red peppers	tomatoes and tomato juice
strawberries	

CAUTION: Vitamin C is perishable. Heat, light or exposure to air can destroy it, and it dissolves in cooking water. To preserve it:
- Cover and refrigerate juices after opening.
- Prepare foods just before cooking.
- Cook vegetables with their skins on.
- Steam or bake (don't boil) fruits and vegetables.
- Keep cooking times as short as possible.
- Eat fruits and vegetables raw as often as possible.

And finally, the brassica vegetables. Not only are they packed with vitamins and minerals, but they seem to have an extra protective effect against cancer risk. Have several servings of these vegetables each week.

Cabbages Are Kings

broccoli	kohlrabi
Brussels sprouts	rutabagas
cabbage	turnips
cauliflower	

4. Keep your weight close to ideal.

Since being significantly overweight (40 percent above ideal) seems to increase cancer risk, it is important to keep your weight as close as possible to ideal. Maintaining normal weight will also benefit your general health and decrease your risk of other serious diseases, such as heart disease and diabetes.

The best way to lose weight (you've heard it before, but it's still true) is to eat less and exercise more. It is the safest method (no dangerous starvation diets), the one most likely to be permanent (no drastic changes you won't be able to keep up), and it has extra benefits (toned muscles, reduced stress). Other points to remember:

- Lose weight slowly, about two pounds/1 kg a week. Anything more puts you in danger of losing essential lean tissue, such as muscle. Depending on physical condition and level of activity, most people can achieve the desired weight loss with about 1,200 calories per day.
- Eat smaller portions.
- Eat less fat. Fat is concentrated calories: one gram of fat has more than twice as many calories as one gram of protein or carbohydrates, so reducing fat intake is the quickest way to cut down on calories. Some fat is essential for nutrition though, so don't try to eliminate it completely. (See pages 10–11 for fat-cutting suggestions.)
- Cut out or cut down on alcohol. Alcohol is the second most concentrated source of calories (see page 11) and is associated with increased cancer risk. As well as being high in calories, the nutritional benefits of alcohol are negligible.
- Avoid foods that are high in sugar.

Choose to Lose

Instead of	Calories	Choose	Calories
doughnut	235	plain muffin	120
peanuts ($\frac{1}{2}$ cup/125 mL)	420	popcorn, unbuttered (2 cups/500 mL)	108
fried chicken (3 oz/90g dark meat with skin)	240	roast chicken (3 oz/90g white meat, skin removed)	145
mayonnaise (2 tbsp/30 mL)	120	low-cal mayonnaise (2 tbsp/30 mL)	40
ice cream ($\frac{1}{2}$ cup/125 mL)	135	low-fat yogurt ($\frac{1}{2}$ cup/125 mL)	75
chocolate bar (2 oz/56 g)	285	frozen yogurt, chocolate-coated (75 mL)	127
rib roast (4 oz/125 g)	300	lean flank steak (4 oz/125 g)	200
spareribs (4 oz/125 g)	450	lean pork tenderloin (4 oz/125g)	275
whole milk (1 cup/250 mL)	150	skim milk (1 cup/250 mL)	85
chocolate cake, iced (1 piece)	310	angel food cake, plain (1 piece)	121

5. If you drink alcohol, drink in moderation.

"Moderation" is generally interpreted as two standard drinks per day or two bottles of beer.

Alcohol, especially when combined with smoking, is implicated in cancer risk and is also a source of "empty" calories: it supplies 7 calories per gram (or about 90 calories per 5oz/155mL dry white wine; 104 calories per 1½ oz/45mL 80-proof Scotch; 150 calories per 12oz/375mL beer, 95 calories for light beer; 193 calories per 8oz/250mL gin and tonic; 335 calories per 4oz/125mL eggnog).

If you drink, consider switching to other beverages occasionally: fruit or vegetable juices, mineral water or club soda with lime or a dash of angostura bitters.

6. Limit your consumption of smoked, salt-cured and nitrite-cured foods.

Since smoked hams and fish, cold cuts, sausages and other cured foods seem to be associated with cancer risk, it's wise to avoid them as much as possible. Even if it is later found that adequate intake of vitamin C reduces the risk, cured foods are high in fat and salt, which are linked to cancer and hypertension.

Menu Planning

All recipes in this book have been chosen on the basis not only of good taste but of good health. They are high in fiber, low (or lower than usual) in fat, and rich in vitamins and minerals, and they emphasize fruits and vegetables, whole-grain products, and the lean kinds and cuts of meat and fish. Sugar and salt have been kept to a minimum. Some of the recipes are classic favorites, which you will recognize, adapted to reflect the goals of the Canadian Cancer Society Diet Guidelines.

Use the recipes for everyday meals or for entertaining. Suggested menus are included throughout the book and are listed in the index.

To help you plan your own menus, each recipe gives you the number of calories and grams of fat per serving, as well as fiber, vitamin and mineral ratings. Remember the daily requirements:

- 20 to 30 grams of fiber
- fat intake not to exceed 30 percent of total calories. (To calculate your fat allowance in grams, refer to Appendix, page 228.)

All recipes in this book were analyzed and tested using 2% milk, low-fat yogurt and 2% cottage cheese.

A helpful tool to simplify calculations is Canada's Food Guide. We've been hearing about it for years, and following it is the fastest and easiest way to ensure a healthy diet. Try to include foods from each of these groups at every meal. The four food groups and recommended daily servings are:

1. Fruits and vegetables (including green and deep yellow vegetables): 4 or 5 servings (serving size 1/2 cup/125 mL)
2. Breads and cereals (including pasta, rice, muffins): 3 to 5 servings (serving size: 1 slice bread, muffin or roll; 1/2 to 1 cup/125 to 250 mL cereal, cooked rice, macaroni)
3. Milk and milk products (including cheese, yogurt): 2 to 4 servings (serving size: 1 cup/250 mL milk, yogurt or cottage cheese; 1 1/2 oz/45 g Cheddar cheese)
4. Meat, fish, poultry and alternates (such as peanut butter, beans, lentils, cheese, eggs): 2 servings (serving size: 2 to 3 oz/60 to 90g cooked lean meat, fish or poultry; 4 tbsp/60 mL peanut butter; 1 cup/250 mL cooked dried peas, beans or lentils; 2 oz/60g Cheddar or cottage cheese; 2 eggs). Three ounces/90g of cooked meat means a piece of sirloin steak about 4 × 2 × 1/2 inches/10 × 5 × 1 cm.

Liquids: A daily intake of 8 to 12 cups/2 to 3 liters of liquid (including soups, juices and beverages) is recommended.

To see if you need to adjust your eating habits, keep track of your diet for several days. Figure out the amount of fat and fiber you are eating, and whether you are fulfilling Canada's Food Guide.

Once you are familiar with which foods are high in fat and fiber and which are low, you can plan your menus with this in mind. For example, if you have a meal with a rich dessert, compensate by choosing other foods low in fat for the rest of the menu: use low-fat salad dressing and broiled chicken instead of a creamy dressing and fried steak. If you aren't getting enough fiber, add a bran muffin, fresh fruit or raw vegetable to your diet.

Once you get used to your new way of eating, you will be able to estimate how you are doing without a lot of calculating.

Comparing Menus

Instead of	Choose
Breakfast	
orange juice	whole orange (more fiber)
cheese omelet (2 eggs, cooked in butter)	Spanish omelet (1 egg, cooked in non-stick pan)
croissant with jam and 1 pat butter or margarine	whole-wheat toast and jam
coffee with cream	milk, or coffee with 2% milk
Fast-Food Lunch	
hot dog	slice of cheese pizza
French fries	Italian vegetable salad
milkshake	2% milk
Dinner	
roast pork and gravy	lean pork tenderloin with meat juices
hash-browned potatoes	baked potato with low-fat yogurt and chives
carrots	carrots
lettuce salad with creamy dressing	spinach salad with diet dressing whole-wheat roll
lemon meringue pie	lemon sherbet
3 glasses wine	1 glass wine spritzer
coffee with cream	coffee with 2% milk

These menus are relatively low in calories. To suit higher calorie needs, serve larger portions and add milk, breads or snacks.

Everyday Family Meals	Grams Fiber/ Serving	Grams Fat/ Serving	Calories	% Calories from Fat
Breakfast Grapefruit ($\frac{1}{2}$)	.72	tr.*	45	
Swiss Fruit Muesli (page 226)	5.83	6	282	
Milk (skim, 1 cup/ 250 mL)	0	tr.	90	
Lunch Oven-toasted cheese sandwich (with skim-milk cheese) ($1\frac{1}{2}$ oz/45g) on whole-wheat bread (2 slices)	4.24	4	226	
Carrot sticks ($\frac{1}{2}$ cup/125 mL)	1.68	tr.	20	
Peaches, packed in water ($\frac{1}{2}$ cup/125 mL)	1.16	tr.	39.5	
Cinnamon Coffee Cake (page 214)	.58	3.8	172	
Dinner Chicken Dijon (page 88)	0	3.89	190	
Brown rice ($\frac{3}{4}$ cup/175 mL)	1.32	2.5	112	
Steamed asparagus (1 cup/250 mL)	1.15	tr.	16	
Whole-wheat roll	1.89	1	125	
Butter (1 tsp/5 mL)	0	4	36	
Rhubarb Crumb Pie (page 216)	2.76	3.6	234	
Milk (skim, 1 cup/ 250 mL)	0	tr.	90	
Totals with skim milk	21.3g	25.8g	1678	13.8%
Totals with 2% milk	21.3g	35.8g	1756	18%
Totals with whole milk	21.3g	43.8g	1812	22%

* tr. = trace

Everyday Family Meals		Grams Fiber/ Serving	Grams Fat/ Serving	Calories	% Calories from Fat
Breakfast	Orange (1)	2.62	tr.	65	
	Breakfast Bran-and-Fruit (pages 222-3) (includes ½ cup/ 125 mL milk)	6.65	7	219	
	with fresh blueberries	5.4	0.5	45	
	Slice whole-wheat toast (1)	1.8	0.5	73	
	Jam or jelly (1 tsp/5 mL)	0	tr.	18	
Lunch	Tri-Color Bean Soup (page 51)	8.95	0.4	120	
	Whole-Wheat Irish Soda Bread (page 181) with 1 tsp/5 mL butter	2.9	5.7	179	
	Yogurt (low-fat, ½ cup/125 mL)	0	3	85	
	Almond-Apricot Squares (page 184)(2)	3.4	8	154	
Dinner	Marinated Flank Steak (page 101)	0	9	200	
	Mashed Potatoes with Onions (page 170)	1.81	2	123	
	Broccoli and Sweet Pepper Stir-Fry (page 156)	2.75	2	40	
	Poached Pears with Chocolate Sauce (pages 190-1)	2.6	8	168	
	Milk (skim, ½ cup/125 mL)	0	0	45	
	Totals with skim milk	39g	38.9g	1498	23%
	Totals with 2% milk	39g	48.9g	1576	28%
	Totals with whole milk	39g	56.9g	1632	31%

Everyday Family Meals		Grams Fiber/ Serving	Grams Fat/ Serving	Calories	% Calories from Fat
Breakfast	Orange juice ($\frac{1}{2}$ cup/125 mL)	0	tr.	64	
	Whole-wheat cereal ($\frac{3}{4}$ cup/ 175 mL) with fresh strawberries ($\frac{1}{2}$ cup/125 mL)	2.23	1.39	145	
	Refrigerator Bran Muffin (page 176) (1 med.)	3.42	5.5	116	
	Jam or jelly (1 tsp/5 mL)	0	tr.	18	
	Milk (skim, 1 cup/250 mL)	0	tr.	90	
Lunch	Bermuda Bean Salad (pages 78-9)	8.28	3.5	201	
	Whole-Wheat Raisin Scone (page 182) (1)	2.43	8	220	
	Prune Cake with Lemon Icing (page 199)	2.58	1.25	182	
	Milk (skim, 1 cup/ 250 mL)	0	tr.	90	
	Banana (1)	3.9	tr.	100	
Dinner	Sole Fillets with Lemon and Parsley (page 119)	0	7	117	
	Brown rice	.82	0.5	105	
	Steamed green beans	1.95	tr.	16	
	Spinach Salad with Buttermilk Herb Dressing* (page 82)	7	12	250	
	Chocolate cake	1	9.5	271	
	Totals with skim milk	33.6g	48.6g	1985	22%
	Totals with 2% milk	33.6g	58.6g	2063	26%
	Totals with whole milk	33.6g	66.6g	2119	28%

*These figures are for the large main-course-size serving of salad; the smaller side-salad size has 4 grams of fat and 83 calories.

Everyday Family Meals		**Grams Fiber/ Serving**	**Grams Fat/ Serving**	**Calories**	**% Calories from Fat**
Breakfast	Stewed prunes (3)	9.98	0.5	156	
	Whole-wheat cereal (1)	2.2	tr.	80	
	Boiled egg (1)	0	6	79	
	Slice whole-wheat toast (1)	1.79	0.5	73	
	Butter ($\frac{1}{2}$ tsp/2 mL)	0	2	18	
	Milk (skim, 1 cup/250 mL)	0	tr.	90	
Lunch	Chicken sandwich on whole-wheat (2) with lettuce or alfalfa sprouts and mayonnaise (1 tsp/5mL)	4.64	6	295	
	Celery sticks ($\frac{1}{2}$ cup/125 mL)	.95	tr.	9	
	Tangerine (1)	2.20	tr.	40	
	Wheat Germ Crispy Cookies (page 186) (2)	.9	6	114	
	Milk (skim, 1 cup/250 mL)	0	tr.	90	
Dinner	Old-Fashioned Meat Loaf (page 105)	0.3	9.5	186	
	Baked potato (1 med.)	4.04	tr.	91	
	Steamed Brussels sprouts ($\frac{1}{2}$ cup/125 mL)	2.38	0.5	29	
	Lemon Ginger Carrots (page 155) ($\frac{1}{2}$ cup/125 mL)	2.54	4	69	
	Butter ($\frac{1}{2}$ tsp/2 mL)	0	4	36	
	Apricot Clafouti (page 210)	2.05	4.4	162	
	Totals with skim milk	34g	43.4g	1527	26%
	Totals with 2% milk	34g	53.4g	1605	30%
	Totals with whole milk	34g	61.4g	1661	33%

Eating Out

There's no reason to throw away your diet resolutions when you eat out or travel. The Canadian Cancer Society Diet Guidelines are flexible enough to accommodate almost any dining situation. Superhuman willpower is not required, only knowledge and foresight—and a little ingenuity.

- Beware of high-fat foods: don't order a succession of rich dishes. Concentrate more on fruits, vegetables and whole-grain foods.
- If you over-indulge on a special occasion, eat moderately for the rest of the day and for a few days after.
- Many restaurants now offer low-calorie or light meals—some even specialize in creating exciting gourmet versions (sometimes called alternative or spa cuisine).
- Ask to have a fried dish steamed or broiled; ask for salads with the dressing on the side so you can serve yourself; ask to have meats served minus rich sauces or gravy. Many restaurants are becoming accustomed to such requests.
- Split a dish, or several dishes, with your dining companion; many restaurants will serve the two half-portions on separate plates.
- Choose a couple of appetizers instead of an entrée, or order soup and a salad.
- Choose clear instead of cream soups.
- Butter bread or rolls sparingly, or not at all.
- Choose fish or chicken dishes, and avoid those with cream sauces.
- Cut all the fat off meats.
- Avoid sautéed and deep-fried foods.
- If choosing a high-fat food, ask for a small portion.

Breakfasts

Choose:
- fresh fruits and juices
- whole-grain breads and cereals, muffins
- poached or boiled eggs (if concerned about cholesterol, limit to 3 per week)
- pancakes or waffles as long as they're not fried in a lot of fat—ask about this—and don't add butter yourself
- yogurt with fresh fruit
- low-fat milk instead of cream or whole milk with cereals and coffee or tea

Avoid:
- Danish pastries or croissants
- bacon, sausages, ham
- too much butter or margarine

Lunches and Dinners

Choose:
- pretzels rather than peanuts
- salads—add the dressing yourself or ask for a wedge of lemon. Choose from the salad bar: include spinach, corn, kidney beans, chick-peas.
- cottage cheese
- clear soups

- pasta dishes with tomato-based or wine-based sauces rather than sauces made with cream, oil or butter
- chicken or fish dishes, broiled or poached (light sauce only)
- fresh fruit desserts, sorbets and sherbets

Avoid, or choose occasionally and in moderate amounts:
- alcoholic drinks (other possibilities are tomato juice, soda or mineral water)
- quiches (pastry is high in fat)
- pâtés and avocados (high in fat)
- French-fries
- butter or sour cream on baked potatoes (ask for yogurt and chives or green onions
- fatty cuts of beef, pork and lamb (especially in large servings), duck and goose
- high-fat cheeses (Cheddar, cream cheeses)
- barbecued foods
- breaded foods (they're usually fried)
- peanuts and potato chips (substitute raw vegetables)
- smoked and heavily salted foods: ham, salami, herring
- chocolates (instead, choose fruit-jelly candy)
- mousses and rich desserts (chocolate, cream)

Cooking Methods

Cooking methods to avoid or use with caution:
Some cooking methods, such as barbecuing, grilling or smoking, may be harmful. To barbecue safely, wrap food in foil or place it high above the coals and cook slowly. It has been suggested that chemicals that are possibly cancer-causing may form when food is charred. For this reason, and because of the added fat, avoid frying, especially at high temperatures.

Cooking methods to choose:
Baking, roasting (use rack), oven-broiling (don't burn or char), microwave cooking, boiling, steaming (see pages 131 and 162), poaching, stewing and stir-frying (see pages 95-6) are good methods. They require little or no additional fat.

Cooking equipment you need:
- steamer: either the double-boiler type or a basket
- heavy nonstick skillet
- heavy Dutch oven

To preserve vitamins in cooking:
Some vitamins are destroyed by heat; others dissolve in the cooking water. To preserve them as much as possible:
- Cook vegetables quickly just until tender-crisp.
- Use as little water as possible and have it boiling before adding vegetables.
- Use any leftover cooking liquid in soups or stews.
- Use cooking methods that require very little or no liquid at all: microwaving, baking, steaming, foil-wrapped in oven and stir-frying using a small amount of oil.

19

To reduce fat in cooking:
- Many recipes begin by sautéing vegetables such as onions in butter. In most cases you can reduce the butter at least by half, often to one teaspoon/5 mL; add a few tablespoons/25 mL of white wine or water and cook the vegetables slowly over low heat. This method brings out the flavors just as effectively as the traditional method.
- If oil, margarine or butter is needed for flavor, add it at the end just before serving; you will get the most flavor for the least amount of fat.
- It is very important to use heavy pans, nonstick where possible. This is one of the best ways to cut down on fat without having foods burn or stick.
- Cut off all visible fat before cooking and drain off fat during cooking; make stews or soups using meats or stocks a day in advance and refrigerate overnight—fat solidifies on top and can be easily lifted off.
- Instead of butter or oil for flavor, use herbs and spices, onions or garlic, ginger, lemon juice, mustard.
- Buy the best-quality vegetables in season: they will have the best natural flavor and won't need as much butter or salt.
- Use vegetable purées (coulis) as a sauce rather than butter-based sauces.
- Use a rack in the roasting pan so that the meat doesn't sit in fat.
- Remove the skin from fowl before cooking or eating.
- Choose lean cuts of meat, such as flank steak or sirloin tip. Avoid prime rib and pork loin.
- Serve four-ounce/125 gram portions, or less, of meats; you can extend them and make them more interesting by cooking them with vegetables in stews, soups and stir-fries or with pasta.
- Cut meats into thin slices; it will look like more.
- Reduce oil in standard marinades, or omit oil altogether (see Marinated Leg of Lamb with Coriander, pages 114-15; Marinated Flank Steak, page 102).
- Use skim or 2% milk instead of whole, yogurt instead of sour cream, wine instead of butter or oil.
- Avoid desserts made with whipping cream; choose desserts based on milk or yogurt.
- Avoid dessert pastries; choose crisps instead (e.g. instead of double-crust apple pie, choose apple crisp).
- If you're making muffins, or cakes or other rich desserts, compare various recipes for fat or oil content and choose the one with the lowest amount.
- Use dessert recipes calling for cocoa rather than chocolate, as long as the cocoa recipe doesn't have additional fat.

Shopping

Check the labels on cans and other containers: they often give the fat and fiber content in grams per serving, plus other nutritional information. When the ingredients are given on a label, they are listed in order of amounts by weight, beginning with the largest amount. Sugars are often listed by kind (invert sugar, glucose, sucrose) and it may be difficult to determine the total amount of sugar.

Choose:
- calorie-reduced or low-fat soups and salad dressings
- low-fat yogurt, milk, ice cream and cheese (see Tables D and E, pages 233 and 234)
- low-fat or whipped butter or margarines for spreading (use regular hard margarines or butter for baking)
- lean types and cuts of meat (see Table C, pages 230-2)
- angel food cakes; Social Teas, Fig Newtons, gingersnaps, arrowroot
- turkey that hasn't been injected with fat, i.e., regular grades, not self-basting
- dark green lettuces or spinach (not iceberg lettuce)
- whole-wheat or stone-ground breads, pita bread, crackers, English muffins, pasta
- whole-grain cereals, cereals with bran or high fiber (see Table F, pages 235-6)
- bran muffins
- fresh fruits and vegetables

Avoid:
- processed meats: hot dogs, bologna, salami (if purchasing, choose fat-reduced kinds such as Schneider's Lite wieners)
- high-fat meats and poultry: duck, goose, regular ground meat, sausages, spareribs (see Table C, pages 230-2)
- side bacon (very occasionally choose lean ham, or peameal or back bacon)
- breaded and fried frozen meats and fish, e.g. fish sticks
- tuna fish packed in oil (instead choose tuna packed in water)
- avocados
- doughnuts, Danish pastries, croissants, pies, pastries, cakes, cookies, brownies
- cereals with sugar and low fiber
- chocolates
- peanuts, potato chips

APPETIZERS

Scrumptious snacks and cocktail party tidbits are irresistible and first courses are often the most innovative and interesting part of a meal. What's more, they can add valuable nutrients to your diet. But beware, they can also be nutritional hazards.

Pâtés, peanuts, potato chips, savory-filled pastries and mayonnaise-based dips are high in fat and should be avoided. Instead, choose crudités (raw vegetables, higher in fiber and vitamins) with a yogurt- or cottage-cheese-based dip, or savories with a bread casing (lower in fat than pastry cases). Appetizers such as Shrimp Wrapped with Snow Peas or Teriyaki Beef Rumaki will be favorites with any crowd and are also low in fat. The recipes in this section of the book will help you plan menus for entertaining that are low in fat and in calories.

Appetizer courses in restaurants can be wonderfully appealing and nutritious. Because some restaurant entrées are very large, appetizers are often just the right size to substitute for a main course.

SHRIMP WRAPPED WITH SNOW PEAS

This colorful, delicious hors d'oeuvre is very easy to prepare. Serve any remaining snow peas with a dip or spread, or split them down the center and fill with cottage cheese. This dish is unusually low in fat and calories.

4 cups	water	1 L
1	thick slice of onion	1
1	clove garlic, halved	1
1	bay leaf	1
2	stalks celery with leaves	2
1 lb	large raw shrimp in shells (about 18)	500 g
$\frac{1}{4}$ lb	snow peas	125 g

In large saucepan, combine water, onion, garlic, bay leaf and celery; bring to a boil. Reduce heat and simmer for 5 minutes; add shrimp and simmer, uncovered, for 3 to 5 minutes or until shrimp turn pink. Drain immediately and chill under cold water. Remove shell and black intestinal vein from each shrimp.

Trim snow peas and blanch in boiling water for 2 minutes or just until peas are pliable. Drain and plunge into a bowl of ice water to prevent further cooking and to set color. Drain.

Wrap a snow pea around each shrimp and secure with a toothpick. Arrange on serving platter or stick into head of cauliflower. Cover and refrigerate until serving time. Makes about 18 (4 servings).

Calories per piece: 14
Grams fat per piece: 0.1
Fiber: Good
Snow peas are a good source of vitamin A and fiber.

Variations:
- Use pita rounds with any of the salads in salad section of book.
- Line pita with alfalfa sprouts and fill with a spoonful of Hummus (page 32); top with Garlic Dip (page 28).
- Substitute cooked or canned salmon or shrimp (not tuna fish packed in oil) for crab.
- Line pita with lettuce and fill with Eggplant Caviar (page 31) or Spinach Dip (page 29).

*Make the full recipe of Parsley Dressing and use the rest of it as a dip—it's delicious!

CRAB-STUFFED MINI-PITAS

Silver-dollar-size pita bread rounds provide quick and easy containers for countless fillings. The packaged varieties are available in the bread sections of some supermarkets and specialty stores. Choose the whole-wheat ones for more flavor and fiber.

1	pkg (7oz/200 g) whole-wheat mini-pitas	1
$\frac{1}{2}$ lb	crab meat (canned, fresh or frozen)	250 g
2 tbsp	minced green onion	25 mL
$\frac{1}{2}$ cup	Parsley Dressing*(page 85)	125 mL
$\frac{1}{2}$ tsp	lemon juice	2 mL
	Salt and freshly ground pepper	
	Leaf lettuce	

Cut pita breads in half. Drain crab meat thoroughly. In bowl, combine crab meat, onion, Parsley Dressing, lemon juice, and salt and pepper to taste; and mix lightly. (Add more Parsley Dressing to taste.) Line pita bread pockets with lettuce. Spoon crab meat mixture into each pita. Refrigerate until needed. Makes 40.

Calories per piece: 16
Grams fat per piece: 0.2
Fiber: 0.26 g per piece

Diet Hint: Reducing fat content in hors d'oeuvres

- Instead of pastry cases, use: bread cases—see Stuffed Mushroom Croustades (page 26)—or whole-wheat mini-pita rounds.
- To hold fillings, use hollowed-out cherry tomatoes, canned lichees and cucumber slices.
- Avoid pâtés and mayonnaise-based dressings.

Photo:

Teriyaki Beef Rumaki (page 27)
Stuffed Mushroom Croustades (page 26)
Cherry Tomatoes Stuffed with Spinach Dip (page 29)
Shrimp Wrapped with Snow Peas (pages 22-3)
Crab-Stuffed Mini-Pitas (page 23)

CRAB-CUCUMBER ROUNDS

Crisp cucumber slices, instead of pastry or bread, make refreshing low-calorie, low-fat canapé bases.

1	seedless English cucumber	1
1	can (6 oz/170 g) crab meat	1
2 tbsp	sour cream	25 mL
2 tbsp	chopped chives or green onion	25 mL
	Salt and freshly ground pepper	
	Paprika	

Run tines of fork lengthwise along cucumber to make decorative edge on slices. Cut cucumber into slices $\frac{1}{4}$ inch/5 mm thick.

Drain crab meat thoroughly. Mix with sour cream chives and salt and pepper to taste. Place small spoonful of crab mixture on each cucumber slice. Sprinkle with paprika. Cover and refrigerate for up to 4 hours. Makes about 36.

Calories per round: 4.3
Gram fat per round: 0.2

Hidden Fat in Foods

We all know that foods such as mayonnaise, whipped cream and Cheddar cheese are high in fat. Here are some other foods that are also deceptively high in fat.

	Grams fat/serving
Peanuts ($\frac{1}{2}$ cup/125 mL)	36
Potato chips (1 small bag)	24
Corn chips (1 small bag)	20
Half an avocado	19
Eggnog, nonalcoholic (1 cup/250 mL)	19
Peanut butter (2 tbsp/25 mL)	16
Olives, black (6 medium)	14
Pâté de foie gras (2 tbsp/25 mL)	13
Ice-cream bar, chocolate-coated (2 oz/60 g)	10
Chocolate bar (1 oz/28 g)	9
Chocolate chip cookies (3 small)	9
Popcorn with butter (1 cup/250 mL)	8
[Popcorn without butter (1 cup/250 mL)	0.7]
French-fried potatoes (10 pieces)	7
[Boiled or baked potato	trace]
Olives, green (8 medium)	6
Egg yolk	5

GREEN BEAN CRUNCH

For a salty, crunchy snack that's low in fat and calories, try Green Bean Crunch instead of peanuts or potato chips. It's sure to be appreciated by dieters who crave salty foods. You can add other raw vegetables such as carrots, kohlrabi, fennel and turnip.

1½ lb	green beans	750 g
½	small head cauliflower	½
1 cup	water	250 mL
1	onion, chopped	1
1	large clove garlic	1
1 tbsp	lemon juice	15 mL
¼ cup	soy sauce	50 mL
¼ cup	water	50 mL
1 tbsp	sunflower oil	15 mL
1 tbsp	sesame seeds	15 mL
8	large leaves Boston lettuce	8

Remove stem end of green beans. Cut cauliflower into small florets. In large saucepan, bring 1 cup/250 mL water to a boil; add onion, garlic, lemon juice, beans and cauliflower. Reduce heat, cover and simmer until vegetables are tender-crisp, about 8 minutes; drain, and discard garlic. Combine soy sauce, ¼ cup/50 mL water and oil; pour over vegetables. Cover and refrigerate for at least 1 hour.

Place sesame seeds on pie plate and toast in 325°F/160°C oven for 5 minutes or until golden brown.

Just before serving, toss vegetable mixture; remove from marinade. Arrange lettuce leaf on each plate. Spoon vegetable mixture onto lettuce and sprinkle with sesame seeds. Makes 8 servings.

Calories per serving: 45
Grams fat per serving: 1.7
Fiber: Good
Vitamin A: Good
Cauliflower is a good source of fiber and of vitamin C.

Spinach-Stuffed Mushrooms
Fresh white mushrooms are delicious raw. Remove their stems and they're easy to stuff. If you're having a party, make the full recipe of Spinach Dip (page 29) or Parsley Dressing (page 85); use 1 cup/250 mL as a stuffing for ½ lb/250 g mushrooms or cherry tomatoes, and the rest as a dip. They're a low-fat, low-calorie appetizer.

Stuffed Cherry Tomatoes
Cherry tomatoes are a colorful, fresh-tasting addition to an hors d'oeuvres platter. To stuff, cut off the top of each tomato, hollow out some of the pulp and fill with Hummus (page 32), Spinach Dip (page 29), or Creamy Fresh Dill Dip (page 30).

Cherry tomatoes are a good source of vitamins A and C and are low in fat.

Photo:

Crudités with Creamy Fresh Dill Dip (page 30)

STUFFED MUSHROOM CROUSTADES

These mushroom appetizers are so delicious, they just melt in your mouth. I first tasted them at Toronto caterer Alison Cummings' home. To keep the fat as low as possible, I reduce the butter and use low-fat cheese. You can also use the croustade cases for other savory fillings—they're much lower in fat and calories than pastry.

24	thin slices bread	24
24	medium-size white mushrooms	24
Stuffing:		
1 cup	fine fresh whole-wheat bread crumbs	250 mL
1	large clove garlic, minced	1
$\frac{1}{4}$ cup	finely chopped fresh parsley	50 mL
	Salt and freshly ground pepper	
4 tsp	butter	20 mL
$\frac{2}{3}$ cup	grated low-fat mozzarella cheese	150 mL

Using $2\frac{1}{2}$-inch/6 cm cookie cutter or glass, cut out 24 rounds of bread. Press bread rounds into small muffin tins. Bake in 300°F/150°C oven for 20 to 25 minutes or until light brown. Remove from oven and let cool. (Croustades may be prepared in advance and stored in covered container for about 1 week or frozen for longer storage.)

Wash mushrooms and dry with paper towels; remove stems (save for use in soups). Store mushrooms in refrigerator until needed.

Stuffing: In food processor or mixing bowl, combine bread crumbs, garlic, parsley, and salt and pepper to taste; process until combined. Add butter and process just until mixed. (If mixing by hand, use soft or melted butter.) Spoon some stuffing into each mushroom cap; top with grated cheese.

Just before serving, place a mushroom into each bread case. Place on baking sheet and bake in 400°F/200°C oven for 10 minutes or until hot. If desired, turn on broiler for last minute. Serve hot. Makes 36.

Calories per piece: 93
Grams fat per piece: 2
Fiber: Two pieces are a good source of fiber.

TERIYAKI BEEF RUMAKI

Wrap tender strips of marinated beef around crunchy water chestnuts for a delectable hot appetizer.

$\frac{3}{4}$ lb	sirloin, round or flank steak (about $\frac{1}{2}$ inch/ 1 cm thick)	375 g
$\frac{1}{4}$ cup	soy sauce*	50 mL
1	clove garlic, minced	1
1 tbsp	minced onion	15 mL
1 tbsp	granulated sugar	15 mL
1 tsp	Worcestershire sauce	5 mL
$\frac{1}{2}$ tsp	ground ginger	2 mL
1	can (10 oz/284 mL) water chestnuts	1

Place meat in freezer for about 30 minutes or until firm for easier slicing. Cut off any fat. Slice meat across the grain into very thin strips about $\frac{1}{8}$ inch/2 mm thick and 3 inches/8 cm long.

In a bowl combine soy sauce, garlic, onion, sugar, Worcestershire sauce and ginger. Add meat and stir to coat strips evenly. Marinate for 30 minutes at room temperature, stirring occasionally, or overnight in refrigerator.

Drain meat. Wrap one strip around each water chestnut and secure with toothpick. Arrange on baking sheet or in shallow glass serving dish. Broil for 3 to 4 minutes or until piping hot and cooked medium-rare (or microwave on High for 3 to 4 minutes, rotating dish $\frac{1}{4}$ turn halfway through cooking time). Makes about 25.

Calories per piece: 37
Grams fat per piece: 0.8
Four pieces of rumaki are a good source of iron.

Cocktail Party for 25
Plan on 6 to 8 pieces per person. Multiply recipes according to number of guests.

Teriyaki Beef Rumaki (page 27)
Crab-Stuffed Mini-Pitas (page 23)
Parsley or Watercress Dressing with raw vegetables (page 85)
Mushrooms stuffed with Spinach Dip (page 29)
Shrimp Wrapped with Snow Peas (pages 22-3)
Salmon Mousse with Dill (page 33)

*Use naturally brewed light or sodium-reduced soy sauce for lower sodium (salt) content.

Variation:
Curry Dip: Add 1 tsp/5 mL each curry powder and cumin to Garlic Dip. Amount of onions and garlic can be reduced.

GARLIC DIP

Serve as a dip with raw vegetables, or as a sauce over baked potatoes, sliced tomatoes or cucumber, steamed green beans or fish fillets.

$1\frac{1}{2}$ cups	plain yogurt	375 mL
$\frac{1}{4}$ cup	chopped green onions or chives	50 mL
2	cloves garlic, minced	2
1 tbsp	vegetable oil	15 mL
$\frac{1}{2}$ tsp	granulated sugar	2 mL

In bowl, combine yogurt, onions, garlic, oil and sugar. Mix thoroughly. Cover and refrigerate until needed. Makes about $1\frac{1}{2}$ cups/375 mL.

	Per 1 tbsp/15 mL	Per $\frac{1}{4}$ cup/50 mL
Calories:	24	96
Grams fat:	2	7

$\frac{1}{3}$ cup / 75 mL dip is a good source of calcium.

Diet Hint: Reducing fat content in finger foods, snacks and first courses

Instead of	Choose
Guacamole or mayonnaise	Cottage cheese- or yogurt-based dips
Peanuts and potato chips	Unbuttered popcorn and pretzels
Buttery crackers	Whole-wheat crackers
Crackers with cheese	Pita bread
Oysters Rockefeller	Raw oysters
Caviar	Shrimp
Lobster Newburg	Lobster pieces
Cocktail sausages or frankfurters	Lean meats
Meat pâté	Vegetable pâté
Cream soup	Gazpacho or consommé
Pasta with cream sauce	Pasta with tomato sauce
Mayonnaise-dressed salads (egg, potato)	Green salads with yogurt dressing
Bloody Mary	Tomato juice

Serve with broccoli, snow peas, asparagus, carrots, turnip, green beans, cauliflower and/or cherry tomatoes for good to excellent fiber.

SPINACH DIP

Perfect for dipping vegetables, this is also delicious as a filling for mushrooms and cherry tomatoes or as a dressing for salads and chilled cooked vegetables. Spinach is an excellent source of fiber and vitamin A (carotene).

1	pkg (10 oz/284 g) frozen chopped spinach, or 1 lb/500 g fresh	1
1 cup	sour cream	250 mL
$\frac{1}{2}$ cup	plain yogurt	125 mL
$\frac{1}{2}$ cup	minced fresh parsley	125 mL
$\frac{1}{4}$ cup	finely chopped green onions (including tops)	50 mL
1 tsp	salt	5 mL
	Freshly ground pepper	

If using fresh spinach, trim tough ends. Boil or steam spinach until wilted; drain thoroughly and chop. If using frozen, squeeze by hand to remove all moisture or wrap in paper towels and squeeze.

In bowl, mix together spinach, sour cream, yogurt, parsley, onions, salt, and pepper to taste. Cover and refrigerate for at least 4 hours or overnight to blend flavors. Makes 2 cups/500 mL dip.

	Per 1 tbsp/15 mL
Calories:	17
Grams fat:	1
Vitamin A:	Good
Folacin:	Good

Spinach is an excellent source of fiber and vitamin A.

CRUDITÉS WITH CREAMY FRESH DILL DIP

Prepare a colorful selection of raw vegetables—cauliflower, carrots, red, yellow and purple peppers, snow peas, baby corn, zucchini, Belgian endive, green and yellow beans, celery, fennel; cut them into strips suitable for dipping and arrange on a large platter with dip in center.

4	carrots	4
2	sweet red, yellow or green peppers	2
$\frac{1}{2}$	small cauliflower	$\frac{1}{2}$
2	Belgian endive	2
$\frac{1}{4}$ lb	mushrooms	125 g
Creamy Dill Dip:		
$\frac{1}{4}$ cup	chopped fresh dill (or 2 tsp/10 mL dried dillweed*)	50 mL
2 tbsp	chopped fresh parsley	25 mL
1 cup	cottage cheese	250 mL
3 tbsp	plain yogurt	45 mL
	Salt and freshly ground pepper	

* If using dried dillweed, add 3 tbsp/45 mL more chopped fresh parsley.

Cut carrots and peppers into strips. Separate cauliflower in florets. Separate endive leaves. Halve mushrooms if large. Refrigerate until serving time.

Creamy Dill Dip: Chop dill and parsley in food processor; add cottage cheese, yogurt, and salt and pepper to taste. Process with on-off turns to mix. Refrigerate.

At serving time, arrange vegetables on platter. Place dip in center. Makes 10 servings (about $1\frac{1}{4}$ cups/300 mL dip).

Per 1 tbsp/15 mL of dip
Calories: 12
Grams fat: 0.25
Fiber will vary depending on vegetables (see chart, page 237).

Compare:	Per $1\frac{1}{4}$ cups/300 mL	
Dip made with:	Calories	Grams fat
plain low-fat yogurt	143	3.4
2% cottage cheese	230	4.4
sour cream	416	40
mayonnaise	1,616	179

EGGPLANT CAVIAR

Often called Poor Man's Caviar, this Mediterranean dip is delicious with raw vegetables or as a spread with melba toast.

1	large eggplant (about $1\frac{1}{4}$ lb/560g)	1
3	green onions, finely chopped	3
1	large clove garlic, minced	1
1	large tomato, peeled and chopped	1
$\frac{1}{2}$	stalk celery, finely chopped	$\frac{1}{2}$
$\frac{1}{4}$ cup	minced green pepper (optional)	50 mL
1 tbsp	fresh lemon juice	15 mL
2 tsp	vegetable oil	10 mL
$\frac{1}{2}$ tsp	salt	2 mL
$\frac{1}{4}$ tsp	freshly ground pepper	1 mL

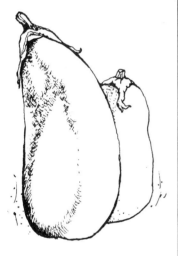

Prick eggplant in several places with a fork. Place on baking sheet and bake in 400°F/200°C oven for 45 minutes or until soft, turning once or twice during baking. Let cool, then peel and chop finely.

In mixing bowl, combine eggplant, onions, garlic, tomato, celery and green pepper if using; toss to mix. Add lemon juice, oil, salt and pepper; mix well. Cover and refrigerate for at least 1 hour to blend flavors. Makes 3 cups/750 mL.

	Per 1 tbsp/15mL	Per $\frac{1}{4}$ cup/50 mL
Calories:	5.8	23
Grams fat:	0.3	1.2

$\frac{1}{2}$ cup/125 mL of Eggplant Caviar is a good source of fiber.

Compare:	Per $\frac{1}{4}$ cup/50 mL	
	Calories	Grams fat
Chicken liver pâté	276	26.4
Eggplant Caviar	23	1.2

HUMMUS (CHICK-PEA DIP)

Serve this Middle Eastern classic with pita bread or vegetables as an appetizer or for lunch, snacks or a picnic. For a casual dinner, add vegetable soup to the menu.

$\frac{1}{4}$ cup	tahini (sesame paste) or peanut butter	50 mL
$\frac{1}{2}$ tsp	(approx) cumin or more to taste	2 mL
$\frac{1}{2}$ tsp	salt	2 mL
2	large cloves garlic, minced	2
2 tbsp	lemon juice	25 mL
3 tbsp	hot water	45 mL
1	can (19 oz/540 mL) chick-peas, drained	1
	Chopped fresh parsley (optional)	

In small bowl, combine tahini, cumin, salt and garlic; while stirring, slowly pour in lemon juice, then hot water. Purée chick-peas in a blender or a food processor, or pass through a food mill; add tahini mixture to purée and process or mix well. Taste and add more cumin and salt if desired. Spread hummus on dinner plate and sprinkle with chopped parsley. Makes $1\frac{1}{2}$ cups/375 mL.

	Per 1 tbsp/15 mL	Per $\frac{1}{4}$ cup/50 mL
Calories:	75	300
Grams fat:	2	8
Fiber: Good—$\frac{1}{4}$ cup/50 mL: 3.4g		

Summer Lunch or Picnic
White wine spritzers
Whole-wheat pita bread filled with Hummus (page 32), topped with alfalfa sprouts or shredded lettuce, and sliced tomatoes or sweet red peppers and a spoonful of yogurt seasoned with curry or cumin.
Strawberries

SALMON MOUSSE WITH DILL

This smooth and creamy spread looks pretty when unmolded and surrounded with crackers, melba toast or fresh vegetables. And because it's made without whipping cream and mayonnaise, it's low in fat and calories. Be sure to use sockeye salmon for its bright red color.

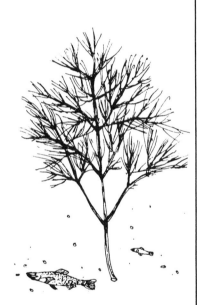

1	envelope unflavored gelatin	1
½ cup	water or clam juice	125 mL
2 tbsp	minced fresh dill or 1 tsp/5 mL dried dillweed	25 mL
2 tbsp	grated onion	25 mL
1 tbsp	lemon juice	15 mL
1 tsp	salt	5 mL
Dash	Tabasco sauce	Dash
¾ cup	plain yogurt	175 mL
½ cup	sour cream	125 mL
½ cup	finely chopped celery	125 mL
2	cans (each 7¾ oz/220 g) sockeye salmon, drained	2

In small saucepan, sprinkle gelatin over cold water or clam juice; let stand until softened, about 5 minutes. Warm over medium heat until gelatin is dissolved. Let cool to room temperature. Stir in dill, onion, lemon juice, salt, Tabasco, yogurt, sour cream and celery. Refrigerate until mixture begins to set.

Remove skin from salmon (but not bones—they're an excellent source of calcium); mash salmon with a fork or process in a food processor. Mix into gelatin mixture. Spoon into 4-cup/1 L mold. Cover and refrigerate until firm, at least 3 hours.

Unmold onto serving plate and surround with crackers, melba toast, or fresh vegetables. Makes about 4 cups/1 L.

	Per 1 tbsp/15 mL
Calories:	18
Grams fat:	1

HONEY-LIME DIP FOR FRUIT

Delicious at the beginning or end of a meal, this refreshing dip can be made with lemon or lime. Choose a colorful variety of fruit: strawberries, grapes, pineapple wedges, apple, mango, papaya, pear, peach, melon, sections of orange or other seasonal fresh fruit. Arrange the fruit on a large platter with the dip in the center and let guests help themselves.

1 cup	plain yogurt	250 mL
	Grated peel of 1 lime	
1 tbsp	lime juice	15 mL
3 tbsp	liquid honey	45 mL

Combine all ingredients and mix well; cover and refrigerate overnight (mixture will thicken upon standing). Makes 1 cup/250 mL dip (enough for 6 servings).

	Per 1 tbsp/15 mL	Per $\frac{1}{4}$ cup/50 mL
Calories:	16	64
Grams fat:	0.2	0.8

Fiber (including $\frac{3}{4}$ cup / 175 mL fresh fruit): Good but will vary depending on kind of fruit
Vitamins A and C: Excellent (depending on kind of fruit)

FIRST COURSES

When planning menus, first decide on the main course. If it is low in fat and calories, you can then consider a hearty or cream soup or a more filling first course such as pasta or fish; if the main course is high in fat and calories, choose a light green salad or a clear soup for a first course. Many of the recipes in the book make delicious first courses. Here are some suggestions.

Soups

Any soup recipe in this book can be a first course, but if it is a filling soup, serve in smaller amounts.

Salads

Roasted Red Pepper, Mushroom and Melon Salad (pages 60-1)

Spinach and Red Cabbage Salad with Blue-Cheese Dressing (page 61)
Greek Salad (page 77)
Arugula and Radicchio Salad with Balsamic Vinaigrette (page 66)
Pasta Salad with Sweet Peppers and Fresh Dill (pages 80-1)
Julienne Vegetable Salad with Lemon Vinaigrette (page 67)
Artichoke-Tomato Salad (page 63)
Melon with Blueberries (page 200)

Fish

Brochettes of Salmon and Shrimp (page 130) (small portions) with Tomato Salsa (page 151) or Dill Mustard Sauce (page 147)
Mussels Sicilian Style (page 122)

Shrimp Wrapped with Snow Peas (pages 22-3) with Garlic Dip (page 28)

Pasta

Capellini with Clam Sauce and Sweet Red Peppers (page 121)
Linguine with Shrimp and Tomato (page 123)
Fettuccine with Fresh Tomatoes and Basil (page 137)
Pasta Salad with Sweet Peppers and Dill (pages 80-1)

Vegetables

Asparagus with Red Pepper Purée (pages 154-5)
Asparagus with Orange Vinaigrette (page 84)
Baked Leeks au Gratin (pages 160-1)
Corn on the Cob (serve, just picked, as a first course)
Broccoli Frittata (pages 132-3)

SOUPS

If I had to choose only one type of food to exist on, I would quickly choose soups. A warming soup in winter is the best comfort food of all, and nothing beats a chilled soup in summer to cool and refresh. Any time of year I love to have a large bowl of soup for either lunch or dinner and need nothing more than thick crusty bread, perhaps a wedge of cheese or a salad, and fresh fruit for dessert. Some soups, such as Portuguese Collard Soup, Summer Garden Italian Soup with Pesto or Split Pea Soup, I can happily eat day after day until a large pot is finished.

Don't forget, when planning your menus, that soups are ideal for lunch or dinner, as either first courses or main courses, for party fare either after the theater or après ski, or for a midnight meal.

Soups are often a good source of vitamins, particularly A and C, and of fiber. Cream soups are usually a good source of calcium, an important addition for adults who don't drink milk and therefore have difficulty meeting their calcium requirements.

Diet Hint: Reducing fat content of soups
When making cream soups, substitute 2% milk or buttermilk for cream or whole milk, and plain low-fat yogurt for sour cream. You can add whipping cream to a hot soup and boil it without the soup curdling, but you cannot do this with the lower-fat substitutes. Here a little care is needed. It is best to warm the milk or yogurt gradually by slowly adding some of the hot mixture to it, then pouring it into the hot soup. The soup can be reheated, but don't let it boil.

See Table E (page 234) for the fat content of milk, yogurt and various creams.

*See page 65 for instructions on cooking beets.

BALKAN BEET CREAM SOUP

Save any leftover cooked beets for this flavorful chilled soup. On a hot summer evening it's perfect for a light meal, along with a refreshing salad and warm bread.

$\frac{1}{2}$ cup	sour cream	125 mL
$\frac{1}{2}$ cup	cottage cheese	125 mL
4 cups	buttermilk	1 L
4	medium beets, cooked, peeled and cut in cubes*	4
2	hard-cooked eggs, peeled and chopped	2
$\frac{1}{2}$	unpeeled English cucumber, diced	$\frac{1}{2}$
$\frac{1}{2}$ cup	chopped fresh parsley	125 mL
$\frac{1}{3}$ cup	sliced radishes	75 mL
3 tbsp	chopped fresh chives or green onions	45 mL
	Salt and freshly ground pepper	

In blender or food processor, combine sour cream and cottage cheese; mix until smooth (or pass through a sieve). Combine with buttermilk; refrigerate.

Just before serving, divide beets among serving bowls. Stir remaining ingredients into buttermilk mixture and pour over beets. Makes 8 large servings (1 cup/250 mL each).

Calories per serving: 125
Grams fat per serving: 5
Calcium, phosphorus and vitamin C: Good

60-Minute Dinner Party
Chilled Melon and Yogurt Soup (page 37)
Chicken with Snow Peas (page 96)
Rice
Tarragon Carrots (page 155)
Frozen Lemon Cream (page 195)

CHILLED MELON AND YOGURT SOUP

A hint of ginger and fresh mint heightens the flavor of this light, refreshing summer soup. Serve it as a first course for brunch, lunch or dinner. Be sure the cantaloupe you use is ripe.

1	ripe cantaloupe	1
1 cup	plain yogurt	250 mL
3 tbsp	lemon juice	45 mL
$\frac{1}{2}$ tsp	peeled and grated fresh ginger root or $\frac{1}{4}$ tsp/1 mL dried ginger	2 mL
2 tbsp	chopped fresh mint leaves	25 mL

Cut cantaloupe in half and remove seeds. Scoop out pulp into container of food processor or blender and purée. You should have about $1\frac{1}{2}$ cups/375 mL purée. Add yogurt, lemon juice and ginger; process to mix. Refrigerate until serving.

Serve soup in small bowls, topped with a sprinkling of fresh mint. Makes 4 servings (about $\frac{1}{2}$ cup/125 mL each).

Calories per serving: 80
Grams fat per serving: 0.3
Vitamins A and C: Excellent
Calcium: Good

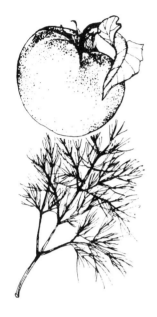

FRESH TOMATO-DILL BISQUE

Make this soup in the summer and fall when fresh dill is available and tomatoes are at their best.

3	large tomatoes, peeled and sliced	3
1	medium onion, sliced	1
1	medium clove garlic, chopped	1
3 tbsp	chopped fresh dill or 2 tsp/ 10 mL dried dillweed	45 mL
1 tsp	salt	5 mL
$\frac{1}{4}$ tsp	freshly ground pepper	1 mL
$\frac{1}{4}$ cup	cold water	50 mL
$\frac{1}{2}$ cup	cooked macaroni	125 mL
1 cup	chicken stock	250 mL
$\frac{3}{4}$ cup	milk	175 mL
2 tbsp	tomato paste (optional)	25 mL
Garnish:		
4 or 5	sprigs fresh dill, chopped	4 or 5
1	large tomato, chopped	1

In saucepan, combine tomatoes, onion, garlic, dill, salt, pepper and cold water. Simmer, covered, for 15 minutes.

Transfer to blender; add macaroni and process for 1 minute. With machine running, add stock, milk and tomato paste (if using). Refrigerate, covered, until thoroughly chilled.

Before serving, taste and adjust seasoning. Garnish each serving with chopped dill and tomato. Makes 4 servings (about $\frac{3}{4}$ cup/175 mL each).

Calories per serving: 74
Grams fat per serving: 1.4
Vitamin C: Excellent
Vitamin A: Good

SPLIT PEA SOUP

This is one of our family's favorite soups. We use the leftover bone from a cooked ham. Many cooks add carrots and other vegetables, but we don't—my mother says they take away from the flavor of the peas. Don't add any salt until just before serving—there is often enough salt in the ham.

1	ham bone from cooked ham	1
$1\frac{1}{4}$ cups	split green peas (12 oz/350 g)	300 mL
8 cups	water	2 L
4	onions, sliced	4
	Salt and freshly ground pepper	

Remove any fat from ham bone, but leave meat. In large saucepan, combine ham bone, peas, water and onions. Bring to a boil and skim off any scum.

Reduce heat and simmer, partially covered, for $1\frac{1}{2}$ to 2 hours or until peas are soft, stirring occasionally. Makes 10 servings (about $\frac{3}{4}$ cup/175 mL each).

Calories per serving: 66
Grams fat per serving: 0.2
Fiber: Good

Compare:
Fresh Tomato-Dill Bisque
made with:

	Grams fat/serving
2% milk	1.4
whole milk	2.8
light cream	8.7
whipping cream	15.4

GAZPACHO

This cold Spanish soup is perfect for hot summer evenings. It's easy to make in a blender, but tastes best when the vegetables are chopped by hand.

1	clove garlic	1
$\frac{1}{2}$	small onion, quartered	$\frac{1}{2}$
$\frac{1}{2}$	green pepper, seeded and cut in chunks	$\frac{1}{2}$
3	tomatoes, quartered	3
1	cucumber, cut in chunks*	1
2 tbsp	wine vinegar	25 mL
2 tbsp	olive oil	25 mL
$\frac{1}{2}$ cup	(approx) chicken stock or water (optional)	125 mL
	Salt and freshly ground pepper	

*Peel cucumber only if skin is tough or waxy.

In blender with machine running, drop garlic into feed tube, then add onion. Turn machine off and add green pepper, tomatoes, cucumber, vinegar and oil. Blend just until chopped. If soup is too thick, add up to $\frac{1}{2}$ cup/ 125 mL chicken stock. Cover and store in refrigerator until serving time. Taste, and add salt, pepper and more vinegar if necessary. Serve cold. Makes 6 servings (about $\frac{3}{4}$ cup/175 mL each).

Calories per serving: 57
Grams fat per serving: 4
Fiber: Good
Vitamin C: Excellent
Vitamin A: Good

CREAM OF BROCCOLI SOUP

This is one of my favorite soups. I like it hot or cold, and sometimes top each serving with a spoonful of sour cream and chopped chives, dill or parsley.

Broccoli is an excellent source of vitamins A and C and of fiber. It's also a brassica vegetable, and people whose diets frequently include brassica vegetables have been shown to have a lower risk of colon cancer. Other brassica vegetables are cabbage, cauliflower, Brussels sprouts, rutabaga, kale and turnips.

1	large onion, coarsely chopped	1
1	medium carrot, sliced	1
1	small stalk celery (with leaves), sliced	1
1	clove garlic, minced	1
3 cups	chicken stock	750 mL
$\frac{1}{4}$ cup	uncooked rice	50 mL
3 cups	coarsely chopped broccoli	750 mL
2 cups	milk	500 mL
1 tsp	salt	5 mL
Pinch	cayenne pepper	Pinch

In large saucepan, combine onion carrot, celery, garlic and chicken stock; bring to a boil. Add rice; cover and simmer for 15 to 20 minutes or until rice is tender. Add broccoli; cover and simmer until broccoli is tender, about 5 minutes. Transfer to blender or food processor and purée (may be done in batches). Return to saucepan; add milk, salt and cayenne. Serve hot. Alternatively, let cool, cover and refrigerate until serving time. Makes 8 servings ($\frac{3}{4}$ cup/ 175 mL each).

Calories per serving: 70
Grams fat per serving: 1.8
Fiber: Good
Vitamins A and C: Excellent

FRESH TOMATO AND BASIL SOUP

This light, flavorful soup is perfect for a first course during tomato season. If fresh basil is not available, use fresh dill; you'll probably want to add more dill than the basil called for here.

1 tbsp	butter	15 mL
1	large clove garlic, minced	1
1	medium carrot, diced	1
1	medium onion, chopped	1
4 cups	chicken stock	1 L
3 cups	peeled and diced ripe tomatoes	750 mL
3 tbsp	chopped fresh basil leaves	45 mL
	Salt and freshly ground pepper	

In heavy saucepan, melt butter; stir in garlic, carrot and onion. Cook over medium-low heat until onion is tender. Add stock; cover and simmer for 20 minutes. Stir in tomatoes and simmer for 10 minutes. Just before serving, stir in basil and salt and pepper to taste. Makes 6 servings (about 1 cup/250 mL each).

Calories per serving: 76
Grams fat per serving: 2.9
Vitamins A and C: Excellent
Niacin: Good

SPA VEGETABLE SOUP

One of the easiest and quickest ways of making soup is simply to cook the vegetables in chicken stock. The trick is to have a colorful and interesting variety of vegetables. Here's a suggestion about what vegetables to use, but you may substitute any you have on hand—squash, turnip, lettuce, potatoes. Add chopped fresh herbs if available.

3 cups	chicken stock	750 mL
1	carrot, diagonally sliced	1
1 cup	broccoli florets	250 mL
1 cup	cauliflower florets	250 mL
½ cup	thinly sliced red cabbage or spinach	125 mL
1	green onion, diagonally sliced	1
	Salt and freshly ground pepper	

Variation:
Seafood Vegetable Soup: After vegetables are tender, add 1 cup/250 mL or 4oz/125 g of cooked or raw shelled shrimp or scallops, or a combination of both, plus 4oz/125 g mussels in shell (optional). Simmer for 2 to 3 minutes longer, or until shrimp and scallops are opaque and mussel shells open. (Discard any mussel if shell doesn't open.)

In saucepan, bring chicken stock to a boil; add carrot and simmer for 10 minutes. Add remaining vegetables and simmer until tender. Season with salt and pepper to taste. Makes 4 servings (about 1 cup/250 mL each).

Calories per serving: 52
Grams fat per serving: 1
Fiber: Good
Vitamins A and C: Good
Niacin: Good

POTAGE VERT

Here is a low-calorie, attractive green vegetable soup that's quick to prepare if you slice the vegetables in a food processor. For a creamy, thick soup, purée in a food processor or blender.

1	large onion, peeled and sliced	1
2	celery stalks sliced	2
2	cloves garlic, minced	2
$\frac{1}{4}$ lb	green beans, cut in 2-inch/5 cm lengths	125 g
1	large carrot, thinly sliced	1
6 cups	chicken stock	1.5 L
$\frac{1}{2}$	head romaine lettuce, sliced, or $\frac{1}{2}$ pkg (10 oz/284 g) fresh spinach	$\frac{1}{2}$
$1\frac{1}{4}$ cups	frozen peas, thawed	300 mL
1 cup	sliced mushrooms (about 4 large)	250 mL
$\frac{1}{2}$ tsp	salt	2 mL
	Pepper	
Pinch	nutmeg	Pinch
$\frac{1}{3}$ cup	finely chopped fresh parsley	75 mL
1 tsp	dried dillweed or 2 tbsp/ 25 mL chopped fresh dill	5 mL

In large saucepan, combine onion, celery, garlic, beans, carrot and chicken stock. Bring to a boil; cover, reduce heat and simmer (at a low boil) for 15 minutes or until vegetables are tender. Add lettuce, peas and mushrooms; cook until tender, 3 to 5 minutes. Add salt, pepper to taste, nutmeg, parsley and dill. Serve hot. (Soup may also be puréed in food processor or blender and served warm or cold. Makes 8 servings (about $1\frac{1}{4}$ cups/300 mL each).

Calories per servings: **74**
Grams fat per serving: 1.3
Fiber: Excellent
Vitamins A and C and niacin: Excellent
Iron: Good

LEEK AND POTATO SOUP

The base for this delicious soup freezes well; just thaw, add cream and serve hot or cold for a first course at a dinner party. For a lunch main course, top soup with garlic croutons and baby shrimp and chopped chives or green onions.

6	medium leeks	6
1	clove garlic, minced	1
4	medium potatoes, peeled, cubed	4
8 cups	chicken stock	2 L
1 cup	light cream	250 mL
	Salt and freshly ground pepper	
3 tbsp	minced fresh parsley or chives	45 mL

Variation:
Family-Style Leek and Potato Soup: Omit the cream and double the potatoes (don't peel them or you will lose fiber). Serve without puréeing. Leftovers can be puréed and frozen. You can also add any other vegetables such as carrots, green beans and broccoli to this soup.

Trim all but about 2 inches/5 cm of green part from leeks. Cut lengthwise halfway into white part. Spread apart and wash under cold running water. Slice thinly by hand or in food processor.

In saucepan, combine leeks, garlic, potatoes and chicken stock; simmer, partially covered, for 30 minutes or until vegetables are tender. Purée in blender or food processor. (Soup can be prepared ahead to this point; let cool, transfer to freezer containers and freeze. Reheat gently before continuing with recipe.)

Just before serving, reheat soup; add cream, and salt and pepper to taste. Remove from heat. Sprinkle with parsley. Makes 12 servings (about 1 cup/250 mL each).

Calories per serving: 91
Grams fat per serving: 3
Vitamin C and niacin: Good

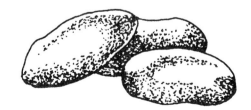

SUMMER GARDEN ITALIAN SOUP WITH PESTO

Pesto, a pungent Italian sauce made with fresh basil and garlic, adds exquisite flavor to soups, pasta and vegetable dishes. This version has less oil than most, without any loss in flavor. If fresh basil isn't available, substitute ¾ cup / 175 mL fresh flat-leafed Italian parsley and 2 tsp / 10 mL dried basil. The flavor isn't the same but is quite acceptable. Add pesto sauce directly to soup before serving, or top each serving with a spoonful.

Pasta with Pesto Sauce: If making pesto to serve with pasta, use pasta cooking liquid instead of soup liquid and add enough to make sauce thick, yet pourable. Spoon about 1 tbsp/ 15 mL over each serving of hot drained pasta and toss to mix.

Compare:
This pesto sauce has less than half the amount of fat of most pesto recipes.

1 cup	dried white beans	250 mL
1 tbsp	vegetable oil	15 mL
2	onions, coarsely chopped	2
3	tomatoes, peeled, seeded and chopped, or 2 cups/ 500 mL canned, chopped	3
4	carrots, thinly sliced	4
2	potatoes, coarsely chopped	2
4	leeks (white part only), coarsely chopped (optional)	4
2	large stalks celery (with leaves), coarsely chopped	2
2 cups	sliced green beans	500 mL
1	medium zucchini, coarsely chopped	1
¾ cup	broken egg noodles or spaghetti	175 mL
	Salt and freshly ground pepper	
Pesto:		
2	large cloves garlic	2
¾ cup	fresh basil leaves (or fresh parsley leaves, plus 2 tsp/10 mL dried basil)	175 mL
½ cup	grated Parmesan cheese	125 mL
2 tbsp	olive oil	25 mL
¼ cup	(approx) hot soup liquid	50 mL

Soak beans in water overnight and drain, or cover beans with cold water and bring to a boil, remove from heat and let stand for 1 hour, then drain.

In saucepan, combine beans with enough water to cover; bring to a boil. Reduce heat and simmer, covered, until beans are tender, about 1 hour; drain.

In skillet, heat oil over medium heat; add onions and cook, stirring, until tender, 6 to 8 minutes. Add tomatoes (if using fresh) and cook until soft, 3 to 4 minutes.

In large pot, bring 8 cups/2 L water to a boil. Add carrots, potatoes, leeks, celery, onion mixture and tomatoes (if using canned); simmer for 15 minutes.

Add green beans, zucchini, egg noodles and cooked white beans; simmer until vegetables are tender, 10 to 15 minutes, adding more water if needed. Add salt and pepper to taste.

Pesto: In food processor, combine garlic and basil; process until chopped. Add Parmesan and olive oil and process until smooth. Add enough warm soup liquid to make mixture the consistency of mayonnaise.

Ladle soup into bowls. Top each serving with a spoonful of pesto. Makes 10 servings (about $1\frac{1}{3}$ cups/325 mL each).

Calories per serving: 162
Grams fat per serving: 5
Fiber: Excellent
Vitamins A and C: Excellent
Iron and niacin: Good

NOVA SCOTIA SEAFOOD CHOWDER

Serve as a main course, along with crusty rolls and a tossed green salad, for an après-ski dinner buffet or an after-theater party. You can make it early in the day to give the flavors a chance to develop. To save time, chop onions, celery and carrots in a food processor.

2 tbsp	butter	25 mL
1 cup	chopped onions	250 mL
2 cups	chicken stock or clam juice	500 mL
1 cup	chopped celery	250 mL
3	carrots, coarsely chopped	3
1 tsp	salt	5 mL
	Freshly ground pepper	
1 lb	haddock fillets	500 g
2 cups	whole milk	500 mL
$\frac{1}{3}$ cup	all-purpose flour	75 mL
1	can (5 oz/142 g) clams, undrained	1
$\frac{1}{4}$ lb	cooked small shrimp or lobster meat	125 g

In large saucepan or soup kettle, melt butter; add onions and cook over low heat for a few minutes until soft. Stir in chicken stock, celery, carrots, salt, and pepper to taste. Bring to a boil; reduce heat and simmer, uncovered, for 20 minutes or until carrots are tender. Add fillets, cover and cook for 5 minutes longer. (The chowder may be prepared ahead to this point and frozen; thaw and reheat before continuing with recipe.)

Stir about half of the milk into the flour to make a smooth mixture. Gradually stir mixture into soup, then stir in remaining milk and simmer until soup thickens slightly. Just before serving, stir in clams and shrimp; heat through. Taste and adjust seasonings. Makes 6 servings (about $1\frac{1}{4}$ cups/300 mL each).

Calories per serving: 225
Grams fat per serving: 6
Calcium: Good
Vitamin A and niacin: Excellent

VEGETABLE BORSCHT

Serve small portions of this colorful, bursting-with-flavor soup for a first course, or larger servings for a main course. Any leftover soup may be frozen.

Diet Hint: Sour cream versus yogurt
Sour cream, the traditional garnish for borscht, has 2.5 grams fat per 1 tbsp/15 mL. If serving this soup as a main course, or as part of a meatless meal, the fat content is probably not significant, and sour cream may be used. If not, either omit the sour cream, or use plain yogurt which has a negligible amount of fat per 1 tbsp/15 mL.

1	onion, chopped	1
2	large fresh beets, peeled and chopped	2
1	medium carrot, sliced	1
1	large potato, peeled and cubed	1
4 cups	beef or chicken stock	1 L
$\frac{1}{4}$	small head cabbage, shredded	$\frac{1}{4}$
1	tomato, chopped	1
2 tbsp	chopped fresh parsley	25 mL
$\frac{1}{2}$ tsp	dried dillweed	2 mL
1 tsp	salt	5 mL
	Freshly ground pepper	
1 tsp	lemon juice	5 mL
Garnish:		
3 tbsp	sour cream or plain yogurt	45 mL

In large saucepan, combine onion, beets, carrot, potato and stock. Bring to a boil; cover and simmer for 30 minutes, skimming foam if necessary. Add cabbage, tomato, parsley and dill; simmer for 30 minutes longer, or until vegetables are tender. Season with salt, pepper to taste and lemon juice. Top each serving with 1 tsp/5 mL of sour cream. Makes 8 servings (1 cup/250 mL each).

Calories per serving: 53
Grams fat per serving: 1.4
Fiber: Good
Vitamins A and C: Good

TOMATO-BEAN CHOWDER

This comforting soup is hearty enough for a cold winter day, yet light enough for a summer supper.

4	onions, finely chopped	4
2 tsp	chili powder	10 mL
1	green pepper, seeded and chopped	1
1	can (28 oz/796 mL) tomatoes, undrained	1
4 cups	beef or vegetable stock	1 L
1	can (19 oz/540 mL) red kidney beans, drained	1
1	can (19 oz/540 mL) chick-peas, drained	1
	Salt and freshly ground pepper	
Garnish:		
$\frac{1}{2}$ cup	finely chopped fresh parsley	125 mL

In large, heavy saucepan, combine onions, chili powder, green pepper, tomatoes and stock; bring to boil, reduce heat and simmer for 15 minutes. Break up tomatoes with back of spoon. Add drained beans and peas; simmer for 10 minutes. Add salt and pepper to taste. Garnish each serving with a sprinkling of parsley. Makes 10 servings (1 cup/250 mL each).

Calories per serving: 233
Grams fat per serving: 2.6
Fiber: Excellent
Vitamin C: Excellent
Iron, vitamin A, phosphorus and niacin: Good

TRI-COLOR BEAN SOUP

This hearty soup is a meal on its own. Serve with homemade bread and a crisp salad.

Rush-Hour Family Dinner
Tri-Color Bean Soup (page 51)
Spinach Supper Salad (page 75)
Whole-wheat rolls
Fresh fruit

*If unavailable, substitute kidney beans, baby lima beans, black-eyed peas or flageolets.

2	large onions, sliced	2
3	cloves garlic, minced	3
4 cups	water	1 L
2	potatoes, cubed	2
3	carrots, cut in $\frac{1}{4}$-inch/5 mm slices	3
1	can (19 oz/540 mL) pinto beans, drained*	1
1	can (19 oz/540 mL) kidney beans, baby lima beans, black-eyed peas or flageolets, drained	1
1	can (19 oz/540 mL) garbanzo beans (chick-peas), drained	1
1 tsp	oregano	5 mL
2 tsp	basil	10 mL
	Salt and freshly ground pepper	

In large saucepan, combine onions, garlic, water, potatoes and carrots; bring to a boil, cover and simmer for 20 minutes or until vegetables are tender. Add all beans, oregano, basil, and salt and pepper to taste. Simmer for 5 to 10 minutes to blend flavors. Makes 12 servings (1 cup/250 mL each).

Calories per serving: 120
Grams fat per serving: 1.6
Fiber: Excellent
Iron and vitamin A: Good

PORTUGUESE COLLARD SOUP

Collard greens are similar in shape to large beet greens but look like dark green, flat cabbage leaves with coarse stems. This soup is so popular in Portugal, the grocery stores sell plastic bags full of thinly sliced collard leaves.

5	large potatoes, peeled and coarsely chopped	5
1	large carrot, cut in thin slices	1
6 cups	water	1.5 L
14	large collard leaves	14
2 oz	chorizo* (sweet smoked pork sausage), about $3\frac{1}{2}$ inches/ 9 cm long	60 g
2 tbsp	olive oil	25 mL
2 tsp	salt	10 mL

In saucepan, combine potatoes, carrot and water; simmer over medium heat until tender. Use a hand-held blender and purée in pot until smooth. (Alternatively, use slotted spoon to transfer potatoes and carrots to food processor, then blend until smooth. Return potato mixture to pan with cooking liquid and stir until combined.)

Remove tough stems from collard leaves. Thinly slice leaves in food processor or by hand into ⅛-inch/2 mm or less strips. (Roll up 4 or 5 leaves, put into food processor and slice crosswise.) You should have about 8 cups/2 L lightly packed sliced collard leaves.

Peel casing from sausage; slice sausage as thinly as possible (1/16 inch/1 mm thick). Add sliced collard leaves and sausage to soup; stir. Simmer, uncovered, for 10 minutes. Add oil and salt. If soup is too thick, add more water. Makes 10 servings (about 1 cup/250 mL each).

Calories per serving: 185
Grams fat per serving: 6.7
Fiber: Excellent
Vitamins A and C: Excellent
Thiamine, calcium and iron: Good

Variation:
Spinach Soup:
Substitute 1 package
(10 oz/284 g) fresh spinach,
thinly sliced, for the collard.

*Chorizo sausages are available in many European meat stores or delicatessens. Sweet means they are not hot and spicy. If chorizo sausages aren't available, use a small pepperoni instead.

For a very low-fat diet, omit oil. Soup will taste fine.

Brown or Red Lentils—Is there a difference?

Yes. When cooked, red lentils are soft, while brown lentils retain their shape. Use red lentils for soups, and dishes (such as patties) where you want the lentils to be soft. Use brown lentils in salads, or in dishes where you want the lentils to retain their shape.

When cooked in a soup, red lentils turn an attractive yellow. Brown lentils are unappealing in soups, unless used in a small amount and combined with other vegetables.

Because lentils are a good source of protein they are often included in meatless meals. One cup /250 mL of lentils is an excellent source of fiber.

RED LENTIL SOUP

Serve this easy-to-make soup with grilled cheese sandwiches or a salad for a quick meal. Be sure to use red lentils, not brown ones, in this soup.

1	pkg (8 oz/250 g) dried red lentils (about 1 cup/250 mL)	1
3	onions, coarsely chopped	3
5 cups	water	1250 mL
1	bay leaf	1
1	large clove garlic, minced	1
1 tsp	dried thyme (or 1 tbsp/15 mL chopped fresh)	5 mL
3	carrots, scraped and thinly sliced	3
3 tbsp	chopped fresh parsley	45 mL
	Salt and freshly ground pepper	

Wash and drain lentils. In large saucepan, combine lentils, onions, water, bay leaf and garlic. Cover and simmer for 1 hour. Add thyme and carrots; simmer, covered, for 30 minutes longer, or until carrots are tender and lentils are soft. Remove bay leaf. Add parsley, and salt and pepper to taste. Serve hot. Makes 8 servings ($\frac{3}{4}$ cup/175 mL each).

Calories per serving: 96
Grams fat per serving: 0.9
Fiber: Good
Vitamin A: Excellent

FISH CHOWDER, FAMILY STYLE

Any fresh or frozen fillets can be used in this recipe, but try monk-fish if it's available. It's sometimes called lobster fish, because it tastes so much like lobster.

2 tbsp	butter	25 mL
1	onion, finely chopped	1
3	potatoes, diced	3
1	carrot, finely chopped	1
2 cups	water	500 mL
2 cups	milk	500 mL
1 lb	monkfish or other fish fillets (fresh or frozen)	500 g
1 cup	kernel corn	250 mL
1 tsp	salt	5 mL
$\frac{1}{8}$ tsp	freshly ground pepper	0.5 mL
	Chopped fresh parsley	

Super Supper
Fish Chowder, Family Style
(page 54)
Whole-wheat buns
Tossed salad
Fresh fruit

In heavy saucepan, melt butter; add onion, potatoes and carrot, and cook over medium heat, stirring occasionally, for 5 minutes. Add water; cover and simmer until vegetables are nearly tender, about 15 minutes.

Stir in milk, fish (if using monkfish, cut into chunks) and corn; simmer for 5 to 10 minutes, or until fish flakes and is opaque. Add salt, pepper, and parsley to taste. Makes about 6 cups/1.5 L ($1\frac{1}{2}$ cups/375 mL main-course serving; $\frac{3}{4}$ cup/175 mL appetizer serving).

Calories per main-course serving: 258
Grams fat per serving: 8
Fiber: Good
Vitamins A and C: Excellent
Calcium, phosphorus and niacin: Good

CURRIED APPLE AND ZUCCHINI SOUP

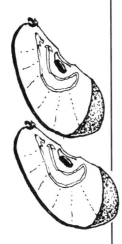

This light cream soup has a lovely delicate flavor. It's a good choice for a first course at a dinner party.

2 tbsp	margarine or butter	25 mL
1	large onion, chopped	1
1	apple, peeled, cored and chopped	1
1 to 2 tsp	curry powder	5 to 10 mL
4 cups	chicken stock	1 L
$\frac{1}{4}$ cup	uncooked rice	50 mL
2 cups	diced unpeeled zucchini ($\frac{1}{2}$ lb/225 g)	500 mL
$\frac{1}{2}$ tsp	salt	2 mL
1 cup	milk	250 mL

In saucepan, melt butter; sauté onion and apple until soft. Sprinkle with curry powder; cook, stirring, for a few seconds. Pour in chicken stock; bring to a boil. Add rice, zucchini and salt. Cover and cook until rice and zucchini are tender, about 30 minutes. Pour into blender and blend until smooth. Return to pan and add milk. Heat through. Serve hot. Makes 8 servings ($\frac{3}{4}$ cup/175 mL each).

Calories per serving: 79
Grams fat per serving: 1.9
Niacin: **Good**

CHICKEN AND LEEK CHOWDER

Here's a delicately flavored yet hearty soup. For a stew, simply thicken liquid with flour and add dumplings to top.

1	chicken (3 lb/1.5 kg)	1
1	onion, coarsely chopped	1
1	stalk celery, chopped	1
8 cups	water	2 L
10	black peppercorns	10
4	large leeks*	4
2	large potatoes, diced	2
3	medium carrots, sliced	3
2	large stalks celery, chopped	2
1 tbsp	chopped fresh thyme leaves or 1 tsp/5 mL dried	15 mL
1 tbsp	chopped fresh tarragon leaves or 1 tsp/5 mL dried	15 mL
1 tbsp	chopped fresh rosemary leaves or 1 tsp/5 mL dried	15 mL
2	bay leaves	2
1 cup	kernel corn (frozen or canned)	250 mL
1 cup	lima beans (frozen or canned)	250 mL
$\frac{1}{2}$ cup	vermicelli or broken spaghetti	125 mL
1 tbsp	butter	15 mL
$1\frac{1}{2}$ cups	milk	375 mL
$\frac{1}{3}$ cup	all-purpose flour	75 mL
$\frac{3}{4}$ cup	chopped fresh parsley	175 mL
2 tsp	salt	10 mL
	Freshly ground pepper	

*If leeks aren't available, substitute 3 onions instead.

Photo:

Balkan Beet Cream Soup (pages 36-7)

Remove as much fat as possible from chicken, and discard. In large saucepan or soup kettle, combine chicken, onion, 1 stalk celery, water and peppercorns. Bring to a boil; reduce heat, partially cover and simmer for 1 to $1\frac{1}{2}$ hours or until chicken is cooked. Let cool.

Remove chicken from pot and discard skin and bones; cut meat into bite-size pieces and set aside. Strain liquid and refrigerate. When cold, remove hardened fat from surface.

Trim leeks, leaving about 3 inches/8 cm, or tender part, of greens attached. Cut stalks in half lengthwise and wash thoroughly under running water, holding leaves apart. Slice crosswise into $\frac{1}{2}$-inch/1 cm slices. In large saucepan, combine leeks, potatoes, carrots and reserved chicken stock (from cooking chicken); bring to a boil and simmer for 15 minutes, stirring occasionally.

Add chopped celery and chicken meat to soup. Add thyme, tarragon, rosemary and bay leaves; simmer for 10 minutes. Add corn, beans and vermicelli; cook for 10 minutes longer, or until vegetables are tender.

Just before serving remove bay leaves and add butter. Stir enough of the milk into the flour to make a smooth, thin paste; gradually add to soup, stirring continuously. Add remaining milk, parsley, salt, and pepper to taste. Makes 10 large servings.

Calories per serving: 232
Grams fat per serving: 5.7
Fiber: Good
Niacin, vitamins A and C: Excellent
Iron: Good

Photo:

**Melon and Bean Salad
(page 72)**

CORN AND TOMATO CHOWDER WITH TARRAGON

*For a completely different but appealing flavor, substitute 1 tsp/5 mL each curry powder and cumin for the tarragon.

Fresh tarragon is a delicious addition to this soup. If it isn't available, but other fresh herbs are, use them instead (try basil, rosemary or oregano). If you can't find any fresh herbs, use dried tarragon. Serve soup hot or cold.

1 tbsp	butter	15 mL
¼ cup	chopped onion	50 mL
1	clove garlic, minced	1
2 tbsp	all-purpose flour	25 mL
1	can (19 oz/540 mL) tomatoes (undrained)	1
2	potatoes, diced	2
1 cup	chicken stock	250 mL
2 cups	milk	500 mL
2 cups	kernel corn (canned, frozen or from cooked cob)	500 mL
1 tbsp	chopped fresh tarragon	15 mL
2 tbsp	chopped fresh parsley	25 mL
2 tbsp	chopped fresh chives or green onions	25 mL
	Salt and freshly ground pepper	

In heavy saucepan, melt butter; add onion and garlic and cook over medium heat until tender. Sprinkle flour into pan and mix well. Stir in tomatoes and bring to a boil, stirring. Add potatoes and stock; boil gently for 15 minutes, or until potatoes are tender.

In separate saucepan or in microwave oven, heat milk until hot but not boiling; pour into tomato mixture and stir in corn.

Just before serving, stir in tarragon, parsley, chives, and salt and pepper to taste. Makes 10 servings (¾ cup/175 mL each).

Calories per serving: 88
Grams fat per serving: 2.3
Fiber: Good
Vitamin C: Excellent
Vitamin A: Good

BUTTERMILK-CUCUMBER BISQUE

A refreshing beginning to a dinner or a picnic, this cream soup is low in calories and fat.

1	English cucumber	1
$\frac{1}{2}$ tsp	salt	2 mL
$1\frac{1}{4}$ cups	buttermilk	300 mL
$1\frac{1}{4}$ cups	chicken stock	300 mL
2 tbsp	minced green onion or fresh chives	25 mL
$\frac{1}{4}$ cup	chopped fresh parsley	50 mL
	Freshly ground pepper	
Garnish:	Thin slices of unpeeled cucumber	
	Cooked shrimp (optional)	

Peel cucumber only if skin is tough; remove seeds and chop cucumber by hand or in food processor. Place in colander; sprinkle with salt. Let drain for 30 minutes; pat dry.

In pitcher or large bowl, combine buttermilk, chicken stock, onion, parsley, pepper to taste and cucumber. Refrigerate for 2 to 8 hours. Taste and adjust seasoning if necessary. To serve, ladle into bowls; garnish with cucumber slice and a few shrimp if using. Makes 4 servings (about 1 cup/250 mL each).

Calories per serving: 46
Grams fat per serving: 1.1

SALADS

Salads are achieving a new status in our meals and deservedly so. Rock-hard tomatoes and flavorless iceberg lettuce are finally being pushed aside by crisp romaine and tender buttery Boston lettuce. We now have so many wonderful fresh ingredients to work with that there has been a break-through in imaginative combinations of foods—the Melon and Bean Salad (page 72) is absolutely delicious. In fact, we could feast on salads for months and never taste the same one twice. Red radicchio lettuce and nutty arugula are special treats to excite your palate. Pasta salads (now much more than macaroni with mayonnaise), Greek Salad, Chick-Pea with Red Onion and Tomato, plus many others, are delicious as a main course as well as a side salad.

Moreover, health-conscious gourmets realize that salads are a good way to get fiber, vitamins and minerals into our diet. When combined with high-fiber vegetables, such as spinach, beans and chick-peas, and tossed with a low-fat dressing, such as Yogurt-Basil (page 85) or Blue Cheese Dressing (page 84), they are low in calories and fat, and high in fiber. This follows the Canadian Cancer Society's recommendations for a low-fat, high-fiber diet.

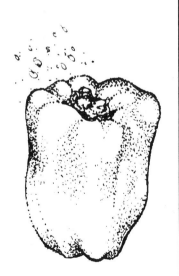

ROASTED RED PEPPER, MUSHROOM AND MELON SALAD

Roasted peppers have a rich, delicious flavor and a soft, yet still firm, texture. If time is short, use the peppers raw. This salad is spectacular as an appetizer or for lunch. Increase the shrimp and serve as a main-course salad for a light supper.

1	large sweet red pepper	1
1	head Boston lettuce	1
1	honeydew melon or cantaloupe	1
12	white mushrooms	12
2	tomatoes, sliced	2
$\frac{1}{2}$ lb	cooked salad shrimp (optional)	250 g
1 cup	Orange Vinaigrette (page 84)	250 mL

Place red pepper on a baking sheet; roast in 375°F/190°C oven for 18 minutes; turn and roast on other side for 18 minutes longer, or until pepper is soft and blistered. Place pepper in paper or plastic bag; close bag and let pepper steam for 10 minutes. Using fingers and small knife, peel skin from pepper (it should come off easily); seed pepper and cut into strips.

Wash lettuce leaves; dry in spinner or with paper towels and refrigerate until needed. Cut melon in half; discard seeds. Peel and cut melon into wedges. Slice mushrooms.

Line 8 individual salad plates with lettuce leaves. Arrange wedges of melon in center; place red pepper strips on top of melon, mushrooms on one side, tomato slices on other and shrimp (if using) over remaining lettuce. Drizzle Orange Vinaigrette over each salad. Makes 8 appetizer servings.

Calories per serving: 82
Grams fat per serving: 0.8
Fiber: Good
Vitamin C: Excellent
Vitamin A, iron and niacin: Good

SPINACH AND RED CABBAGE SALAD WITH BLUE CHEESE DRESSING

Red cabbage on dark green spinach is a striking color combination. Team it with Blue Cheese Dressing (page 84) to add extra flavor and a creamy texture.

3 cups	packed spinach leaves (5 oz/140 g)	750 mL
1 cup	grated red cabbage	250 mL
$\frac{2}{3}$ cup	Blue Cheese Dressing	150 mL

Wash spinach; discard tough ends and tear large leaves into 2 or 3 pieces. Just before serving, toss spinach with cabbage and dressing. (Alternatively, line individual plates with spinach, arrange cabbage in rings on top. Place spoonful of dressing in center of each plate.) Makes 4 servings (about 1 cup/250 mL each).

Calories per serving: 56
Grams fat per serving: 2
Fiber: Good
Vitamins A and C: Excellent

Menu-Planning Tip for Busy Cooks

Once a week, make a large amount of a hearty soup, such as Tri-Color Bean Soup (page 51), Summer Garden Italian Vegetable Soup with Pesto (page 46) or Nova Scotia Seafood Chowder (page 48), and a salad that keeps well, such as Bermuda Bean Salad (pages 78-9), Tabbouleh (page 64) or Chick-Pea Salad with Red Onion and Tomato (page 78). Along with thick fresh bread or toast, you'll be ready for rush-hour meals. Or serve either the salad or the soup with open-face grilled sandwiches, such as mozzarella on whole-wheat buns sprinkled with oregano for a fast, nutritious meal.

BROCCOLI BUFFET SALAD

Serve this colorful winter salad as a first course, or as a main course with an omelet, soup or grilled meat or chicken. It's ideal for a buffet table because you can make it ahead. For a variation, make the salad with Tomato-French Dressing (page 86) instead of the vinaigrette.

Winter Family Supper
Broccoli Buffet Salad (page 62)
Omelet à la Jardinière
(page 135)
Old-Fashioned Molasses Bread
(page 180)
Cinnamon Applesauce
(page 219)

1	bunch broccoli (1 lb/500 g)	1
1	red onion, thinly sliced and separated into rings	1
$\frac{1}{4}$ lb	small mushrooms	125 g
$\frac{1}{4}$ lb	feta cheese, crumbled	125 g
2 tbsp	toasted sliced almonds	25 mL
Vinaigrette Dressing:		
2 tbsp	olive oil	25 mL
2 tbsp	lemon juice	25 mL
3 tbsp	water	45 mL
1	clove garlic, minced	1
$\frac{1}{2}$ tsp	oregano	2 mL
	Salt and freshly ground pepper	

Trim ends of broccoli. Cut into florets. Peel stalks and cut into 1-inch/12.5 cm long strips about $\frac{1}{4}$ inch/5 mm wide. You should have about 6 $\frac{1}{2}$ cups/1.5 L of broccoli.

In large pot of rapidly boiling water, cook broccoli for 2 minutes; drain, and refresh under cold running water to prevent further cooking and to set color; drain and dry with paper towels. (If preparing a day in advance, do not cook broccoli; use raw.)

In salad bowl, toss broccoli with onion, mushrooms and cheese.

Vinaigrette Dressing: Combine oil, lemon juice, water, garlic and oregano; mix well. Pour over vegetables and toss to mix. Season with salt and pepper to taste. Toss again. Sprinkle almonds over top. Serve immediately, or cover and refrigerate for up to 3 hours. Stir before serving. Makes about 8 servings (1 cup/250 mL each).

Calories per one-cup serving: 120
Grams fat per serving: 7.8
Fiber: Excellent
Calcium, phosphorus, riboflavin and niacin: Good
Vitamins A and C: Excellent

For Perfect Hard-Cooked Eggs:
For tender hard-cooked eggs without a dark ring, cover eggs with cold water and bring to a boil. Remove pan from heat; cover and let stand for 20 minutes before rinsing eggs in cold water. Hard-cooked eggs can be stored for up to 1 week in the refrigerator.

ARTICHOKE-TOMATO SALAD

Tasty chunks of artichoke heart combine with cucumbers, tomatoes and green onions for a sensational summer salad. Serve with soup or cheese and fresh bread for lunch or supper.

2 tbsp	red wine vinegar	25 mL
$\frac{1}{2}$ tsp	Dijon mustard	2 mL
1	clove garlic, minced	1
$\frac{1}{4}$ cup	vegetable or olive oil	50 mL
4	green onions, chopped	4
1	long seedless cucumber, cut in chunks	1
5	tomatoes, coarsely chopped	5
1	can (14 oz/398 mL) artichoke hearts, drained and quartered	1
2	hard-cooked eggs, grated or chopped	2
	Salt and freshly ground pepper	
	Lemon juice	

In large salad bowl, mix together vinegar, mustard and garlic. Gradually whisk in oil. Add following ingredients in layers: onions, cucumber, tomatoes and artichokes. Sprinkle eggs over top. Cover and refrigerate.

About 15 minutes before serving, toss salad and add salt, pepper and lemon juice to taste. Makes 6 large servings (about 1 cup/250 mL each).

Calories per serving: 134
Grams fat per serving: 10
Fiber: Good
Vitamin C: Excellent
Vitamin A: Good

	Per $3\frac{1}{2}$ oz/100g
Compare:	Grams fiber
Lettuce (iceberg, romaine or Boston)	1.5
Cabbage (red, green or Savoy)	3.4
Spinach	3.9

TABBOULEH

This Mediterranean salad is one of my favorite summer salads. It's delicious as part of a salad plate for picnics or lunches, and keeps well in the refrigerator. Bulgur, or cracked wheat, adds a nutty flavor and texture, and fresh mint lends a special touch. If mint isn't in season, simply omit it.

1 cup	bulgur (cracked wheat)	250 mL
$\frac{1}{3}$ cup	olive oil	75 mL
$\frac{1}{3}$ cup	lemon juice	75 mL
1 cup	finely chopped green onions	250 mL
2 cups	lightly packed chopped fresh parsley	500 mL
$\frac{1}{4}$ cup	chopped fresh mint	50 mL
3	tomatoes, diced	3
1	cucumber, peeled, seeded and chopped	1
1 tsp	salt	5 mL
	Freshly ground pepper	

Soak bulgur in enough warm water to cover for 1 hour; drain well. Toss with oil, lemon juice, onions, parsley, mint, tomatoes and cucumber. Cover and refrigerate for at least 1 hour or overnight. Add salt, and pepper to taste. Makes 10 servings (about $\frac{2}{3}$ cup/150 mL each).

Calories per serving: 148
Grams fat per serving: 7
Fiber: Good
Vitamins A and C: Excellent

Picnic Salad Supper
White Kidney Bean Salad
(page 74)
Pasta Salad with Sweet Peppers
and Dill (page 80)
Tabbouleh (page 64)
Whole-wheat pita bread
Fresh peaches

Bulgur and Cracked Wheat
Bulgur and cracked wheat add a new dimension in texture, a nutty flavor, good nutrients and fiber to dishes. They are both made from wheat berries and can be used interchangeably in most recipes. Cracked wheat is basically made from wheat berries that have been cracked, then coarsely milled. Bulgur is made from wheat berries that have been crushed, then either parboiled (European) or steamed (American), then dried. When made from club wheat or hard red winter wheat it has much more fiber than when it's made from white wheat. Three and a half ounces/100 grams of bulgur made from hard red winter wheat has 7 grams of dietary fiber.

Bulgur and cracked wheat are available in some supermarkets, but you can always find them in health food stores. Use in salads (Tabbouleh, page 64) or stuffings, or mix with other grains or vegetables. To cook, combine with twice as much water as grain and simmer bulgur for about 15 minutes, cracked wheat for about 25 minutes, or until tender but not mushy.

To Cook Beets:

Cut tops from beets, leaving at least 1 inch/2.5 cm of greens attached; don't trim off tapering root. (If beets are trimmed too close, color and vitamins are lost in the water.) Cook beets in boiling water or steam for 1 hour or longer or until beets are tender when pierced with a fork. Drain; under cold running water, slide off skins. Serve hot or let cool and add to salads.

Beet Greens

Don't throw out the beet tops. Cooked beet greens are an excellent source of vitamin A and folic acid, and a good source of vitamin C, riboflavin, calcium and fiber. They're delicious steamed, boiled or used instead of collard leaves in Portuguese Collard Soup (page 52).

Beet greens are best when cooked fresh from the garden or within a day or two of picking. They are prepared and cooked like spinach, but require a longer cooking time.

To prepare and cook beet greens: Cut off and discard tough stems or blemished leaves. Either steam in covered steamer over simmering water for 10 to 15 minutes or until wilted and tender, or boil, covered, in ½ inch/1 cm of water in large saucepan for 10 to 15 minutes or until tender. Drain, and season with salt, pepper, lemon juice and a dab of butter.

DANISH CUCUMBER SALAD

Danes serve this salad often, especially with chicken or as a topping for open-face sandwiches. Sprinkling the cucumbers with salt draws out the water and makes the cucumbers crisp. The dressing has virtually no fat. When I had this dish in Denmark, it was beautifully garnished with blue cornflowers.

2	English cucumbers	2
1 tbsp	salt	15 mL
1 cup	granulated sugar	250 mL
1 cup	vinegar	250 mL
	Salt and freshly ground pepper	
	Chopped fresh dill	

Thinly slice unpeeled cucumbers and place in bowl or sieve. Sprinkle with salt and let stand for 1 hour. Pour off liquid and pat dry; transfer to bowl.

In a small saucepan or microwave-safe dish, combine sugar and vinegar; stir over low heat or heat in microwave until sugar is dissolved; remove from heat and let cool. Pour over cucumbers; let stand for 30 to 60 minutes. Drain cucumbers; season with salt and pepper to taste. Garnish with chopped dill. Makes 6 to 8 servings.

Calories per serving: 40
Grams fat per serving: trace
Vitamin C: Good

* Available in some supermarkets and most specialty food
stores.

ARUGULA AND RADICCHIO SALAD WITH BALSAMIC VINAIGRETTE

*Arugula is a tender lettuce with a delightful buttery-nutty fla-
vor—it's very special and very expensive. Radicchio, a red leaf lettuce, is much like a small cabbage in appearance. Together they
make an elegant salad. The flavors are wonderful, so it isn't necessary to add a lot of other ingredients.*

1	small head radicchio	1
1	bunch arugula or lamb's lettuce	1
1	head Boston or Bibb lettuce	1
1	orange (optional)	1
$\frac{1}{4}$ cup	coarsely chopped fresh parsley	50 mL
2 tbsp	balsamic vinegar *	25 mL
2 tbsp	olive oil	25 mL
	Salt and freshly ground pepper	

Separate lettuce leaves and wash thoroughly. Spin, or
pat dry on paper towels. Wrap and refrigerate until serving
time. Cut off rind and white pith from orange (if using), cut
into thin slices.

Just before serving, tear lettuces into large pieces. Combine with orange slices in glass salad bowl. (Alternatively,
arrange lettuce on individual salad plates. Arrange orange
slices on top.) Sprinkle with parsley, vinegar, oil, salt and
pepper, and toss to mix. Makes 6 servings.

Calories per serving: 56
Grams fat per serving: 4
Vitamin C: Excellent
Vitamin A: Good

JULIENNE VEGETABLE SALAD WITH LEMON VINAIGRETTE

White or yellow turnip or tender parsnips cut into julienne, or matchstick-size, strips are delicious additions to this salad.

1 cup	julienne strips of carrot	250 mL
1 cup	julienne strips of zucchini	250 mL
1 cup	green beans, in $1\frac{1}{2}$-inch/ 4 cm lengths	250 mL
1 cup	julienne strips of celery	250 mL
	Salt and freshly ground pepper	
Lemon Vinaigrette:		
1 tbsp	olive or walnut oil	15 mL
$\frac{1}{4}$ cup	lemon juice	50 mL
2 tbsp	chopped fresh parsley	25 mL
2 tbsp	chopped green onion tops or fresh chives	25 mL
1	clove garlic, minced	1

In bowl, combine carrot, zucchini, green beans and celery.

Lemon Vinaigrette: In small bowl, combine oil, lemon juice, parsley, green onions and garlic; mix thoroughly. Pour over vegetables and toss to mix. Add salt and pepper to taste. Cover and refrigerate until serving time. Makes 6 servings ($\frac{2}{3}$ cup/150 mL each).

Calories per serving: 45
Grams fat per serving: 2.4
Fiber: Good
Vitamins A and C: Excellent

Making the Most of Salad Oils
1 tbsp/15 mL oil contains 14 grams of fat, so use it sparingly. A heavier oil, such as olive or walnut, gives more of an oil flavor.

COLESLAW WITH APPLE AND ONION

This is a good everyday summer salad, using new-crop, mild-flavored, crisp cabbage, and a fine winter salad when lettuce and tomatoes aren't plentiful or flavorful.

To reduce the fat content and to give a lighter flavor and texture, substitute low-fat yogurt for mayonnaise in salad dressing recipes, or use half yogurt and half sour cream.

2 cups	finely shredded cabbage	500 mL
1	medium carrot, grated	1
$\frac{1}{2}$	green pepper, chopped	$\frac{1}{2}$
1	apple, chopped	1
2	green onions, chopped	2
	Salt and freshly ground pepper	
Yogurt Dressing:		
3 tbsp	plain yogurt	45 mL
2 tbsp	sour cream	25 mL
1 tbsp	mayonnaise	15 mL
1 tsp	lemon juice	5 mL
$\frac{1}{4}$ tsp	dillweed	1 mL

    In serving bowl, combine cabbage, carrot, green pepper, apple and onions.

    Yogurt Dressing: Combine yogurt, sour cream, mayonnaise, lemon juice and dillweed; mix well. Pour over salad and toss to mix. Add salt and pepper to taste. Makes 4 servings (about $\frac{1}{2}$ cup/125 mL each).

Calories per serving: 70
Grams fat per serving: 2.7
Fiber: Good
Vitamin A: Excellent
Vitamin C: Good

TOMATO RAITA

Raita is an East Indian type of salad. Delicious with curries, it adds a colorful note to the meal.

1	medium cucumber	1
1 tsp	salt	5 mL
2	medium tomatoes	2
1 tbsp	finely chopped onion	15 mL
1 cup	plain yogurt	250 mL
$\frac{1}{4}$ cup	chopped fresh parsley	50 mL
2 tbsp	chopped fresh coriander or cilantro	25 mL
1 tsp	cumin	5 mL

Peel cucumber. Cut in half lengthwise and remove seeds. Cut into thin slices by hand or in food processor; sprinkle with salt and let stand for about 40 minutes. Drain cucumber, squeezing slightly to remove excess liquid.

Core tomatoes; cut into $\frac{1}{2}$-inch/1 cm cubes. Toss together tomatoes, cucumber and onion; drain off any liquid. Combine yogurt, parsley, coriander and cumin; pour over vegetables and mix with a spoon. Cover, and refrigerate until ready to serve. Makes 4 servings (about $\frac{3}{4}$ cup/175 mL each).

Calories per serving: 59
Grams fat per serving: 0.3
Calcium : Good
Vitamin C: Excellent
Vitamin A: Good

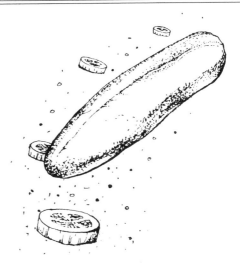

RED POTATO SALAD WITH SOUR CREAM AND CHIVES

Red-skinned potatoes add color, but any kind of new potato can be used. Be sure to leave the skin on, for additional flavor and fiber. Sour cream and yogurt combine to make a light yet creamy dressing that is much lower in fat than traditional mayonnaise.

6	medium-large red-skinned potatoes	6
$\frac{1}{2}$ cup	sour cream	125 mL
$\frac{1}{2}$ cup	plain yogurt	125 mL
$\frac{1}{4}$ cup	finely chopped fresh chives or green onions	50 mL
1 tsp	salt	5 mL
	Freshly ground pepper	

Scrub potatoes (don't peel). If large, cut in half or in quarters. Boil potatoes in their skins until fork-tender; drain. Shake pan over medium heat for a few seconds to dry potatoes. Cut into $\frac{1}{2}$-inch/1 cm cubes; let cool.

Combine sour cream, yogurt and chives; toss with potatoes. Add salt, and pepper to taste. Refrigerate until serving. Makes 10 servings ($\frac{1}{2}$ cup/125 mL each).

Calories per serving: 130
Grams fat per serving: 4
Fiber: Good
Vitamin C: Excellent

Compare:

	Per $\frac{1}{2}$ cup/125 mL	
	Calories	Grams fat
Potato salad made with:		
mayonnaise	235	18
yogurt and sour cream	130	4

CHICKEN AND MELON SALAD

For an elegant but easy lunch, serve this delicious main-course salad. The chicken can be cooked and all ingredients chopped a day in advance; then simply assemble the salad before serving. Instead of grapes or honeydew melon, you can substitute other melons, papaya, pineapple, mushrooms or water chestnuts.

*For 6 cups/1.5 L cubed cooked chicken, use two 2½-lb/1.25 kg roasting chickens or 8 chicken breasts. To cook whole chicken in microwave oven, put chicken in microwave dish, cover dish with plastic wrap, folding back corner to vent steam. Microwave on High for about 17 minutes or until juices run clear when thigh is pierced. To cook conventionally, simmer whole chicken in water to cover for 1 hour or until tender, skimming off scum occasionally.

1	small honeydew melon or canteloupe	1
6 cups	cubed cooked chicken*	1.5 L
2 cups	chopped celery	500 mL
2 cups	seedless green or red grapes	500 mL
1 cup	sliced water chestnuts (optional)	250 mL
½ cup	sour cream	125 mL
½ cup	plain yogurt	125 mL
1½ tsp	curry powder	7 mL
	Salt and freshly ground pepper	

Cut melon in half and remove seeds. With melon baller, scoop out pulp (alternatively, cut into cubes). In large bowl, combine melon balls, chicken, celery, grapes, and water chestnuts (if using).

In small bowl, mix together sour cream, yogurt and curry powder; stir gently into salad. Season with salt and pepper to taste. Makes 10 servings (about 1 cup/250 mL each).

Calories per serving: 237
Grams fat per serving: 6
Vitamin C and niacin: Excellent
Phosphorus: Good

MELON AND BEAN SALAD

Red kidney beans, juicy melon balls and strips of sweet red pepper are a delicious combination that will perk up any meal from cold turkey to meat loaf and sandwiches.

1	cantaloupe or honeydew melon	1
1	can (19 oz/540 mL) red or white kidney beans, drained	1
2	green onions (including tops)	2
1	small red pepper	1
1	clove garlic, minced	1
2 tbsp	chopped fresh parsley	25 mL
2 tbsp	lemon juice	25 mL
2 tbsp	olive oil	25 mL
	Salt and freshly ground pepper	

Cut melon in half, scoop out seeds. With melon baller, scoop out pulp (alternatively, cut into cubes). You should have at least 2 cups/500 mL. Place melon balls in salad bowl and toss with kidney beans. Cut onions and red pepper into thin strips about 1 to $1\frac{1}{2}$ inches/2.5 to 4 cm long; add onion, peppers, garlic and parsley to melon-kidney bean mixture; toss to mix.

Whisk together lemon juice and oil; pour over salad. Add salt and pepper to taste; toss to mix. Cover and refrigerate until serving time. (Salad may be refrigerated for up to 3 days.) Makes 8 servings (about $\frac{1}{2}$ cup/125 mL each).

Calories per serving: 114
Grams fat per serving: 3
Fiber: Excellent
Vitamins A and C: Excellent

CRACKED WHEAT WITH PEAS AND ONIONS

Serve this as a salad or instead of a starchy vegetable such as potatoes. It's good with beef, chicken and fish. Bulgur, or cracked wheat, is available at some supermarkets and most health food stores. Sesame oil is used for flavor, but taste the dish first, and if you like it without oil, then omit it altogether.

$\frac{3}{4}$ cup	bulgur (cracked wheat)	175 mL
2 cups	green peas (fresh or frozen)	500 mL
$\frac{1}{2}$ cup	chopped green onions	125 mL
3 tbsp	lemon juice	45 mL
$\frac{1}{2}$ cup	chopped fresh parsley	125 mL
	Salt and freshly ground pepper	
1 tbsp	sesame oil	15 mL

Pour enough boiling water over bulgur to cover by at least 1 inch/2.5 cm; let stand for 20 to 30 minutes or until tender and doubled in volume. Drain throughly, pressing out excess water. Cook peas in boiling water for 1 minute; drain.

In salad bowl, combine bulgur, peas, onions, lemon juice, parsley, and salt and pepper to taste. Sprinkle with oil and toss to mix. Serve cold or at room temperature. Makes 8 servings ($\frac{1}{2}$ cup/125 mL each).

Calories per serving: 125
Grams fat per serving: 2
Fiber: Excellent
Vitamin C: Excellent

WHITE KIDNEY BEAN SALAD

Summer Salad Plate
White Kidney Bean Salad
(page 74)
Devilled eggs
Spinach greens with Butter-
milk Herb Dressing (page 82)

Jiffy White Kidney Bean Salad
Keep a can of white kidney beans on hand for a salad you can make at a moment's notice. Toss 1 can (19 oz/540 mL) well-drained white kidney beans with 2 tbsp/25 mL olive oil, 2 cloves garlic, minced, 1 cup/250 mL chopped fresh parsley, and salt, pepper and lemon juice to taste. Makes 4 servings.

10-Minute August Supper
Corn on the cob
Sliced tomatoes
Jiffy White Kidney Bean Salad
(page 74)
Whole-wheat bread
Fresh blueberries or peaches
Milk

Cannellini or white kidney beans make a delicious salad when teamed with summer garden vegetables. Add cucumber and tomato and you have a salad with a gazpacho-like flavor. If white kidney beans are not available, use red. Serve as part of a salad plate, with hamburgers or cold chicken, or toss with spinach for a substantial salad.

1	can (19 oz/540 mL) white kidney beans, drained (about 2 cups/500 mL)	1
$\frac{2}{3}$ cup	chopped cucumber	150 mL
$\frac{2}{3}$ cup	chopped Spanish or sweet onion	150 mL
1	sweet green pepper, chopped	1
1	large tomato, chopped	1
2 tbsp	lemon juice	25 mL
1 tbsp	olive oil	15 mL
Pinch	cumin	Pinch
	Salt and freshly ground pepper	
	Lettuce (optional)	

In medium bowl, combine beans, cucumber, green pepper, tomato, lemon juice, oil and cumin. Taste, and add more lemon juice, cumin, and salt and pepper to taste. Cover and refrigerate until serving. Serve alone or on lettuce. Makes 6 servings ($\frac{2}{3}$ cup/150 mL each).

Calories per serving: 120
Grams fat per serving: 3
Fiber: Excellent
Vitamin C: Excellent
Iron: Good

SPINACH SUPPER SALAD

On a hot summer night, this is a perfect light meal with French bread, cold soup and, for dessert, fresh fruit. This salad is also delicious with Oil-and-Vinegar Dressing (page 83).

4 cups	torn spinach leaves (4 oz/125 g)	1 L
$\frac{1}{2}$	head leaf lettuce, in bite-size pieces	$\frac{1}{2}$
2 cups	alfalfa sprouts	500 mL
$\frac{1}{4}$ lb	mushrooms, sliced	125 g
1	large tomato, cut in chunks	1
2	green onions, chopped	2
$\frac{1}{2}$ cup	crumbled feta cheese (2 oz/60 g)	125 mL
1	hard-cooked egg, peeled, and coarsely chopped	1
$\frac{1}{4}$ cup	Buttermilk Herb Dressing (page 82)	50 mL

In large shallow salad bowl, toss spinach, lettuce and alfalfa spouts, or arrange on individual salad plates. Sprinkle mushrooms, tomato, green onions, feta cheese and egg over top. Drizzle dressing over all. Makes 2 main-course or 6 side-salad servings.

Main-course serving	Without dressing	With Buttermilk Herb Dressing
Calories per serving:	231	250
Grams fat per serving:	10.3	12
Fiber: Excellent		
Calcium, phosphorus, iron, vitamins A and C, riboflavin, niacin and thiamine: Excellent		

	Oil-and-Vinegar Herb Dressing	Buttermilk Herb Dressing
Side-salad-size serving:		
Calories per serving:	92	83
Grams fat per serving:	5.6	4

MEDITERRANEAN LENTIL SALAD

Brown lentils instead of red are better for salads. They retain their shape after cooking and are tender but not mushy. This salad keeps well in the refrigerator and is delicious served on salad plates with sliced tomatoes, artichoke hearts, green beans or asparagus in a vinaigrette.

1 cup	brown lentils	250 mL
1 cup	diced carrots	250 mL
1 cup	diced red onion	250 mL
2	large cloves garlic, minced	2
1	bay leaf	1
$\frac{1}{2}$ tsp	dried thyme	2 mL
2 tbsp	olive oil	25 mL
2 tbsp	lemon juice	25 mL
$\frac{1}{2}$ cup	diced celery	125 mL
$\frac{1}{4}$ cup	chopped fresh parsley	50 mL
1 tsp	salt	5 mL
$\frac{1}{4}$ tsp	freshly ground pepper	1 mL

In saucepan, combine lentils, carrots, onion, garlic, bay leaf and thyme. Add enough water to cover by at least 1 inch/2.5 cm. Bring to a boil; reduce heat and simmer, uncovered, until lentils are tender but not mushy, 15 to 20 minutes. Drain and remove bay leaf. Add oil, lemon juice, celery, parsley, salt and pepper; toss to mix. Serve at room temperature. Makes 8 servings ($\frac{1}{2}$ cup/125 mL each).

Calories per serving: 100
Grams fat per serving: 3
Fiber: Good
Vitamins A and C: Good

GREEK SALAD

This salad is wonderful made with home-grown sun-ripened tomatoes that haven't seen the inside of a refrigerator. Serve with soup or an omelet or as part of a salad plate.

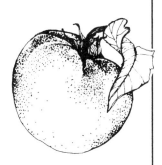

3	large ripe tomatoes, chopped	3
2	cucumbers, peeled, and chopped	2
1	small red onion or 2 green onions, chopped (optional)	1
$\frac{1}{4}$ cup	olive oil	50 mL
4 tsp	lemon juice	20 mL
$1\frac{1}{2}$ tsp	crumbled dried leaf oregano	7 mL
	Salt and freshly ground pepper	
1 cup	crumbled feta cheese (4 oz/ 125 g)	250 mL
6	black olives (preferably Greek), sliced	6

In shallow salad bowl or on serving platter, combine tomatoes, cucumber and onion. Sprinkle with oil, then with lemon juice, oregano, and salt and pepper to taste. Sprinkle feta cheese and olives over salad. Makes 6 servings (about $\frac{3}{4}$ cup/175 mL each).

Calories per serving: 126
Grams fat per serving: 9
Vitamin C: Excellent
Vitamin A, calcium and riboflavin: Good

CHICK-PEA SALAD WITH RED ONION AND TOMATO

Chick-peas, or garbanzo beans, are popular in the south of France and make a delicious substantial salad. Serve as part of a salad plate with a green salad and dark bread for a light yet high-fiber lunch or supper. It's ideal as part of a meatless meal—chick-peas are high in protein as well as in fiber and iron.

1	can (19 oz/540 mL) chick-peas, drained	1
2 tbsp	finely chopped red onion or green onions	25 mL
2	cloves garlic, minced	2
1	tomato, diced	1
½ cup	chopped fresh parsley	125 mL
3 tbsp	olive oil	45 mL
1 tbsp	lemon juice	15 mL
	Salt and freshly ground pepper	

In salad bowl, combine all ingredients and toss. Chill for 2 hours to blend and develop flavors before serving. Taste and adjust seasoning. Makes 4 servings (about ½ cup/125 mL each).

Calories per serving: 361
Grams fat per serving: 14
Fiber: Excellent
Vitamin C and iron: Excellent
Vitamin A, niacin, thiamine and phosphorus: Good

Summer Picnic in the Park
Broccoli Buffet Salad (page 62)
Red Potato Salad with Sour Cream and Chives (page 70)
Sliced cucumbers
Chick-Pea Salad with Red Onion and Tomato (page 78)
Whole-Wheat Irish Soda Bread (page 181)
Fresh peaches

BERMUDA BEAN SALAD

This salad is good with just about any meal, especially hamburgers. It keeps well in the refrigerator, and is handy at a picnic or the cottage for crowd-size entertaining. The recipe can easily be halved by using 10-ounce/284 mL cans of beans and half a pound/250 g each of fresh beans, but make the same amount of marinade. Bermuda onions—white and slightly flattened at the ends—have a wonderful sweet, mild flavor.

1 lb	fresh wax beans	500 g
1 lb	fresh green beans	500 g

1	can (19 oz /540 mL) red kidney beans, drained	1
1	can (19 oz/540 mL) lima or broad beans, drained	1
1	can (19 oz/540 mL) chick-peas, drained	1
1	can (19 oz/540 mL) pinto, romano or white kidney beans, drained	1
2	sweet green peppers, chopped	2
2	Bermuda onions, thinly sliced into rings	2
Marinade:		
$\frac{1}{2}$ cup	red wine vinegar	125 mL
$\frac{1}{4}$ cup	vegetable oil	50 mL
$\frac{1}{3}$ cup	granulated sugar	75 mL
$\frac{1}{3}$ cup	packed brown sugar	75 mL
1 tsp	freshly ground pepper	5 mL
$\frac{1}{2}$ tsp	salt	2 mL

Snap ends off fresh beans and cut into $1\frac{1}{2}$-inch/4 cm pieces. Cook beans in rapidly boiling water for 3 minutes; plunge into cold water until cool, then drain and pat dry. In large bowl, combine cooked beans, kidney beans, lima beans, chick-peas, green peppers and onions.

Marinade: Combine vinegar, oil, both sugars, pepper and salt; stir into bean mixture. Marinate in refrigerator overnight. Makes 20 servings ($\frac{1}{2}$ cup/125 mL each).

Calories per serving: 248
Grams fat per serving: 4
Fiber: Excellent
Vitamin C: Excellent
Iron, thiamine, niacin and phosphorus: Good

PASTA SALAD WITH SWEET PEPPERS AND DILL

You can add any of the usual salad ingredients to this dish except lettuce. It's a terrific salad to have in the refrigerator for a quick and easy summer meal or a picnic. Vegetables can be crisply cooked, but I like the crunch of them raw. To serve as a main course, add julienne strips of ham, chicken and/or cheese.

* If fresh dill isn't available, substitute fresh parsley and 1 tsp/5 mL each dried dillweed and either basil or oregano.

3½ cups	rotini (corkscrew-shaped pasta) or ½ lb/250 g flat egg noodles	875 mL
¼ lb	snow peas or green beans	125 g
3 cups	cauliflower, in small pieces	750 mL
1 cup	thinly sliced carrots	250 mL
2	sweet peppers (red, yellow, green or purple, or combination), chopped	2
2	green onions, chopped	2
¼ cup	chopped fresh dill *	50 mL
Dressing:		
2	cloves garlic, minced	2
⅓ cup	red wine vinegar	75 mL
1 tbsp	granulated sugar	15 mL
⅓ cup	corn oil	75 mL
3 tbsp	water	45 mL
	Salt and freshly ground pepper	

In large saucepan of boiling water, cook pasta until al dente (tender but firm—start tasting after 2 minutes for fresh pasta, 5 minutes for dry); drain, rinse under cold running water and drain again.

Blanch snow peas or green beans in boiling water for 2 minutes. Drain; rinse under cold running water and drain again. Cut diagonally into 2-inch/5 cm lengths.

In large bowl, combine cauliflower, carrots, peppers, green onions, dill, snow peas and pasta; toss to mix.

Dressing: In food processor or bowl, combine garlic, vinegar and sugar; mix well. While whisking or processing, gradually add oil and water; mix well. Pour over salad and toss to mix. Add salt and pepper to taste. Makes about 10 servings (1 cup/250 mL each).

Lunch Menus for Entertaining

Spring
Chicken and Melon Salad
(page 71)
Tossed green salad
Asparagus with Orange Vinaigrette (page 84)
Old-Fashioned Molasses Bread
(page 180)
Lemon Charlotte with
Strawberries (page 202)

Summer
Pasta Salad with Sweet Peppers
and Dill (page 80)
Sliced tomatoes with basil
Whole-Wheat Raisin Scones
(page 182)
Peaches with Raspberry Coulis
(page 193)

Fall
Nova Scotia Seafood Chowder
(page 48)
Artichoke-Tomato Salad (page
63)
Whole-Wheat Irish Soda Bread
(page 181)
Apple Cinnamon Sorbet (page
194)
Almond Meringues (page 179)

Winter
Tex-Mex Chili (page 104) or
Fettuccine with Clam Sauce
(page 108)
Whole-wheat toast
Broccoli Buffet Salad (page 62)
or Spinach and Red Cabbage
Salad (page 61)
Applesauce Whole-Wheat
Cake (page 215)
Grapefruit Ice (page 196)

Calories per serving: 288
Grams fat per serving: 7.7
Vitamins A and C and thiamine: Excellent
Iron and niacin: Good
Fiber: Good, when made with whole-wheat noodles (otherwise fair)

SALAD DRESSINGS

Beware of salad dressings: when made with mayonnaise, cream or oil, they can add a wicked amount of fat to your diet. You can make delicious dressings with low-fat yogurt or buttermilk, and just a touch of oil, with fresh herbs, mustard or garlic for added flavor.

To reduce the fat in your usual recipes, substitute plain low-fat yogurt or buttermilk for half of the mayonnaise or sour cream you usually use. You'll be surprised at the results—the dressing will be lighter and have added flavor.

Try some of our dressings—most of them are very low in fat compared to traditional recipes for dressings. If buying commercial varieties, choose the calorie-reduced kind.

Diet Hint: Reducing fat content of salad dressings

1. Instead of using mayonnaise, sour cream or whipping cream in creamy dressings, substitute half or more of the quantity called for with yogurt, buttermilk or cottage cheese and process in blender or food processor for a smooth texture.
2. Instead of using all the oil called for in an oil-and-vinegar dressing, use half the amount and make up the difference with water, orange juice, tomato juice or beef stock (if the vinegar flavor is too strong, add a little sugar).
3. Use only enough dressing to lightly coat the salad ingredients. Don't let them drown!
4. Nuts are deceptively high in fat, although they are an excellent source of fiber. When the rest of the menu is high in fat, substitute water chestnuts for nuts in salads to achieve a crunchy texture.

BUTTERMILK HERB DRESSING

Buttermilk, made from low-fat milk, has only a trace of fat, yet it gives body and a wonderful flavor to this creamy salad dressing.

1 cup	buttermilk	250 mL
$\frac{2}{3}$ cup	plain yogurt	150 mL
$\frac{1}{4}$ cup	vegetable oil	50 mL
1 tbsp	white vinegar	15 mL
1 tsp	dried dillweed or 3 tbsp/45 mL chopped fresh dill	5 mL
1 tsp	Dijon mustard	5 mL
$\frac{1}{2}$ tsp	salt	2 mL
1	clove garlic, minced	1
	Freshly ground pepper	
$\frac{1}{3}$ cup	chopped fresh parsley	75 mL

In mixing bowl or large measuring cup, combine all ingredients. Using whisk or fork, mix well. Cover and refrigerate for up to 1 week. Makes 2 cups/500 mL.

Calories per 1 tbsp / 15 mL: 18
Grams fat per 1 tbsp / 15mL: 1.5

Herb Vinaigrette: Add $\frac{1}{4}$ tsp/1mL each crumbled dried thyme leaves and celery seed, and 1 tbsp/15 mL chopped fresh herbs or parsley.

A classic oil-and-vinegar dressing uses 3 parts oil to 1 part vinegar (e.g., $\frac{3}{4}$ cup/175 mL oil and $\frac{1}{4}$ cup/50 mL vinegar), and has about 10 grams fat per 1 tbsp/15 mL. To reduce the fat content, replace half the oil with water, orange juice, or beef or chicken stock, and add a pinch of sugar.

OIL-AND-VINEGAR DRESSING

Use this delicious dressing on green salads, pasta salads, as a marinade for vegetables, or with any salad for which you want a vinaigrette dressing. It has about half the fat content of a home-made oil-and-vinegar dressing, but use it sparingly—it is still high in fat.

2 tbsp	vinegar	25 mL
$\frac{1}{2}$ tsp	Dijon mustard	2 mL
1	clove garlic, minced (optional)	1
	Salt and freshly ground pepper	
$\frac{1}{4}$ cup	salad or olive oil	50 mL
3 tbsp	water	45 mL
$\frac{1}{2}$ tsp	granulated sugar (optional)	2 mL

In small bowl or food processor, combine vinegar, mustard, garlic (if using), and salt and pepper to taste, and mix well. While whisking or processing, gradually add oil. Add water; taste, and add sugar if desired. Makes about $\frac{1}{2}$ cup/ 125 mL.

Calories per 1 tbsp / 15 mL: 51
Grams fat per 1 tbsp / 15 mL: 6

Compare:

	Per 1 tbsp/15 mL	
Salad Dressings	Grams fat our recipe	Grams fat conventional recipe
Blue Cheese	0.8	8
Buttermilk Herb	1.5	6
Oil-and-Vinegar	6	10
Orange Vinaigrette	2.8	—
Parsley Dressing	0.5	—
Tomato-French	1.4	6
Yogurt-Basil	0.1	—
Thousand Island		8
Mayonnaise		11
Half mayonnaise, half plain low-fat yogurt	6	—

ORANGE VINAIGRETTE

Use this citrusy oil-and-vinegar dressing with tossed salads or as a marinade for vegetables.

1	clove garlic	1
2 tbsp	chopped fresh parsley	25 mL
2 tbsp	white vinegar	25 mL
1 tsp	granulated sugar	5 mL
$\frac{1}{2}$ tsp	salt	2 mL
	Freshly ground pepper	
$\frac{1}{4}$ cup	orange juice	50 mL
2 tbsp	vegetable oil	25 mL

In food processor or blender, chop garlic and parsley. Add vinegar, sugar, salt, and pepper to taste; process to mix. With motor running, gradually add orange juice and oil. Makes about $\frac{1}{2}$ cup/125 mL.

Calories per tbsp / 15 mL: 32
Grams fat per tbsp / 15 mL: 2.8

Spring Appetizer
Enjoy tender-crisp asparagus with a touch of tangy flavor. Sprinkle $\frac{1}{2}$ cup/125 mL Orange Vinaigrette over $1\frac{1}{4}$ lb/625g cooked asparagus. Makes 4 servings.

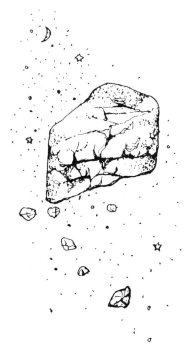

BLUE CHEESE DRESSING

Using yogurt instead of traditional mayonnaise in this dressing makes a lighter but equally good-tasting dressing that's much lower in both fat and calories. Use with green and spinach salads.

$\frac{1}{2}$ cup	crumbled blue cheese (about $2\frac{1}{2}$ oz/70 g)	125 mL
1 cup	plain yogurt	250 mL
1	clove garlic, minced	1
Pinch	dry mustard	Pinch
	Freshly ground pepper	

In small bowl, use a fork to cream half of the cheese. Stir in yogurt, garlic, mustard and pepper to taste; mix well. Stir in remaining cheese. Cover and store in refrigerator. Makes about $1\frac{1}{3}$ cups/325 mL.

Calories per 1 tbsp / 15 mL: 16
Grams fat per 1 tbsp / 15 mL: 0.8

PARSLEY DRESSING

This thick, creamy dressing is one of my favorites. It's good with spinach and green salads, and can also be served as a dip for vegetables.

$\frac{1}{2}$ cup	chopped fresh parsley	125 mL
1 cup	2% cottage cheese	250 mL
1 tsp	Dijon mustard	5 mL
1	egg	1
1 tsp	lemon juice	5 mL
	Salt and freshly ground pepper	

Variation:
Watercress Dressing: Substitute watercress leaves (stems removed because they have too strong a flavor, and also won't chop finely in food processor) for the parsley.

In food processor, chop parsley. Add cottage cheese, mustard, egg, lemon juice, and salt and pepper to taste; process until well mixed. Cover and refrigerate until needed (will keep for a few days). Makes 1 cup/250 mL.

Calories per 1 tbsp / 15 mL: 16
Grams fat per 1 tbsp / 15 mL: 0.5
Cottage cheese is a good source of calcium.

YOGURT-BASIL DRESSING

Use this low-fat dressing with green salads, cooked vegetable and pasta salads.

$\frac{1}{4}$ cup	plain yogurt	50 mL
$\frac{1}{4}$ cup	cottage cheese	50 mL
$\frac{1}{2}$ tsp	dried basil, or 1 tbsp/15 mL chopped fresh	2 mL
$\frac{1}{2}$ tsp	granulated sugar	2 mL
2 tsp	lemon juice	10 mL
	Salt and freshly ground pepper	

In a food processor or blender, combine all ingredients; blend until smooth. Makes about $\frac{1}{2}$ cup/125 mL.

Calories per 1 tbsp / 15 mL: 9
Grams fat per 1 tbsp / 15mL: 0.1

For other salad dressing recipes, see:
Balsamic Vinaigrette (page 66)
Creamy Dill Dressing (page 30)
Lemon Vinaigrette (page 67)
Yogurt Dressing (page 68)

TOMATO-FRENCH DRESSING

This is one of the best low-calorie, low-fat vinaigrette dressings that I've tasted—keep it handy in your refrigerator.

½ cup	tomato juice	125 mL
1 tsp	cornstarch	5 mL
1 tbsp	red wine vinegar	15 mL
1 tbsp	olive oil	15 mL
½ tsp	Dijon mustard	2 mL
1	small clove garlic, minced	1
½ tsp	dried tarragon, thyme or basil, or chopped fresh herbs to taste	2 mL
	Salt and freshly ground pepper	

In small saucepan or microwave container, whisk together tomato juice and cornstarch. Cook, stirring, over medium heat or at high until mixture comes to a boil and thickens. Boil 1 minute, stirring constantly. Remove from heat and whisk in remaining ingredients. Transfer to jar with screw-top lid. Refrigerate until needed. Shake before using. Makes about ⅔ cup/150 mL.

Calories per 1 tbsp / 15 mL: 16
Grams fat per 1 tbsp / 15 mL: 1.4

Portable Lunch Menus
Whole-wheat pita bread filled
with Hummus (page 32),
leaf lettuce and alfalfa sprouts
Apple
Milk

Refrigerator Bran Muffin
(page 176)
Raw vegetables (carrots, sweet
green and red peppers, zuc-
chini, cauliflower) with Creamy
Fresh Dill Dip (page 30) or
Parsley Dressing (page 85)
Banana
Milk

Green Bean Crunch (page 25)
or carrot sticks
Whole-wheat bagel with low-
fat cream cheese
Date Square (page 183)
Orange
Milk

Pita bread filled with Tabbouleh (page 64) or Hummus
(page 32)
Cantaloupe wedge
Milk

Chicken sandwich on whole-
wheat bread
Fresh grapes or figs
Milk

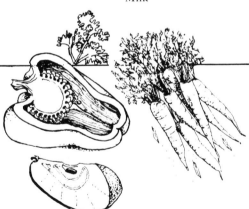

POULTRY

From coq au vin to tandoori, chicken is a mainstay of cuisines around the world. Its flavor appeals to children as well as to adults and it lends itself to a wide range of seasonings and sauces.

For the health-conscious cook, chicken has the added benefit of being a low-fat source of animal protein. To keep the fat at a minimum, remove the skin and any visible fat from chicken pieces before cooking; from whole chickens cut the skin away before eating (whole chickens take longer to cook and would dry out if skin were removed before cooking). Roast chicken with skin has 53 percent fat calories, while roast chicken without skin has 31 percent fat calories.

Obviously, frying chicken adds to the fat intake; baking and broiling are far better cooking methods. Dark meat has considerably more fat than white meat. Small broilers or fryers have the least amount of fat, stewing hens the most. The larger and older the bird, the higher the fat content. When baking chicken, place pieces or whole bird on a rack so the fat drips off and the chicken doesn't roast in it. Though turkey and chicken are both low in fat, duck and goose have a much higher fat content.

CHICKEN DIJON

Crisp and juicy, this chicken can be prepared ahead of time and served hot, warm or cold.

6	chicken breasts	6
	Salt and freshly ground pepper	
$\frac{1}{4}$ cup	Dijon mustard	50 mL
$\frac{1}{3}$ cup	plain yogurt	75 mL
$\frac{1}{2}$ cup	fine fresh bread crumbs	125 mL
1 tsp	thyme	5 mL

In the Chicken Dijon the skin is removed to reduce the fat content. Because of the mustard mixture and bread-crumb coating, the chicken stays moist. Use whole-wheat bread crumbs if possible. They are quick to make using a food processor.

Remove skin from chicken. Sprinkle chicken lightly with salt and pepper. Mix mustard into yogurt. In another bowl, mix bread crumbs, thyme, $\frac{1}{2}$ tsp/2 mL salt and $\frac{1}{4}$ tsp/1 mL pepper.

Spread each piece of chicken with mustard mixture, then roll in bread-crumb mixture. Place chicken in single layer on lightly greased baking sheet. Bake in 350°F/180°C oven for 45 to 50 minutes for bone-in chicken, 30 to 35 minutes for boneless, or until golden brown and meat is no longer pink. Makes 6 servings.

Photo:

Spinach and Red Cabbage Salad (page 61) with Blue Cheese Dressing (page 84)

Calories per serving: 190 (with skin on—241)
Grams fat per serving: 3.9 (with skin on—8.4)
Niacin: Excellent

CRISPY HERBED CHICKEN

I keep a small jar of herb-seasoned flour on hand so I can make this chicken dish quickly—it's one of my children's favorites. To make only enough seasoned flour for one meal, combine 2 tbsp / 25 mL flour with 2 tsp / 10 mL of dried herbs, and salt and pepper.

6	chicken pieces (about 2 lb/1 kg, bone-in)	6
2 tbsp	Herb-Seasoned Flour*	25 mL
$\frac{1}{3}$ cup	(approx) warm water	75 mL

Remove skin from chicken; rinse chicken under cold running water and pat dry with paper towels. Place chicken in single layer in lightly greased shallow roasting pan or baking dish. Use small sieve or spoon to sprinkle Herb-Seasoned Flour over chicken. Pour warm water down side of pan, not directly over chicken.

Bake, uncovered, in 375°F/190°C oven for 40 to 50 minutes or until chicken is no longer pink inside, basting occasionally with liquid in pan to brown top of chicken. Add more water if there's not enough liquid in pan for basting. Makes 6 servings.

Calories per serving: 200
Grams fat per serving: 3.2
Niacin: Excellent

August Dinner Menu
Fresh Tomato and Basil Soup (page 42)
Chicken Dijon (page 88)
Herbed Green Beans with Garlic (page 160)
Cracked Wheat and Basil Pilaf (page 173)
Melon with Blueberries (page 200)

*Herb-Seasoned Flour
In small jar with lid, combine $\frac{1}{2}$ cup/125 mL all-purpose flour, 2 tsp/10 mL each of salt, dried basil and thyme, 1 tsp/5 mL each of dried oregano, tarragon and paprika and $\frac{1}{2}$ tsp/ 2 mL pepper. Cover and shake to mix; store at room temperature. Makes about $\frac{2}{3}$ cup/150 mL.

Compare:

	%fat calories
Roast chicken with skin on	53
Roast chicken without skin	31

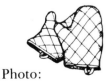

Photo:
Orange-Ginger Chicken with Leeks (page 94)

1 pound/500 g of boneless chicken will usually serve four people; since the chicken in this recipe is cut into thin slices, it looks like a lot more, and you should be able to serve five people instead of four.

LEMON CHICKEN SCHNITZEL

Serve this easy-to-make, moist and tender chicken to family and guests. You can use boneless turkey instead of chicken.

1 lb	boneless skinless chicken breasts	500 g
	Juice of 1 lemon	
$\frac{1}{4}$ cup	all-purpose flour	50 mL
$\frac{1}{2}$ tsp	salt	2 mL
$\frac{1}{2}$ tsp	thyme	2 mL
$\frac{1}{2}$ tsp	celery salt	2 mL
1	egg	1
1 tsp	water	5 mL
$\frac{1}{2}$ cup	fine dry bread crumbs	125 mL

Cut chicken horizontally into $\frac{1}{4}$-inch/5mm thick slices. Place between 2 pieces of waxed paper and flatten chicken, using the flat side of cleaver or bottom of bottle. Sprinkle chicken with lemon juice; let stand for 10 minutes.

In shallow dish, combine flour, salt, thyme and celery salt; mix well. In another shallow dish, lightly beat egg with water. Dip chicken pieces into flour mixture, then into egg mixture, then into bread crumbs. Place on lightly greased baking sheet or in microwave dish. Bake in 400°F/200°C oven for 10 to 15 minutes, or microwave, uncovered, on High for 4 minutes, or until chicken is no longer pink. Makes 5 servings.

Calories per serving: 274
Grams fat per serving: 7.2
Niacin: Excellent
Iron: Good

SAUTÉED CHICKEN WITH YOGURT AND MUSHROOMS

A flavorful dish for company or guests; serve with broiled tomatoes, a green vegetable and rice. Any kind of mushrooms can be used—domestic, wild or dried (soak dried mushrooms for about 30 minutes). Try shiitake, cepe, oyster, or a combination.

6	chicken pieces (about 2 lb/1 kg bone-in)	6
1 tbsp	all-purpose flour	15 mL
4 tsp	butter	20 mL
2	onions, thinly sliced	2
$\frac{1}{4}$ lb	mushrooms, sliced	125 g
$\frac{1}{2}$ cup	water (or half water and half white wine)	125 mL
$\frac{1}{2}$ cup	plain yogurt	125 mL
	Salt and freshly ground pepper	

Remove skin from chicken. Sprinkle chicken lightly with flour. In large nonstick skillet, melt butter over medium-high heat; cook chicken until browned all over, about 5 minutes on each side. Reduce heat to medium or medium-low and cook for 10 minutes longer on each side or until meat is no longer pink. Remove from pan and keep warm.

Add onions and mushrooms to pan and cook, stirring often, until tender, 5 to 10 minutes. Stir in water and bring to a full boil, loosening any brown bits on bottom of pan to flavor sauce. Remove from heat and stir in yogurt, and salt and pepper to taste. Return chicken to pan and spoon sauce over it. Makes 6 servings.

Calories per serving: 200
Grams fat per serving: 6
Niacin: Excellent
Calcium, phosphorus and riboflavin: Good

BREAST OF CHICKEN FLORENTINE

This recipe may look lengthy but it isn't hard to make. Because most of the preparation can be done in advance, it's ideal for a dinner party. It takes only minutes to cook, so complete the dish just before serving while you reheat the sauce and spinach. Serve with Two-Cabbage Stir-Fry (page 159) or broiled tomato halves and brown rice.

$\frac{1}{4}$ cup	all-purpose flour	50 mL
$\frac{1}{2}$ tsp	salt	2 mL
$\frac{1}{2}$ tsp	thyme	2 mL
	Pepper to taste	
1	egg, lightly beaten	1
1 tbsp	water	15 mL
$\frac{1}{2}$ cup	fine dry bread crumbs	125 mL
$\frac{1}{4}$ cup	grated Parmesan cheese	50 mL
4	boneless skinless chicken breasts (about 1 lb/500 g)	4
	Tarragon and Mushroom Sauce (page 150) or enoki mushrooms for garnishing (optional)*	
1 lb	spinach	500 g
1 tsp	fresh lemon juice	5 mL
1 tsp	butter	5 mL
	Salt and freshly ground pepper	

On plate, combine flour, salt, thyme, and pepper to taste; mix well. In shallow bowl, combine egg and water; mix well. On another plate, combine bread crumbs and cheese. Coat chicken pieces with seasoned flour; shake off excess. Dip into beaten-egg mixture, then roll in cheese-crumb mixture. Refrigerate for 20 minutes or up to 2 hours.

Prepare Tarragon and Mushroom Sauce, if desired.

On lightly greased baking sheet or microwave dish, bake chicken in 400°F/200°C oven for 15 minutes, or microwave, uncovered, on High for 4 to 5 minutes, or until chicken is no longer pink. If microwaving, let stand for 1 to 2 minutes (cooking time will vary, depending on thickness of chicken).

Trim stems from spinach. Wash and place in saucepan

*Enoki mushrooms have long, thin stems and small, round heads. They add a woodsy flavor to salads, and are lovely as a garnish on cooked meats and chicken. They are available in some supermarkets and specialty vegetable stores. Eat them raw or cooked.

with just the water clinging to leaves. Cover and cook over medium-high heat until spinach has wilted. Drain thoroughly, and chop coarsely; toss with lemon juice, butter, and salt and pepper to taste. Place on warm dinner plates or platter and keep warm in 200°F/100°C oven until chicken is cooked.

Place chicken on top of spinach and garnish with a few spoonfuls of Tarragon and Mushroom Sauce or raw enoki mushrooms. Makes 4 servings.

Calories per serving: 260
Grams fat per serving: 6.2
Fiber: Excellent
Vitamins A and C and niacin: Excellent
Iron and phosphorus: Good
Spinach is an excellent source of fiber.

Compare:	Per $3\frac{1}{2}$ oz/100 g
	Grams fat
Kentucky-fried chicken (1 piece)	17
Broiled chicken without skin (1 piece)	4

ORANGE-GINGER CHICKEN WITH LEEKS

A quickly prepared dish for guests or family. To make it special, garnish with slices of fresh mango or grapes and cooked snow peas. Serve over Chinese vermicelli.

$1\frac{1}{4}$ lb	boneless skinless chicken breasts	625 g
2	large leeks	2
1 tbsp	butter	15 mL
2	green onions, chopped	2
$\frac{1}{4}$ cup	dry white wine	50 mL
1 tbsp	grated fresh ginger root	15 mL
1	tomato, peeled, seeded and chopped	1
$\frac{1}{2}$ cup	fresh orange juice	125 mL
$\frac{1}{2}$ tsp	grated orange rind	2 mL
1 tbsp	all-purpose flour	15 mL
$\frac{1}{4}$ tsp	granulated sugar	1 mL
1 cup	seedless green grapes	250 mL
	Salt and freshly ground pepper	

Chinese rice vermicelli, or rice sticks, are available in some supermarkets and Chinese grocery stores. They take only a few minutes to boil or, for a special occasion, drop a few noodles at a time into hot oil in a wok and watch them explode to six times their volume.

Cut chicken into 1-inch/2.5 cm cubes. Cut off and discard tough green part of leeks. Cut leeks in half and wash thoroughly under cold water. Cut into matchstick-size julienne strips.

In large, heavy skillet, melt butter. Cook chicken over high heat, for 2 to 3 minutes or until lightly browned; remove chicken to side plate. Stir in leeks and onions and cook 1 minute, or until leeks are wilted. Stir in wine, ginger and tomato, scraping up any brown bits from bottom of pan.

In measuring cup, combine orange juice, rind, flour and sugar; mix until smooth. Pour into hot mixture, stirring constantly. Bring to a boil, stirring constantly, and simmer 2 to 3 minutes. (Dish may be prepared in advance to this point. Reheat sauce.) Return chicken to pan. Stir in grapes, and salt and pepper to taste. Makes 4 servings.

Calories per serving: 337
Grams fat per serving: 13
Vitamin C, niacin and phosphorus: Excellent
Iron: Good

Stir-frying

Stir-frying is a quick and easy way to cook meats, poultry, seafood and vegetables. By frying in a small amount of oil over high heat and stirring continuously and vigorously, foods are seared and quickly cooked. Vegetables are crisp, and meats are very tender. You can control the temperature by moving the pan on and off the heat.

Use a wok or heavy skillet. Heat the oil before adding the ingredients; otherwise, the food will absorb the oil.

Because stir-frying is so fast, have all your food chopped and measured before you start to cook. The food should be evenly shredded, diced or cut into thin slices so it will cook in a short time. By cutting meats and vegetables on the diagonal, meats will be tenderized, and the largest possible surface area of the food is exposed to the heat.

To add flavor and tenderize the meat, marinate it in advance; using cornstarch in the marinade helps to tenderize the meat and thicken the dish.

When using vegetables that require a longer cooking time, add a little water, chicken stock or rice vinegar, then cover and steam for a few minutes. When preparing a large quantity of stir-fried vegetables, blanch the longer-cooking vegetables first (blanch cut vegetables in boiling water, then cool under cold running water, to prevent further cooking).

*To toast almonds, roast on pie plate in 350°F/180°C oven for 5 minutes or until golden.

ALMOND CHICKEN

Stir-frying is a great way to make one pound of chicken serve four people and look like a lot. It's a great family dish that's pretty enough for casual entertaining. Serve over rice or noodles.

4 tsp	cornstarch	20 mL
2 tbsp	soy sauce	25 mL
1 lb	boneless skinless chicken breast, cut into strips	500 g
½ cup	chicken stock	125 mL
2 tbsp	vegetable oil	25 mL
2 cups	thinly sliced celery	500 mL
2 cups	diagonally cut green beans or snow peas	500 mL
1 cup	thinly sliced carrots	250 mL
1	large onion, halved and thinly sliced	1
2	cloves garlic, minced	2
2 tbsp	water	25 mL
	Salt and freshly ground pepper	
2 tbsp	toasted sliced almonds*	25 mL

In medium bowl, combine 3 tsp/15 mL of cornstarch and soy sauce; mix well. Add chicken and toss to coat; set aside. Stir remaining 1 tsp/5 mL cornstarch into chicken stock; set aside.

Heat wok or heavy skillet over medium-high heat. When hot, add oil, then chicken, and stir-fry for 4 minutes or until chicken is opaque. Remove chicken and set aside. To wok, add celery, beans, carrots, onion and garlic; stir-fry for 1 minute. Add water, cover and cook for 2 minutes. Stir chicken stock mixture into pan. Return chicken to pan; cook, stirring, for another minute or until mixture boils and vegetables are tender-crisp. Season with salt and pepper to taste. Sprinkle with toasted almonds. Makes 4 servings.

Calories per serving: 340
Grams fat per serving: 13.7
Fiber: Excellent
Niacin and vitamin A: Excellent
Iron: Good

CHICKEN WITH SNOW PEAS

Keep this stir-fried dish in mind for when you want a special meal but have only a few minutes to prepare it.

1 lb	boneless chicken breasts	500 g
3 tbsp	dry sherry	45 mL
4 tsp	cornstarch	20 mL
2 tbsp	low-sodium soy sauce*	25 mL
1 tsp	granulated sugar	5 mL
2 tbsp	vegetable oil	25 mL
4	cloves garlic, minced	4
2 tsp	peeled and grated ginger root, or $\frac{3}{4}$ tsp/4 mL dried ginger	10 mL
2	onions, coarsely chopped	2
$\frac{1}{2}$ lb	snow peas	250 g
$\frac{1}{2}$ cup	water	125 mL

Remove skin from chicken. Cut chicken into 1-inch/ 2.5 cm cubes. In bowl, combine 2 tbsp/25 mL of the sherry and 3 tsp/15 mL of the cornstarch; mix well. Stir in chicken. Cover, and marinate in refrigerator for at least 1 hour.

In small bowl, combine soy sauce, remaining sherry, remaining cornstarch and sugar; set aside.

In large heavy skillet or wok, heat oil over high heat until hot but not smoking. Add chicken and stir-fry for 2 minutes. Remove chicken from pan and set aside.

Add garlic and ginger to pan; stir well, then add onions, snow peas and water. Stir-fry for 2 minutes. Return chicken and soy-sauce mixture to pan and stir rapidly over high heat until hot. Serve with rice or noodles. Makes 4 servings.

Calories per serving: 307
Grams fat per serving: 13
Fiber: Good
Niacin: Excellent
Iron and Vitamin C: Good

Step-by-Step Stir-Frying:
1. Have all ingredients cut and measured.
2. Heat wok or heavy skillet over high heat.
3. Add corn or salad oil and when hot (but not smoking), add foods in the order listed in the recipe (or the ones requiring the longest cooking time first).
4. Use a long-handled spatula or wooden spoon to continuously stir the foods.
5. Add chopped garlic, ginger or onions along with vegetables; soy sauce, sherry or vinegar at the end for flavor.
6. Mix 1 to 2 tsp/5 to 10 mL cornstarch with 3 tbsp/45 mL cold water or stock and add to wok to thicken dish if desired.

Once you have tried a few recipes for stir-frying, you'll find it easy to improvise and make up your own. I make a stir-fried dish for dinner at least once a week, rarely following a recipe. This lets me use up all the small quantities of raw vegetables hiding in the back of the refrigerator. Stir-frying is an excellent way to stretch a small amount of meat, chicken or seafood; and, along with the vegetables, stir-fries are ideal for low-fat main dishes.

*Soy sauce is very high in sodium. If possible, use a sodium-reduced soy sauce. If unavailable, look for naturally brewed soy sauce. The highest amount of sodium is found in chemically brewed soy sauce.

How to Microwave Whole Poultry

Microwaving is an easy, quick and moist way to cook chicken or turkey when you want to remove the meat from the bone to use in salads, such as Chicken and Melon (page 71), or other dishes such as Casserole of Turkey with Melon and Curry Sauce (page 98).

- Tie wings and legs tightly to body.
- Place bird in shallow microwave dish; cover with plastic or waxed paper, folding back one corner to allow steam to escape.
- Microwave chicken on High for about 17 minutes for a $2\frac{1}{2}$ lb/1.2 kg chicken (6 to 7 minutes per pound/500g), turning dish occasionally depending on your microwave.
- For 12 lb/6 kg turkey, microwave breast-side down, covered loosely with waxed paper or plastic wrap, on Medium-High for 24 minutes, draining liquid once or twice. Turn breast-side up and microwave on Medium-High for $\frac{3}{4}$ to 1 hour or until meat registers 190°F/90°C (older ovens may take a longer time). Drain off juices every 15 minutes.
- Pour juices from chicken into container and refrigerate or freeze—fat will rise to the surface and solidify; lift fat off and discard. Use remaining liquid for stock or for making sauces or soups.
- Let chicken stand for 10 to 15 minutes, turkey for 20 minutes, before using.

MICROWAVE TARRAGON CHICKEN WITH JULIENNE VEGETABLES AND YOGURT HOLLANDAISE

Leeks are particularly good when cooked in this way with chicken, but carrots, zucchini or celery, or a combination of these, also work well. The sauce adds a rich flavor, yet it is deceptively low in fat and calories.

3 cups	julienned carrots, leeks, celery or zucchini (in thin matchstick strips)	750 mL
4	chicken breasts	4
	Salt and freshly ground pepper	
2 tsp	butter	10 mL
$\frac{1}{4}$ tsp	dried tarragon or 4 sprigs fresh tarragon or rosemary	1 mL
$\frac{1}{2}$ cup	Yogurt Hollandaise (pages 150-1)	125 mL

In baking dish just large enough to hold chicken in a single layer, sprinkle half the vegetables. Remove skin from chicken. Place chicken on top of vegetables and season lightly with salt and pepper. Top with remaining vegetables and dot with butter. Sprinkle with tarragon, and salt and pepper to taste.

Cover with plastic wrap, turning back one corner to vent; microwave on High for 6 minutes if boneless, 8 to 10 minutes bone-in, or until chicken is no longer pink. Spoon Yogurt Hollandaise over and serve.

	Without Sauce	With Sauce
Calories per serving:	194	228
Grams fat per serving:	5.2	7

Fiber: Good
Niacin and vitamin A: Excellent
Vitamin C and phosphorus: Good

This is a lovely buffet casserole. It's easy to eat without a
knife and can be prepared in
advance. (Add melon just
before serving.) It can be easily
doubled or tripled for a larger
number of guests. You can substitute chicken for the turkey
and can also include shrimp.
Plan on about $\frac{1}{4}$ lb/125 g snow
peas per person or use less and
serve another vegetable as
well.

**Hard-Cooked Eggs with Curry
Sauce**
Here's a delicious dish at an
Easter buffet. In a large skillet,
prepare Curry Sauce
(page 171). Add peeled, halved
hard-cooked eggs (about $1\frac{1}{2}$
eggs per person) to Curry
Sauce and warm over low heat
until heated through, about 5
minutes. Serve over rice.

*You can substitute chicken for
the turkey. See page 97 for
microwave instructions.

CASSEROLE OF TURKEY WITH MELON AND CURRY SAUCE

*Juicy melons, mangoes or peaches add a festive touch and cooling
flavor to this curry dish. The sauce is also good with shrimp or
hard-cooked eggs. If using the sauce for shrimp, use half chicken
stock and half clam juice.*

3 cups	chopped cooked turkey (in large chunks)*	750 mL
2 cups	melon balls, sliced mango or sliced peaches	500 mL
Curry Sauce:		
$\frac{1}{4}$ cup	butter	60 mL
1	onion, chopped	1
1	clove garlic, minced	1 mL
4 tsp	curry powder	20 mL
$\frac{1}{2}$ tsp	chili powder	2 mL
$\frac{1}{2}$ tsp	cumin	2 mL
$\frac{1}{3}$ cup	all-purpose flour	75 mL
2 cups	chicken stock	500 mL
$\frac{1}{2}$ tsp	salt	2 mL
	Freshly ground pepper	

Curry Sauce: In flameproof casserole or saucepan,
melt butter. Stir in onion, garlic, curry powder, chili
powder and cumin; cook, stirring, over medium-low heat
until onion is tender. Stir in flour and mix well. Stir in
stock; bring to a boil, stirring, and simmer, uncovered, for
5 minutes. Add salt and pepper to taste.

Stir in turkey. (Casserole may be prepared in advance to
this point, covered, and refrigerated for up to 2 days.
Reheat gently before continuing with recipe.) Add melon
and cook, stirring, until heated through, 5 to 10 minutes.
Makes 6 servings.

Calories per serving: 209
Grams fat per serving: 7
Iron, niacin and vitamin C: Excellent
Phosphorus: Good
*Cantaloupe is an excellent source of vitamin A and a good source
of vitamin C.*

To Roast Turkey or Chicken

- Truss bird, with kitchen twine or string, tying wings and legs close to body (do not use synthetic twine).
- Place bird on rack in roasting pan. This makes it easier to remove the bird and keeps it from cooking in its own juices and fat.
- Cover turkey lightly with lid or foil (shiny side down); remove foil during last hour of roasting to brown top.
- Bird is cooked when it reaches an internal temperature of 185°F/90°C, drumstick moves easily in socket and juices from thigh run clear when pierced.
- Remove from oven and transfer to platter; let stand for 15 minutes before carving.
- Roast turkey in 325°F/160°C oven for 4 to 5 hours for 12 to 14 lb/5.5 to 6.5 kg bird (20 to 25 minutes per pound/500g if small; 15 minutes per pound/500g if over 18 lb/9 kg).
- Roast chicken in 350°F/180°C oven for about 1½ hours for 4 lb/2 kg chicken.

Diet Hint: Reducing fat content when roasting chicken or turkey

- Avoid recipes for stuffing that use oil or butter.
- Instead of stuffing poultry, slip garlic slivers, fresh herbs, sliced fresh ginger root under the skin (between flesh and skin) or place in cavity.
- Stuff cavity with apple slices, onion wedges, mushrooms and/or orange sections.
- If making a bread stuffing, use fairly fresh bread, or moisten stale bread with chicken stock; add chopped onions, celery and apple instead of oil or butter.
- Instead of gravy, serve pan juices with fat removed, Blackberry Sauce (page 147) or cranberry sauce (you can add flavor and interest with chutney, port or brandy).
- Discard skin before serving.

MEAT

Meat can be a high source of fat in our diet. One way of reducing our intake of fat is to eat lean cuts of meat, and to cut down on the amount of meat we eat. Remember: Cut down, DON'T *cut out*. Meat is an important source of complete protein; this means it has all the essential amino acids, the building blocks of protein. Meat is also an important source of iron in a form the body can easily use, as well as a good source of B vitamins and minerals. Just $3\frac{1}{2}$ ounces/100 g of cooked lean beef (such as flank steak or lean hamburger) provides 30 g of protein and nearly 4 mg of iron. This constitutes more than half of an adult's average daily requirement for protein and half of a male adult's average daily requirement for iron (teenagers, and women aged 16 to 49, require up to 14 mg of iron a day).

The problem is that we don't often limit our meat portions to 3 to 4 ounces/90 to 125 g. We eat fatty marbled as well as lean meat. To help us eat more healthily, the meat industry is producing leaner beef and pork.

To keep the size of portions down, yet still make them appear satisfying, use meat in mixed dishes such as stir-fries, stews and soups, or in sauces such as spaghetti sauce. Canadians still aren't used to eating only 4-ounce/ 125 g portions of steak, but if you slice the steak in thin slices before serving, a 4-ounce/125 g portion will look like much more.

BEEF AND VEGETABLE STEW

Stews are an ideal way to serve a 4-oz/125 g portion of meat without appearing skimpy. With the addition of vegetables, this not only stretches the meat but increases the fiber; add a potato (boiled with skin) per person and the fiber content is up to 10 g per serving.

When making any kind of stew, make it a day in advance and refrigerate. Any fat will solidify on the surface and then can easily be removed.

This savory stew tastes even better the second day when flavors have had a chance to blend. Serve with mashed or boiled potatoes or over hot noodles.

$1\frac{1}{4}$ lb	boneless stewing beef	625 g
2 tbsp	all-purpose flour	25 mL
1 tbsp	vegetable oil	15 mL
2 cups	water	500 mL
3	onions, quartered	3
1	bay leaf	1
1 tsp	thyme	5 mL
$\frac{1}{2}$ tsp	marjoram or oregano	2 mL
1 tsp	salt	5 mL

See Table C, pages 230-2, for fat content of various meats.

Diet Hint: Reducing fat content in meat and meat dishes
- Buy lean cuts of meat such as flank, sirloin tip and lean ground beef.
- Trim all visible fat from meat.
- When browning meat or cooking ground meat, pour off all fat before adding other ingredients.
- Cook stews and simmered meat dishes a day in advance and refrigerate overnight. The next day you can easily remove hardened fat from the surface.
- Cut off any fat from cooked meat before eating.
- Processed meats such as salami, bologna, hot dogs and sausages are usually high in fat as well as salt, nitrates and nitrites. They should be avoided, or eaten in only small amounts.

$\frac{1}{4}$ tsp	freshly ground pepper	1 mL
1 tsp	grated orange rind	5 mL
1	small turnip (about 1 lb/ 500 g)	1
5	carrots	5
1 cup	frozen peas	250 mL
$\frac{1}{4}$ cup	chopped fresh parsley	50 mL
	Salt and freshly ground pepper	

Cut all visible fat from beef and discard. Cut beef into about 1-inch/2.5 cm cubes. Coat beef with flour, using up all flour.

In heavy pan, heat oil over medium-high heat. Add beef and cook, stirring, until brown on all sides.

Pour in water and bring to a boil, scraping up any brown bits on bottom of pan. Add onions, bay leaf, thyme, marjoram, salt, pepper and orange rind. Cover, and simmer for $1\frac{1}{2}$ hours.

Peel turnip and cut into $\frac{3}{4}$-inch/2 cm pieces (you should have about 3 cups). Scrape carrots and cut into 1-inch/2.5 cm pieces. Add carrots and turnip to pan; simmer, covered, for 40 minutes or until vegetables are tender. Add peas, parsley, and salt and pepper to taste. Simmer until peas are hot. Makes 6 servings.

Calories per serving: 220
Grams fat per serving: 9
Fiber: Excellent
Niacin and vitamins A and C: Excellent
Iron: Good

Making the Most of Pan Juices
Pan juices from roasting meats are flavorful and make a wonderful sauce. To remove fat, either use a large spoon and skim from surface, or add a tray of ice cubes to the juices (the fat will cool and harden, and can then be easily removed). Bring the juices to a boil; boil for a few minutes to evaporate extra water and reduce sauce to desired consistency.

Pan juices and brown bits on the bottom of the pan after broiling or sautéing meats, chicken and fish make a good base for a savory sauce. Simply spoon off the fat, add a large spoonful or two of wine, vinegar or fruit juice and bring to a boil, scraping up all brown bits from bottom of the pan. Add other flavorings, such as garlic, onions, shallots and parsley, if desired. Remove from heat and stir in a little yogurt.

MARINATED FLANK STEAK

This is my son John's favorite steak. It's tender, flavorful and one of the leanest cuts of beef.

September Dinner
Balkan Beet Cream Soup
(pages 36-7)
Marinated Flank Steak
(page 102)
Tomatoes Florentine
(page 153) or Tarragon
Carrots (page 155)
Barley and Parsley Pilaf
(page 165)
Lemon and Fresh Blueberry
Tart (pages 204-5)

1 lb	flank steak	500 g
$\frac{1}{4}$ cup	soy sauce	50 mL
$\frac{1}{4}$ cup	vegetable oil	50 mL
2 tbsp	vinegar	25 mL
2 tbsp	sugar or honey	25 mL
1 tbsp	peeled and grated fresh ginger root or 1 tsp/5 mL ground ginger	15 mL

Score one side of the steak by making shallow cuts in a crisscross pattern. Place meat in a shallow dish or plastic bag. Combine soy sauce, oil, vinegar, sugar and ginger; pour over meat. Cover, and refrigerate for 1 to 3 days, or at room temperature for up to 3 hours.

Remove meat from marinade and broil for 4 to 5 minutes on each side. Slice thinly on an angle across the grain. Serve hot or cold. Makes 4 servings.

Calories per serving: 200
Grams fat per serving: 9
Niacin: Excellent
Iron, riboflavin and niacin: Good

STUFFED BABY PEPPERS WITH TOMATO-BASIL SAUCE

Tiny sweet peppers are available in small grocery stores. For a truly attractive dish, use a variety of colors. If the tiny ones are not available, substitute regular-size peppers.

24	baby red, green, yellow or purple peppers (or 12 medium)	24
$\frac{3}{4}$ lb	medium ground beef	375 g
1	onion, finely chopped	1
2 cups	cooked rice (1 cup/250 mL raw)	500 mL
$1\frac{1}{2}$ cups	drained canned or chopped fresh tomatoes	375 mL
$\frac{1}{2}$ cup	tomato sauce*	125 mL
1 tbsp	Worcestershire sauce	15 mL
1 tsp	salt	5 mL
$1\frac{1}{2}$ cups	Tomato-Basil Sauce (page 149)	375 mL

Slice top off each pepper; chop tops and save to add to filling. Remove core, seeds and white membranes from peppers. Blanch peppers in boiling water for 3 minutes; drain and set aside.

In large skillet or heavy saucepan, cook beef, onion and chopped pepper until beef is browned and onions are tender. Drain off any fat. Stir in rice, tomatoes, tomato sauce, Worcestershire and salt; simmer for 2 minutes. Spoon meat mixture into peppers. (Recipe may be prepared ahead to this point and refrigerated or frozen.) Bake in 350°F/180°C oven for 20 minutes or until hot. Serve with Tomato-Basil Sauce to spoon over. Makes 6 servings.

Calories per serving: 213
Grams fat per serving: 6
Vitamins A and C and niacin: Excellent
Iron, riboflavin and phosphorus: Good

September Family Supper
Stuffed Baby Peppers with Tomato-Basil Sauce (page 103)
Steamed carrots
Whole-wheat bread
Peach Blueberry Crisp (page 208)

Stuffed peppers can be frozen. Cook frozen or thawed peppers in a microwave or in a conventional oven.

*Instead of tomato sauce, you can use $\frac{1}{4}$ cup/50 mL each tomato paste and water (mixed), or $\frac{1}{2}$ cup/125 mL catsup.

Variation:
Instead of Tomato-Basil Sauce, sprinkle stuffed peppers with grated Parmesan cheese or low-fat mozzarella cheese before baking.

TEX-MEX CHILI

Tex-Mex is hot and spicy Mexican food adapted to a North American palate. You can add cooked brown beans or any other type of beans.

1 lb	lean ground beef	500 g
2	large onions, coarsely chopped	2
2	large cloves garlic, minced	2
2 tbsp	(approx) chili powder	25 mL
1 tsp	ground cumin	5 mL
½ tsp	oregano	2 mL
½ tsp	crushed red chili peppers	2 mL
1	can (28 oz/796 mL) tomatoes	1
4 cups	cooked red kidney beans, or 2 cans (each 19 oz/540 mL), drained	1 L
1 tsp	salt	5 mL
1½ cups	kernel corn (canned, frozen or fresh)	375 mL

In large heavy saucepan or nonstick skillet, cook beef for about 5 minutes or until brown. Pour off any fat. Add onions, garlic, chili, cumin, oregano and red pepper; cook, stirring, over low heat until onions are tender (about 5 minutes). Stir in tomatoes, kidney beans and salt; bring to a boil, reduce heat and simmer for 20 minutes, or until desired consistency is reached. Add corn, and cook until corn is heated through. Makes 6 servings.

Calories per serving: 349
Grams fat per serving: 8.5
Fiber: Excellent
Iron, niacin, vitamins A and C: Excellent
Thiamine: Good

OLD-FASHIONED MEAT LOAF

Adding bran to a family favorite is an easy way to add a little fiber to your meals. Serve this traditional meat loaf with baked potatoes and a green vegetable.

1 lb	lean beef	500 g
1	large onion, finely chopped	1
$\frac{1}{4}$ cup	natural bran	50 mL
1	slice whole-wheat bread, crumbled	1
$\frac{1}{2}$ tsp	thyme	2 mL
$\frac{1}{2}$ tsp	salt	2 mL
Dash	Worcestershire sauce	Dash
	Freshly ground pepper	
1 cup	tomato juice or tomato sauce	250 mL
1	egg, lightly beaten	1
1 tbsp	chopped fresh herbs—thyme, rosemary, savory, sage (optional)	15mL

In mixing bowl, combine beef, onion, bran, bread crumbs, thyme, salt, Worcestershire, and pepper to taste. Stir in tomato juice, egg and herbs (if using); mix lightly. Turn into 9 × 5-inch/2 L loaf pan or baking dish. Bake in 350°F/180°C oven for 45 minutes, or until brown and firm to the touch.

Remove from oven; pour off fat. Makes 5 servings.

	Using lean ground beef	Using regular ground beef
Calories per serving:	186	267
Grams fat per serving:	9.5	17
Niacin: Excellent		
Iron and phosphorus: Good		

Compare:
Lean ground beef contains not more than 17% fat.
Medium ground beef contains not more than 23% fat.
Regular ground beef contains not more than 30% fat.

Lean, Medium or Regular
• Use medium or regular ground beef when you can pour fat from pan after browning the meat.
• Use medium ground beef where some fat is needed for tenderness and juiciness (hamburgers).
• Use lean ground beef when you can't pour off the fat (shepherd's pie, or stuffing for pasta), or where other fats are in same dish, so more fat is not needed for tenderness or flavor.

Be sure to pour off any fat in pan before serving meat loaf.

HAMBURGERS AU POIVRE

Dress up peppery hamburgers with this shallot-yogurt sauce.

1 lb	lean ground beef	500 g
2 tsp	peppercorns	10 mL
1 tbsp	vegetable or corn oil	15 mL
1 tbsp	finely chopped shallots*	15 mL
1 tbsp	red wine vinegar	15 mL
$\frac{1}{4}$ cup	yogurt or sour cream	50 mL
1 tbsp	minced fresh parsley	15 mL

*If shallots are unavailable, use cooking onions.

Divide meat into 4 portions and shape into hamburger patties.

Put peppercorns on large piece of waxed paper or foil. Using bottom of heavy skillet or pan, crack peppercorns coarsely. Spread peppercorns out, and place patties on top. Press patties down; turn patties over and sprinkle any remaining peppercorns over top. Press peppercorns so they stick to meat.

In large skillet, heat oil over high heat. Add patties and cook over high heat for 2 to 3 minutes or until browned; turn and cook other side for 1 to 2 minutes or until browned, and at desired degree of doneness (reduce heat if necessary to prevent burning).

Transfer patties to warm serving plate. Pour off fat in pan; add shallots and wine vinegar and cook over medium heat, scraping up brown bits from bottom of pan. Remove from heat; add yogurt and stir to mix well. Stir in parsley. Place patties on individual plates, then spoon sauce over them. Makes 4 servings.

Calories per serving: 244
Grams fat per serving: 13
Niacin: **Excellent**
Iron and phosphorus: **Good**

POT-AU-FEU

This French savory classic consists of a pot roast of beef and various vegetables slowly simmered together. The heavenly broth can be served as a first course, and the meat and vegetables as the main course. Or, the meat and vegetables can be served as the main course, then any leftovers added to the broth and served for dinner another night. It's best to start this a day in advance and refrigerate it overnight so the fat will solidify on top for easy removal. Serve with boiled potatoes and Horseradish Sauce (page 147).

4 lb	(approx) boneless rib, blade or sirloin tip roast	2 kg
8 cups	water	2 L
3	large carrots	3
3	large onions	3
2	small white turnips (or half a yellow rutabaga)	2
2	stalks celery	2
1	small cabbage	1
	Salt and freshly ground pepper	

Be sure roast is securely tied. Place in large, deep saucepan or flameproof casserole and add water. Bring to a boil over medium heat; remove any scum. Simmer for 1½ hours.

While stock is heating, peel carrots, onions and turnips; cut into even-sized chunks and add to hot stock. Cut celery into similar-sized pieces and add to stock. Cover, and simmer for another hour or until vegetables are nearly tender. Skim off fat or refrigerate overnight, then remove fat.

Reheat if necessary. Quarter cabbage and add to pot. Cook for 15 minutes or until tender. Season with salt and pepper to taste. Remove meat to platter; let stand for 10 minutes before carving. Keep vegetables warm, and serve broth as a first course (save a little broth to pour over meat and vegetables). Makes 10 servings.

Calories per serving (including broth): 420
Grams fat per serving: 20
Fiber: Good
Vitamins A and C, iron and niacin: Excellent

TOMATO SAUCE PROVENÇAL WITH VEAL ON PASTA

Thin strips of tender veal combine with tomatoes and Provençal seasonings of garlic and parsley in this easy dish. The small amount of veal keeps the cost within reason and the fat content down.

1 tbsp	butter	15 mL
1	large onion, chopped	1
2 tbsp	(approx) water	25 mL
$\frac{1}{2}$ lb	whole-wheat noodles	250 g
1	can (28 oz/796 mL) plum tomatoes, drained	1
$\frac{1}{2}$ lb	lean veal	250 g
4	cloves garlic, minced	4
$\frac{1}{2}$ cup	minced fresh parsley	125 mL
	Salt and freshly ground pepper	

Fettuccine with Clam Sauce
For a delightfully easy pasta dish, substitute 1 can (5 oz/ 142 g) of clams, drained, for the veal in Tomato Sauce Provençal with Veal on Pasta. Toss with hot, drained fettuccine. For 2 to 3 people, use the same basic recipe but substitute 1 can (19 oz/540 mL) tomatoes for the larger can; use slightly less pasta (toss any leftover noodles with sauce and reheat the next day in a microwave or a saucepan).

In large heavy skillet, melt butter over medium heat; cook onion until tender. Add water to prevent onion from burning (add more if necessary).

In large pot of boiling water, cook noodles until al dente (tender but firm). (Dry whole-wheat noodles require a longer cooking time than regular noodles or fresh pasta; follow package directions and taste every few minutes.)

Coarsely chop tomatoes and add to onion in skillet. Cut veal into 2-inch/5 cm strips about $\frac{1}{4}$ inch/5 mm wide; add to skillet and cook over medium heat, stirring occasionally, until veal is cooked (about 2 minutes). Add garlic and parsley.

Drain noodles and arrange on hot dinner plates or platter. Season sauce with salt and pepper to taste; spoon over noodles. Serve immediately. Makes 4 main-course servings, 6 appetizer servings.

Calories per main-course serving: 574
Grams fat per main-course serving: 12
Fiber: Good
Iron, vitamins A and C and niacin: Excellent
Thiamine and riboflavin: Good

MEXICAN PORK STEW

Pork cut in cubes cooks much faster than chops or a roast, making this ideal for a quick family dinner. Add dried hot chili peppers to taste and other vegetables, such as eggplant or zucchini in season. Serve with boiled potatoes or over hot noodles.

1 lb	boneless pork (butt, shoulder)	500 g
1 tsp	vegetable oil	5 mL
1	large onion, coarsely chopped	1
1	clove garlic, minced	1
1	can (19 oz/540 mL) tomatoes	1
1	small sweet green pepper, coarsely chopped	1
2 tbsp	chopped fresh parsley	25 mL
$\frac{1}{2}$ tsp	crumbled dried cumin	2 mL
$\frac{1}{2}$ tsp	leaf oregano	2 mL
$\frac{1}{4}$ tsp	thyme	1 mL
	Salt and freshly ground pepper	

Cut off any visible fat from pork. In heavy saucepan or skillet, heat oil over medium-high heat; add pork a few pieces at a time and cook until lightly browned on all sides. (There should be enough fat in pork to prevent burning—a heavy or nonstick pan is important.) Add onion and garlic; cook, stirring, until onion is tender, about 2 minutes.

Stir in green pepper, tomatoes, parsley, cumin, oregano, thyme, and salt and pepper to taste. Bring to a boil; reduce heat and simmer, covered, for 15 minutes. Makes 4 servings.

Calories per serving: 252
Grams fat per serving: 13.6
Vitamins A and C, niacin and thiamine: Excellent
Iron and phosphorus: Good

Shopping Tip
Boneless pork shoulders are often featured in supermarket specials. Cut the meat into cubes or strips, discarding fat, and use in stews and stir-fries or on skewers. Package them in 1 lb/500g portions (or a size to suit your household) and freeze until needed.

Fresh Ginger

Whenever possible, use fresh, not ground, ginger in recipes calling for fresh—the flavor is far superior. Fresh ginger can elevate an ordinary dish into something really delicious. Use it in stir-fries, with vegetables, and in stuffings, stews and other savory dishes. This brown, knobby root is available in the vegetable section of most supermarkets and fruit and vegetable stores.

To buy: Buy young ginger with pale brown skin. Shriveled skin is a sign of age. Avoid buying ginger with cracks, mold or a musty smell.

To store: Wrap ginger in a plastic bag to prevent drying out and store in a cool place or refrigerate for a few weeks. For longer storage, freeze ginger, or peel, place in a jar and cover with sherry or vodka; seal and refrigerate.

To use: With a vegetable peeler or knife, peel skin from portion of root you plan to use. Depending on the recipe, either grate or chop it before adding to the dish. Sometimes a slice of fresh ginger is added to a marinade or stew, then discarded before serving.

CHINESE PORK AND VEGETABLES

My children enjoy this dish because it isn't very spicy. You may want to add sherry, dried chili peppers or perhaps more ginger to taste. Serve on a bed of hot fluffy rice.

1 tbsp	cooking oil	15 mL
1 lb	lean boneless pork, cut in thin strips	500 g
2	cloves garlic, minced	2
1	onion, sliced	1
5	stalks celery, diagonally sliced	5
4	carrots, diagonally sliced	4
1 tbsp	peeled and grated fresh ginger root	15 mL
1 cup	hot chicken stock	250 mL
2 tbsp	low-sodium soy sauce	25 mL
$\frac{1}{4}$ tsp	freshly ground pepper	1 mL
1	small head cabbage	1
1 tbsp	cornstarch	15 mL
2 tbsp	cold water	25 mL
	Lemon juice	
	Salt and freshly ground pepper	

In wok or large heavy skillet, heat oil over high heat. Add pork and stir-fry until pork is no longer pink. Add garlic, onion, celery, carrots and ginger; stir-fry until onion is tender. Add stock, soy sauce and pepper. Cover, and simmer for 5 minutes.

Shred cabbage (you should have about 4 cups/1 L packed shredded cabbage). Stir into skillet and cook for 3 to 4 minutes longer or until vegetables are tender-crisp. Blend cornstarch with cold water; gradually add to skillet, stirring constantly, until sauce thickens. Add lemon juice, salt and pepper to taste. Makes 5 servings.

Calories per serving: 279
Grams fat per serving: 14
Fiber: **Excellent**
Thiamine, niacin and vitamins A and C: **Excellent**
Iron, riboflavin, and phosphorus: **Good**

PORK TENDERLOIN WITH ROSEMARY AND THYME

Pork tenderloin is the leanest cut of pork with little fat. This very quick and easy-to-prepare dish is ideal for a casual Friday night dinner party. In fall, serve with squash or sweet peppers, in summer with Tomatoes Provençal (page 153), in spring with Asparagus with Red Pepper Purée (pages 154-5) and in winter with Braised Red Cabbage (page 157).

2 tbsp	Dijon mustard	25 mL
1 tsp	rosemary	5 mL
$\frac{1}{2}$ tsp	thyme	2 mL
$\frac{1}{4}$ tsp	whole black peppercorns, crushed	1 mL
1 lb	pork tenderloin	500 g

In small bowl, combine mustard, rosemary, thyme and peppercorns and mix. Spread over pork. Place in roasting pan. Roast in 350°F/180°C oven for 35 to 45 minutes or until no longer pink inside. Garnish with fresh rosemary. To serve, cut in thin slices. Makes 3 servings.

Calories per serving: 248
Grams fat per serving: 14
Iron, thiamine and niacin: Excellent
Phosphorus: Good

To reduce fat:
- Buy lean cuts of pork.
- Trim visible fat before cooking.

Compare:	4oz/125 g serving Grams fat
Spareribs	44
Pork chop—lean and fat	42
Pork chop—lean only, fat removed	14
Pork tenderloin	14

SHERRY-BRAISED HAM WITH CURRIED FRUIT

This is one of my favorite entertaining dishes for a large group. If you remove the fat before cooking, there will be less salt as well as less fat. Cooking ham in liquid makes it very juicy and tender.

1	cooked ham (9 lb/4 kg)	1
1	large onion, sliced	1
2	carrots, sliced	2
2½ cups	beef stock	625 mL
½ cup	sherry	125 mL
1	bay leaf	1
½ tsp	thyme	2 mL
1	bunch watercress	1
	Curried Fruit with Rice (page 171)	

Remove skin and all but a very thin layer of fat covering ham. Place ham in roasting pan; arrange vegetables around it. Pour beef stock and sherry over ham; add bay leaf and thyme. Bring to a boil on top of stove. Cover and bake in 325°F/160°C oven for 2½ hours, basting 3 or 4 times during roasting. Uncover and cook for 15 minutes longer. Remove from oven; transfer to platter and let stand for at least 15 minutes before carving (discard vegetables in pan).

Slice ham into thin slices. Garnish platter with watercress and be sure to include a sprig on each person's plate. Arrange hot curried fruit and rice on another plate. Makes about 18 servings.

Calories per serving 3 oz/90g: 186
Grams fat per serving: 8.1
Vitamin A, iron, niacin and thiamine: Excellent
Riboflavin: Good

Easter Dinner
Crudités with Creamy Fresh Dill Dip (page 30)
Sherry-Braised Ham with Curried Fruit (page 112)
Rice
Green beans
Lemon Charlotte with Strawberries (page 202)

Warning: Because of the nitrites in most hams, ham should be eaten only occasionally and in moderation.

GINGER-APRICOT STUFFED LAMB WITH KUMQUATS

Bright orange, grape-sized kumquats are a most attractive edible garnish for this dish. Make it in the spring when kumquats are readily available.

1	boneless leg or shoulder of lamb (3lb/1.5 kg), ready for stuffing (about 5 lb/ 2.2 kg, bone-in)	1
Stuffing:		
1 tsp	butter	5 mL
1	small onion, chopped	1
$\frac{2}{3}$ cup	coarsely chopped dried apricots	150 mL
1 tbsp	peeled and grated fresh ginger root	15 mL
1 tsp	grated lemon rind	5 mL
	Salt and freshly ground pepper	
Glaze:		
2 tbsp	apricot jam	25 mL
$\frac{1}{2}$ tsp	Dijon mustard	2 mL
$\frac{1}{4}$ tsp	ground ginger	1 mL
Garnish:		
8	apricots (fresh or canned), halved and pitted	8
8	sprigs fresh rosemary or watercress	8
8	small ripe kumquats (optional)	8

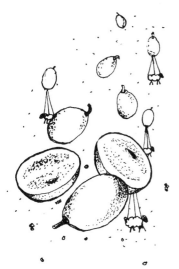

Stuffing: In small skillet, melt butter over medium heat; add onion and cook until soft. Stir in apricots, ginger, lemon rind, and salt and pepper to taste. Place stuffing in lamb cavity and sew or tie together. Place on rack in baking pan. Roast in 325°F/160°C oven for 1½ hours.

Glaze: Combine jam, mustard and ginger; mix well. Brush over outside of lamb and continue roasting for 15 minutes longer or until lamb is brown outside and pink inside. Transfer to serving platter and let stand for 15 minutes before carving. Arrange halved apricots, rosemary sprigs and whole unpeeled kumquats around lamb. Makes 8 servings.

Calories per serving: 326
Grams fat per serving: 10
Fiber: Good
Vitamin A and niacin: Excellent
Iron, thiamine, phosphorus and riboflavin: Good

MARINATED LEG OF LAMB WITH CORIANDER

Boneless butterflied legs of lamb are available in the frozen-food sections of many supermarkets or fresh at butcher stores. This marinade is also delicious with lamb chops and rack of lamb. An easy dish to prepare in advance, marinated leg of lamb is also easy to transport (in a plastic bag) to the cottage or camp.

1	boneless butterflied leg of lamb (about $3\frac{1}{2}$ lb/1.7 kg)	1
	Salt and freshly ground pepper	
	Dijon mustard or Horseradish Sauce (page 147)	
Marinade:		
1 tbsp	coriander seeds	15 mL
$\frac{1}{2}$ cup	lemon juice	125 mL
2 tbsp	vegetable oil	25 mL
1	small onion, chopped	1
1 tbsp	grated fresh ginger root	15 mL
2	cloves garlic, chopped	2
1 tsp	black peppercorns, crushed	5 mL

Should lamb be rare or well-done?

As with beef, this is a matter of personal taste. However, if it is too rare, it can be tough. If overcooked, it will be dry. The safest is medium-rare—it will be tender, juicy and pink on the inside.

Marinade: In skillet, toast coriander seeds over medium heat for 5 minutes, shaking pan occasionally. Remove from heat; let cool, then crush seeds. Combine crushed seeds, lemon juice, oil, onion, ginger, garlic and peppercorns.

Cut off any fat from lamb and discard. If meat is not of even thickness, slash thickest section and open up, book fashion. Place lamb in glass or ceramic dish or plastic bag and coat both sides of meat with marinade. Cover and refrigerate for 48 hours, turning once. Remove lamb from refrigerator about 1 hour before cooking.

Drain lamb and wipe dry. Place on broiler rack and broil about 6 inches/15 cm from heat for about 12 minutes on each side for medium-rare, 15 to 20 minutes on each side for well-done. Meat thermometer should register 140°F/60°C for rare, 160°F/70°C for medium and 180°F/80°C for well-done. Remove from heat; let stand for 5 minutes, season with salt and pepper to taste, then slice thinly across the grain. Serve with Dijon mustard or Horse-radish Sauce (page 147). Makes 8 servings.

Calories per (5oz / 140g) serving: 393
Grams fat per serving: 11
Iron, riboflavin, phosphorus, niacin and thiamine: Excellent
Vitamin C: Good

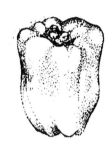

SOUVLAKIA OF LAMB

Greece is famous for its souvlakia or skewered lamb, which the Greeks season with lemon juice and oregano. They don't usually have vegetables on the skewers, but it's more colorful when you include them and they add extra flavor. Boneless lamb loins and lamb tenderloin are available in the frozen-food sections of super-markets if you can't find fresh lamb. Serve the skewers on hot rice.

1 lb	boneless lamb loin	500 g
2 tbsp	lemon juice	25 mL
1 tsp	crumbled leaf oregano	5 mL
	Salt and freshly ground pepper	
8	small onions	8
1	small red pepper	1
1	small yellow or green pepper	1

Cut lamb into 1-inch/2.5 cm cubes. Place in glass dish or plate and sprinkle with lemon juice, oregano, and salt and pepper to taste. Blanch onions in boiling water for 10 to 15 minutes or until almost tender; drain. When cool enough to handle, cut off root ends of onions and squeeze off skins. Seed peppers and cut into 1½-inch/4 cm pieces.

Thread lamb alternating with vegetables onto flat-bladed metal skewers or wooden skewers that have been soaked in water.

Preheat broiler. Place skewers on broiler rack and broil about 5 inches/13 cm from heat, turning every 3 to 4 minutes, for 12 minutes or until meat is brown outside but still pink inside. Makes 4 servings.

Calories per serving: 224
Grams fat per serving: 7
Fiber: Good
Niacin and vitamins A and C: Excellent
Iron and phosphorus: Good

Start this a day in advance and refrigerate overnight. The fat will solidify on top and be easy to remove. Combining meat with vegetables in one dish allows you to get away with serving less meat.

*Bouquet Garni: 2 sprigs fresh parsley, 1 sprig thyme, 1 bay leaf, 1 stalk celery tied with a sprig of parsley or a piece of string, or in cheesecloth tied with string (if you don't have fresh thyme, use ½ tsp/2 mL dried thyme).

NAVARIN OF LAMB

When the International Association of Cooking Professionals held their annual conference in Toronto in 1984, sixteen food writers and teachers entertained delegates in their homes for dinner. We all served the same menu and the main course was Lucy Waverman's beautifully flavored Navarin of Lamb and wild rice. This version is adapted from her recipe. The garlic is sweet and mild, and fresh rosemary adds a very special flavor. Serve with rice noodles or potatoes.

2 lb	lean boneless lamb (e.g. leg)	1 kg
1 tsp	granulated sugar	5 mL
	Salt and freshly ground pepper	
1 tbsp	vegetable oil	15 mL
2 tbsp	all-purpose flour	25 mL
2 cups	beef or lamb stock	500 mL
1	clove garlic, minced	1
1 tbsp	tomato paste	15 mL
	Bouquet garni*	
1	long strip orange rind (orange part only)	1
1 tbsp	fresh rosemary leaves or 1 tsp/5 mL dried	15 mL
Vegetables:		
5	carrots	5
3	small white turnips or 1 yellow rutabaga (about 1 lb/ 500 g)	3
10	small onions or 1 cup/ 250 mL pearl onions	10
Garlic Garnish:		
4	heads garlic	4
½ cup	milk	125 mL

Trim any fat from lamb; sprinkle with sugar, and salt and pepper. In large heavy Dutch oven or nonstick pan, heat oil over medium heat until hot. Add meat a few pieces at a time and brown well.

Remove meat from pan and pour off all fat. Return meat to pan; add flour and cook over medium heat, stirring constantly, for 1 minute or until flour has browned. Add stock, garlic, tomato paste, bouquet garni and orange rind. Bring to a boil, stirring to scrape up all the flavorful brown bits from bottom of pan. Cover and bake in 325°F/160°C oven for 1 hour. Let cool, then refrigerate overnight or until cold.

Remove fat from surface of stew; discard orange rind and bouquet garni.

Vegetables: Scrape carrots; peel turnips and onions. If using pearl onions, blanch in boiling water for 1 minute; drain, then cut off root end and gently squeeze to remove skin. Cut carrots and turnips into $\frac{3}{4}$-inch/2 cm pieces.

Garlic Garnish: Separate garlic heads into cloves. Combine garlic with milk in small saucepan. Bring to a boil and boil for 2 minutes. Reduce heat to low; cover, and simmer until garlic cloves are soft. Drain. When cool, gently squeeze cloves to remove skins. Set aside.

About 45 minutes before serving, gently reheat lamb mixture, stirring to prevent scorching. Add vegetables and simmer, covered, for 30 minutes or until vegetables are tender; add water if necessary. (For a thicker gravy, add 2 tbsp/25 mL flour mixed with $\frac{1}{2}$ cup/125 mL water or stock; bring to a boil and cook, stirring, until thickened slightly.) Add rosemary and garnish with garlic cloves. Makes 8 servings.

Calories per serving: 261
Grams fat per serving: 11
Fiber: Good
Vitamins A and C and niacin: Excellent
Iron and phosphorus: Good

Winter Dinner Party
Cream of Broccoli Soup (page 41)
Navarin of Lamb (pages 116-17)
Tiny boiled potatoes
Arugula and Radicchio Salad with Balsamic Vinaigrette (page 66)
Apple Cinnamon Sorbet (page 94) or Grapefruit Ice (page 196)
Coconut-Oatmeal Cookies (page 185)

Spring Dinner Buffet
Asparagus with Orange Vinaigrette (page 84)
Navarin of Lamb (pages 116-17)
Tiny boiled potatoes
Tossed green salad with Watercress Dressing (page 85)
Rhubarb Crumb Pie (page 216)

FISH

When it comes to fish, Canadians on the east and west coasts don't know how lucky they are. I grew up in Vancouver, and it wasn't until I moved to Ontario that I realized inexpensive fresh fish was a rare commodity to many people. And when I say fresh, I mean no more than a day or two out of the water. Be careful with the meaning of the word fresh. Sometimes we say fresh to mean not frozen, but just because a fish has not yet been frozen it's not necessarily fresh—it may have been out of the water for days.

The best test of a fresh fish is its smell. It should be very mildly fishy, nothing stronger. Don't hesitate to ask to smell the fish; a reputable store will encourage your scrutiny, and you'll discover it pays to find a store you can rely on.

If you can't get good fresh fish, don't let that prevent you from enjoying fish. Frozen fish is available right across the country. Part of the trick of cooking frozen fish is defrosting it properly. Don't put it out on the counter hours before you plan to cook it. It's important to keep fish cold so the outside portions don't deteriorate while the inside is still frozen. The best method of defrosting it is to place fish in the refrigerator. Often we don't have the time, so the next best way is to immerse the package in cold water for about 1½ hours. That way the outside thawed portion stays cold while the center is still defrosting. Before cooking, separate the fish into fillets if it has been frozen in a block; it looks more appealing that way.

There is an unnecessary mystique about cooking fish—too many people are afraid to take the plunge when in fact fish is one of the easiest foods to cook. With fish, the simpler the better. Most fish has a delicate flavor that you don't want to mask with strong seasonings or heavy sauces. A sprinkling of lemon juice and chopped fresh parsley is a classic, delicious preparation. Just try Sole Fillets with Lemon and Parsley (page 119).

And thanks to the Department of Fisheries and Oceans, the Canadian method of cooking fish—as the Americans call it—means we no longer have to guess how long to cook a piece of fish. It's very simple: measure the thickness of the fish at the thickest part; for each inch/2.5 cm of thickness, allow 10 minutes of cooking time at 400°F/200°C; add 5 minutes if the fish is wrapped in foil and double the time if the fish is still frozen. Perfectly cooked fish is opaque and flakes slightly. Avoid overcooking; it dries the fish out.

Best of all, fish is healthy—it's low in fat and calories and high in protein, and for cooks on the run it's one of the fastest foods around.

SOLE FILLETS WITH LEMON AND PARSLEY

This is such a simple recipe, yet it's one of the very best ways to make tender, moist fish fillets. If using frozen fillets, try to thaw and separate them before cooking for best results.

*Pacific perch, snapper or cod may be substituted for the sole.

Fish is an excellent source of protein and is low in fat and calories.

1 lb	sole fillets*	500 g
	Salt and freshly ground pepper	
2 tsp	butter, melted	10 mL
2 tbsp	chopped fresh parsley	25 mL
1 tbsp	lemon juice	15 mL

Place fillets in lightly oiled baking dish just large enough to hold them in single layer. Sprinkle with salt and pepper to taste. Combine butter, parsley and lemon juice. Drizzle over fish. Bake, uncovered, in 450°F/230°C oven for 8 to 10 minutes (10 minutes per inch thickness for fresh fish) or until fish is opaque and flakes easily. To microwave: Cover with plastic wrap and turn back corner to vent for steam; microwave on High for $3\frac{1}{2}$ to $4\frac{1}{2}$ minutes. Makes 4 servings.

Calories per serving: 117
Grams fat per serving: 7

SOLE FLORENTINE

This colorful dish is a little fancier than Sole Fillets with Lemon and Parsley. You can prepare it in advance, then bake it just before serving.

$1\frac{1}{4}$ lb	sole fillets	625 g
1	onion, chopped	1
$\frac{1}{2}$	bay leaf	$\frac{1}{2}$
2 tbsp	lemon juice	25 mL
3	peppercorns	3
$\frac{1}{2}$ tsp	salt	2 mL
$\frac{3}{4}$ cup	dry white wine	175 mL
1 lb	fresh spinach	500 g
4 tsp	butter	20 mL
2 tbsp	all-purpose flour	25 mL
$\frac{1}{2}$ cup	milk	125 mL
	Salt and freshly ground pepper	
1 tbsp	grated Parmesan cheese	15 mL

Roll up fillets and secure with toothpicks. Arrange rolls in skillet or pan just large enough to hold them in single layers; add onion, bay leaf, lemon juice, peppercorns and salt. Pour in wine; bring to a boil. Cover, reduce heat and simmer for 5 minutes. Remove fillets from liquid, reserving liquid.

Wash spinach; cook, covered, in saucepan in just the water clinging to leaves. Drain, and squeeze out excess water; chop finely.

Place spinach in shallow greased dish just large enough to hold the fish rolls. Place fish on top of spinach.

Strain reserved poaching liquid; measure 1 cup/250 mL (add water if necessary). In small saucepan, melt butter; add flour and stir over low heat for 1 minute. Whisk in poaching liquid, milk, and salt and pepper to taste. Bring to a boil, stirring constantly. Remove from heat. (It may be prepared ahead to this point and reheated.)

Pour sauce over fish and sprinkle with Parmesan cheese. Bake in 375°F/190°C oven for 10 to 20 minutes or until bubbly. Makes 4 servings.

Calories per serving: 226
Grams fat per serving: 7
Fiber: Excellent
Vitamins A and C: Excellent
Iron and riboflavin: Good

Photos:

Chicken Dijon (page 88)
Two-Cabbage Stir-Fry (page 159)
Mashed Turnips with Carrot and Orange (page 168)

Navarin of Lamb (pages 116-17)

CAPELLINI WITH CLAM SAUCE AND SWEET RED PEPPERS

Capellini are the thinnest of noodles, but this recipe works well with any kind of noodle. Whole-wheat noodles are good because of their higher fiber content. Serve this extremely easy-to-make dish with steamed snow peas or tossed spinach salad. It's an emergency-shelf type of recipe; the ingredients keep well, and it's so fast to prepare—perfect for unexpected company.

2	sweet red peppers	2
2 tbsp	butter	25 mL
3	cloves garlic, minced	3
	Salt and freshly ground pepper	
1 cup	dry white wine	250 mL
1	can (5 oz/142 g) clams, drained	1
1 tsp	fresh thyme leaves or $\frac{1}{4}$ tsp/ 1 mL dried	5 mL
$\frac{1}{2}$ cup	minced fresh parsley	125 mL
$\frac{1}{2}$ lb	capellini (fresh or dried)	250 g
3 tbsp	grated Parmesan cheese	45 mL

Core and seed red peppers; cut into thin strips.

In heavy skillet, melt half the butter; add red peppers and 1 clove of minced garlic. Cook over medium heat, stirring often, until peppers are tender, about 10 minutes. Season with salt and pepper to taste.

In saucepan, melt remaining butter over medium heat; add remaining garlic and cook, stirring, for 1 minute. Add wine, clams and thyme; simmer for 5 minutes. Add parsley, and salt and pepper to taste.

Meanwhile, in large pot of boiling water, cook capellini until al dente (tender but firm); drain. Spoon capellini onto warmed dinner plates. Pour sauce over it. Arrange sautéed red peppers around pasta. Sprinkle pasta with Parmesan. Serve immediately. Makes 3 main-course or 6 appetizer servings.

	Main Course	Appetizer
Calories per serving:	275	138
Grams fat per serving:	9	4.5
Iron: Excellent		
Vitamins A and C and phosphorus: Good		

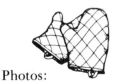

Photos:

Pork Tenderloin with Rosemary and Thyme
(page 111)
Asparagus with Red Pepper Purée
(pages 154-5)

Sole Fillets with Lemon and Parsley (page 119)
Herbed Green Beans with Garlic (page 160)
Cracked Wheat and Basil Pilaf (page 173)

MUSSELS SICILIAN STYLE

For a delightfully easy supper, buy fresh mussels on your way home from work and serve this dish with fresh bread and salad. If you buy cultured mussels, they take only minutes to clean and supper can be ready in 15 minutes.

2 lb	fresh mussels (about 36)	1 kg
1 tsp	olive oil	5 mL
1	small onion, finely chopped	1
1	large clove garlic, minced	1
Pinch	each dried thyme and oregano	Pinch
1	can (14 oz/398 mL) or 2 fresh tomatoes, coarsely chopped	1
$\frac{1}{4}$ cup	dry white wine	50 mL
$\frac{1}{4}$ cup	chopped fresh parsley	50 mL

Scrub mussels under cold water and pull off hairy beards. In large heavy saucepan, heat oil over medium heat; add onion and garlic and cook for 2 to 3 minutes or until tender. Stir in thyme and oregano; add tomatoes, breaking up tomatoes with back of spoon. Bring to a boil and boil for about 2 minutes to reduce liquid. Add wine and return to a boil. Add mussels; cover and cook for 5 minutes or until shells open and mussels are cooked. Discard any shells that don't open. Sprinkle with parsley.

Ladle mussels into large soup bowls, spooning tomato mixture over them. Eat with a fork and a spoon—the fork to pull the mussels out of their shells, the spoon to consume the heavenly broth. Or, sop up remaining broth with bread. Makes 2 servings.

Calories per serving: 223
Grams fat per serving: 6
Fiber: Good
Vitamins A and C, iron, niacin and phosphorus: Excellent
Calcium and thiamine: Good

How to Buy and Store Mussels

It's unbelievable that shellfish as tender and delicious as mussels are so inexpensive. Buy medium-sized (about 18 to the pound/500g) cultured mussels—they're much easier to clean and have more meat than the wild ones. Only buy mussels that have closed shells. The fresher the mussels, the better they taste. However, they can be kept in a bowl or paper (not plastic) bag in the refrigerator for two or three days. Serve as a first course or a main course.

LINGUINE WITH SHRIMP AND TOMATO

The idea for this recipe came from Toronto caterer Dinah Koo. The shrimp and tomato should be quickly cooked over high heat to preserve flavor and texture. If using fresh pasta, make sauce first, because the pasta cooks so quickly.

¼ lb	linguine or whole-wheat noodles	125 g
1 tbsp	vegetable oil	15 mL
1	large clove garlic, minced	1
2 tbsp	finely chopped shallots	25 mL
2	large tomatoes, coarsely chopped	2
¼ tsp	dried basil, or fresh, chopped, to taste	1 mL
¼ lb	small or medium shrimp (raw or cooked)	125 g
1 or 2	green onions, chopped	1 or 2
	Salt and freshly ground pepper	

In a large pot of boiling water, cook linguine until al dente (tender but firm) or according to package directions; drain.

Meanwhile, in heavy skillet, heat oil over high heat. Add garlic and shallots; cook, stirring, for about 30 seconds. Add tomatoes and basil; cook, stirring, for about 1 minute. Add shrimp and cook, stirring, until shrimp are hot and, if using raw, they turn pink. Sprinkle with green onions and season with salt and pepper to taste. Spoon over hot linguine. Makes 2 servings.

Calories per serving: 395
Grams fat per serving: 8
Fiber: Good
Iron, thiamine, niacin and vitamin C: Excellent
Vitamin A and phosphorus: Good

Cooking Pasta

Cook pasta in a large pot of boiling salted water, using about 16 cups/4 L of water for every pound/500 g of pasta. Add pasta a little at a time so the water doesn't stop boiling, and stir with a fork to make sure noodles don't stick together.

Fresh pasta cooks quickly, sometimes in as little time as 2 minutes. Dried pasta takes longer, usually at least 7 minutes, sometimes 10 to 12 minutes. Begin tasting to see whether pasta is done before the suggested cooking time; pasta is cooked when it's al dente (tender but firm—not mushy) and has lost its raw starch taste. Drain in a colander, then toss immediately with sauce, butter or oil as specified in recipe to prevent pasta from sticking together. Because pasta cools quickly, it's important to warm the platter or individual plates it's to be served on. For cold pasta salad, rinse pasta under cold running water to prevent sticking.

Be sure to have the sauce ready before the pasta is finished cooking (overcooked, soft, gluey pasta isn't appealing); then toss pasta with sauce and serve immediately.

SCALLOPS AND SHRIMP IN WINE BOUILLON WITH JULIENNE VEGETABLES

Special Spring Dinner
Asparagus with Red Pepper Purée (pages 154-5)
Scallops and Shrimp in Wine Bouillon with Julienne Vegetables (pages 124-5) or Sole Florentine (page 120)
Strawberries with Raspberry-Rhubarb Sauce (page 220)

Serve this elegant nouvelle cuisine dish for a special dinner. It's the only recipe in the book with whipping cream; the cream is optional, but it does add a delicious smoothness and rich flavor. Luckily, the rest of the ingredients are low in fat.

$\frac{3}{4}$ lb	large raw shrimp	375 g
16	mussels (optional)	16
2	medium carrots	2
1	sweet red pepper	1
2	leeks (white part only)	2
1	small zucchini	1
4 tsp	butter	20 mL
3	shallots, finely chopped	3
2	large cloves garlic, minced	2
$\frac{1}{2}$ cup	white wine	125 mL
$\frac{1}{2}$ lb	scallops	250 g
1 cup	finely chopped fresh parsley	250 mL
$\frac{1}{2}$ cup	whipping cream (optional)	125 mL
	Salt and freshly ground pepper	
3 cups	hot cooked rice	750 mL

Shell shrimp and remove intestinal tract running down back. Scrub mussels and pull off hairy beards. Peel carrots. Seed pepper. Cut leek lengthwise halfway, then wash under cold running water. Cut ends from zucchini. Cut all vegetables into julienne strips (like matchsticks). Blanch vegetables in boiling water for 2 minutes; drain. Plunge into a bowl of ice water to cool; drain.

In large heavy saucepan or flameproof casserole, melt the butter; stir in shallots and garlic and cook over medium-low heat, stirring, for 3 to 5 minutes or until tender. Add wine; bring to a boil. Add shrimp, mussels, scallops and parsley; cover, and simmer for about 3 minutes or until shrimp turn pink and scallops are opaque. Discard any mussels that do not open. Be careful not to overcook or seafood will be tough. Pour in cream (if using) and vegetables and cook until hot.

Taste liquid in pan and add salt and pepper. If liquid is too thin, thicken it by adding 2 tsp/10 mL cornstarch mixed with 2 tbsp/25 mL water; stir and bring to a boil.

Serve in shallow bowls or with rice or noodles. Makes 4 servings.

	Without cream	With cream
Calories per serving:	415	515
Grams fat per serving:	6.5	14.5
Fiber: Good		
Vitamin A, niacin and iron: Excellent		
Thiamine and calcium: Good		

Be very careful not to over-cook scallops. They cook very fast and in just a minute can change from tender to tough and rubbery. They're cooked when they become opaque.

Although scallops are low in fat, they are high in choles-terol. Therefore, they shouldn't be eaten too often.

$\frac{1}{2}$ cup/125 mL whipping cream added to the sauce is scrump-tious but adds 8 grams fat per serving.

BAKED SALMON WITH HERBS

One of my favorite dinner party menus is a baked whole salmon. It's about the easiest main-course dish to prepare, and it is elegant and delicious. When serving four to six people, arrange hot cooked vegetables such as green beans or snow peas on a platter alongside the salmon. It will look like a sumptuous feast.

1	whole salmon or piece about $2\frac{1}{2}$ lb/1.2 kg*	1
$\frac{1}{2}$ cup	chopped fresh parsley	125 mL
2 tbsp	combination of chopped fresh herbs— dill, chives, chervil, basil, sage (optional)	25 mL
	Salt and freshly ground pepper	
1 tbsp	water	15 mL
1 tbsp	lemon juice	15 mL
Garnish (optional):		
	Cucumber slices, parsley, dill or watercress	

*Plan on about $\frac{1}{2}$ lb/250 g per person for a salmon under 4 lb/2 kg; or about $\frac{1}{3}$ lb/166 g per person for a salmon over 4 lb/2 kg or a chunk piece. Of the various types of Pacific salmon, chum has the lowest fat content, spring salmon the highest. Sockeye salmon is the reddest in color, and thus best for mousse recipes.

When buying a whole fish, ask the fishmonger to clean and scale it. If you don't want the head left on, ask him to cut it off. If you want fillets, the fishmonger will usually fillet the fish for you, and sometimes will even remove the backbone and yet leave the fish whole. (Fillets are boneless pieces of fish cut from either side of the backbone; steaks are cut crosswise and include some bone.)

Place salmon on foil; measure thickness at thickest part. Sprinkle parsley and herbs, and salt and pepper to taste inside cavity. Mix water with lemon juice and sprinkle over outside of salmon. Fold foil over and seal.

Place wrapped salmon on baking sheet and bake in 450°F/230°C oven for 10 minutes for every 1 inch/2.5 cm thickness of fish, plus an additional 10 minutes' cooking time because it's wrapped in foil (35 to 40 minutes' total cooking time), or until salmon is opaque. Unwrap salmon and discard skin; most of it should stick to foil. Place salmon on warmed platter. Garnish with cucumber, parsley, dill or watercress (if using). Alternatively, arrange cooked vegetables on platter with salmon.

Serve warm with Yogurt Hollandaise (page 150), Creamy Fresh Dill Dip (page 30) or lemon wedges.

To serve cold: While salmon is still warm, discard skin and scrape off any dark fat. Brush salmon lightly with oil and cover with foil. Refrigerate until serving time. Makes about 4 servings.

Calories per serving: 391
Grams fat per serving: 16
Vitamin C, niacin and phosphorus: Excellent
Thiamine, calcium, iron and vitamin A: Good
These are large-size servings: 3 oz / 90 g of cooked (steamed or baked) salmon has 7 grams fat.

Dinner Party for Six
Fresh Tomato-Dill Bisque
(page 38)
Baked Salmon with Herbs
(pages 126-7)
Rice or tiny potatoes in skins
Herbed Green Beans with Garlic (page 160)
Frozen Lemon Cream (page 195) with Raspberry Coulis
(page 193)

SOLE POACHED WITH TOMATOES, ARTICHOKES AND MUSHROOMS

You can use any type of white fish fillets or steaks, such as cod, halibut or haddock, in this moist and savory fish dish. Serve over pasta or rice.

1 tbsp	butter	15 mL
1½ cups	thickly sliced mushrooms	375 mL
1	clove garlic, minced	1
3	tomatoes, seeded and cut in chunks	3
½ tsp	basil	2 mL
Pinch	thyme	Pinch
1 lb	sole fillets	500 g
1	can (14 oz/398 mL) artichoke hearts, drained and halved	1
	Salt and freshly ground pepper	
	Granulated sugar (optional)	

In heavy saucepan or skillet, melt butter; cook mushrooms and garlic over medium-high heat, shaking pan or stirring, until mushrooms are tender.

Add tomatoes, basil and thyme; bring to a simmer. Add sole and artichokes; cover and simmer for 3 minutes. Uncover and cook for 5 minutes longer or until fish is opaque. Season with salt and pepper to taste (add pinch of sugar if tomatoes are too acidic). Makes 4 servings.

Calories per serving: 141
Grams fat per serving: 5
Vitamin C: Excellent
Vitamin A: Good

MICROWAVE FILLETS PROVENÇAL

Use any lean fish fillets—red snapper, rockfish, Pacific Ocean perch, sole, cod, flounder, haddock or monkfish. It's best to use fresh fillets if available, but you can use frozen.

1	can (19 oz/540 mL) tomatoes	1
1 lb	fish fillets	500 g
	Salt and freshly ground pepper	
$\frac{1}{4}$ cup	chopped fresh parsley	50 mL
$\frac{1}{4}$ cup	fine fresh bread crumbs	50 mL
2 tbsp	minced green onions (including tops)	25 mL
1 tbsp	butter, melted	15 mL
2	cloves garlic, minced	2

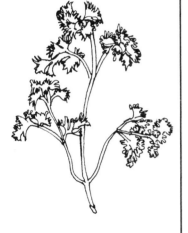

Drain and coarsely chop tomatoes. In microwave dish just large enough to hold fillets in single layer, spoon half the tomatoes. Arrange fillets on top and sprinkle with salt and pepper to taste. Top with remaining tomatoes.

In small bowl, combine parsley, bread crumbs, onions, butter and garlic; sprinkle over tomatoes. Partially cover and microwave on High for 9 to 12 minutes or until fish is opaque. Let stand for 3 minutes before serving. Makes 4 servings.

Note: To cook in conventional oven, bake in 450°F/230°C oven for 20 minutes for fresh fillets, 40 minutes for frozen, or until fish is opaque.

Calories per serving: 244
Grams fat per serving: 9
Vitamins A and C, niacin and phosphorus: Excellent

For other fish dishes, see:
Fish Chowder, Family Style
(page 54)
Nova Scotia Seafood Chowder
(page 48)
Fettuccine with Clam Sauce
(page 108)

BROCHETTES OF SALMON AND SHRIMP

Serve these skewers of salmon and shrimp over a bed of rice.
Either add the vegetables to the skewers or arrange them artisti-
cally around the plate. Creamy Fresh Dill Dip (page 30) goes well
with this.

1½ lb	salmon, skin removed, cut in ¾-inch/2 cm cubes	750 g
16	raw shrimp (about 1 lb/ 500 g)	16
8	stalks asparagus or 16 cherry tomatoes	8
16	large mushrooms	16
16	large seedless green grapes	16
3 tbsp	vegetable oil	45 mL
1 tbsp	lime juice	15 mL
1	clove garlic, minced	1
	Salt and freshly ground pepper	

Snap off tough ends of asparagus. Peel stalks if
desired. Blanch in boiling water for 3 minutes; drain. Cut
into 1½-inch/4 cm lengths. On thin (preferably wooden)
skewers, thread pieces of salmon and shrimp, alternating
with asparagus, mushrooms and grapes.

Combine oil, lime juice, garlic, and salt and pepper to
taste; brush over skewers. Broil for about 10 to 15 minutes
or until fish is opaque. Alternatively, place skewers on wire
rack set over boiling water in broiling pan; cover with foil
and steam for 10 to 15 minutes or until fish is opaque.
Sprinkle with salt and pepper. Makes 6 main-course or 8
appetizer servings.

Calories per main-course serving: 233
Grams fat per main-course serving: 9.3
Niacin: Excellent
Iron, phosphorus and calcium: Good

Types of Fish

Lean fish
— red snapper
— rockfish (silver gray, canary)
— Pacific Ocean perch
— sole
— lingcod, cod (Pacific and Atlantic)
— walleye pollock
— Pacific lake flounder
— haddock, smelt, monkfish

Medium-fat fish
— halibut
— dogfish
— black cod
— tuna
— skate

Fat fish
— herring
— turbot
— shad
— swordfish
— salmon
— mackerel
— catfish

Buying Fresh Fish
When possible buy fish the day you want to cook it. The best test for freshness is to use your nose—the fish should have a mild fishy or seawater odor. Anything stronger means the fish has been out of the water for too long.

Look for:
• mild smell
• glistening, firm flesh that springs back when touched
• very firmly attached scales
• clear, bright, convex eyes (not sunken)

Buying Frozen Fish
Look for:
• glazed fish coated with ice
• shiny, solidly frozen flesh with no signs of drying or freezer burn (white spots)
• tightly wrapped package with no sign of frost or ice crystals inside

Storing Fresh Fish
• If not cleaned, clean as soon as possible.
• Wipe with a damp cloth, wrap in waxed paper and place in covered container.
• Store in coldest part of the refrigerator.
• Cook as soon as possible (same day for store-bought, within 4 days if freshly caught).

Storing Frozen Fish
• Keep fish at 0°F/−18°C or lower for ideal storage.
• Store fat fish (salmon, mackerel, lake trout) for a maximum of 2 months.
• Store lean fish (cod, haddock, ocean perch, pike) for a maximum of 6 months.

How To Cook Fish
• Measure fish at the thickest part (stuffed or not).
• Allow 10 minutes' cooking time per inch/2.5 cm thickness for fresh fish; double the time if fish is frozen. If wrapped in foil, add 5 minutes for fresh, 10 minutes for frozen. This applies to all fish and all cooking methods (if in oven, cook at 450°F/230°C).

Methods of Cooking Fish
Steaming (top of stove)
Pour 2 inches/5 cm of water in a steamer and bring to a boil. Season and wrap fish securely in cheesecloth. Place on a rack over boiling water. Cover and begin timing (see above).

Oven steaming
Preheat oven to 450°F/230°C. Place fresh or frozen fish on lightly greased foil. Season to taste with salt, pepper and herbs (parsley, dill, chives or basil). Sprinkle with lemon juice or white wine. Wrap securely. Place on a baking sheet and bake for required cooking time (see above), adding 5 minutes for fresh and 10 minutes for frozen fish because of being wrapped in foil.

Poaching
Place fish on greased heavy-duty foil. Season with salt and pepper and add chopped onion and celery. Wrap, using double folds to make package water-tight. Place in rapidly boiling water. Cover pan and return to boil; reduce heat and simmer for required cooking time (see above). (Fish may also be wrapped in cheesecloth and poached in court bouillon or fish stock.)

To microwave fish
Place fish in glass dish. Season with salt and pepper to taste. Cover with plastic wrap and turn back corner to allow steam to escape. Estimate cooking time at 3 to 4 minutes per pound/500 g, plus 2 to 3 minutes' standing time. Microwave on High or according to appliance manual.

Fish is cooked when it flakes and separates into solid moist sections when firmly prodded with a fork, and flesh is opaque.

MEATLESS ENTRÉES

Meatless entrées are nothing new. Macaroni and cheese and scrambled eggs have been family favorites for generations, and people who would never call themselves vegetarians often enjoy pizza without pepperoni.

It's becoming increasingly apparent that from both a health and a cost point of view one or more meatless dinners a week can be very beneficial. Also, meatless meals include a surprising variety of foods—everything from vegetables and pasta to eggs and cheese. For the inventive cook, the tasty combinations are endless. For the health-conscious, meatless meals often offer lower fat and higher fiber and vitamin content than meat dishes, and, after all, that kind of eating is what this book is about. For other meatless main-course recipes, be sure to check our soup, salad and vegetable suggestions.

BROCCOLI FRITTATA

This Italian open-faced omelet is delicious for supper or brunch. Unlike a French omelet, which is cooked quickly over high heat and is creamy in the center, a frittata is cooked slowly and is set or firm in the center.

1	bunch broccoli	1
1 tbsp	vegetable oil	15 mL
1 cup	sliced onions	250 mL
2	cloves garlic, minced	2
6	eggs, lightly beaten	6
1 tsp	salt	5 mL
Pinch	each nutmeg and freshly ground pepper	Pinch
$\frac{1}{2}$ cup	grated mozzarella cheese	125 mL

Light Supper for a Winter's Day
Broccoli Frittata (pages 132-3)
Danish Cucumber Salad (page 65)
Whole-Wheat Irish Soda Bread (page 181)
Baked apples

Trim tough ends from broccoli and peel stems. Cut stems and florets into $\frac{3}{4}$-inch/2 cm pieces (you should have about 4 cups/1 L). Steam or cook broccoli in boiling water for 3 to 5 minutes or until crisp-tender; drain thoroughly.

In 10-inch/25 cm skillet, preferably nonstick, heat oil; add onion and garlic and cook over medium heat until onion is tender. Stir in broccoli.

Beat together eggs, salt, nutmeg and pepper; pour over

Broccoli is an excellent source of vitamins A and C and is associated with reduced risk of cancer of the colon.

broccoli mixture and sprinkle with cheese. Cover, and cook over medium-low heat for 5 to 10 minutes or until set but still slightly moist on top. Place under broiler for 2 to 3 minutes to lightly brown top. (If the skillet handle isn't ovenproof, wrap it in foil; since the oven door is open, most of the handle will not be directly under the heat.) Loosen edges of frittata and cut into pie-shaped wedges. Makes 4 servings.

Calories per serving: 181
Grams fat per serving: 10
Fiber: Excellent
Vitamins A and C: Excellent
Riboflavin and niacin: Good

EGGS FLORENTINE

This delicious dish is perfect for brunch, lunch or a light supper. The eggs can be poached in advance, cooled in ice water to prevent further cooking and refrigerated in a bowl of water. Reheat them by placing in a pan of simmering water for about 30 seconds. The spinach and sauce can also be prepared in advance and gently reheated.

¾ cup	Yogurt Hollandaise (pages 150-1)	175 mL
2	pkg (10 oz/284 g each) spinach	2
1 tsp	butter	5 mL
	Salt and freshly ground pepper and freshly grated nutmeg	
2 tbsp	white vinegar	25 mL
6	eggs	6

Prepare Yogurt Hollandaise as directed and keep warm.

Wash spinach and discard stems; place leaves in saucepan. Cover and cook in just the water clinging to leaves over medium-high heat until spinach is wilted. Drain thoroughly and chop spinach coarsely; toss with butter, and salt, pepper and nutmeg to taste. Return to saucepan, cover and keep warm. (If preparing in advance, drain, then cool under cold running water and drain again; reheat over low heat.)

Nearly fill a large shallow pan or skillet with water and bring to a boil; add vinegar. Break eggs over pan and gently drop into water; reduce heat until water is barely simmering and cook eggs for 3 to 5 minutes or until whites are firm and yellows are still soft; spoon water over top of yolk occasionally to cook it slightly.

Spoon spinach onto warmed plates or serving dish. Remove eggs from water with slotted spoon. Place 1 egg over each portion of spinach. Spoon about 2 tbsp/25 mL of sauce over each egg and serve immediately. Makes 6 servings.

Calories per serving: 130
Grams fat per serving: 9
Fiber: Excellent
Vitamins A and C: Excellent
Iron and niacin: Good

Brunch or Lunch Menu
Grapefruit Juice Spritzer (page 134)
Eggs Florentine (page 134)
Tomatoes Provençal (page 153)
Tossed green salad
Toasted English muffins
Raspberry Meringue Torte (page 206) or Pear Crisp with Rolled Oats Topping (page 209)

Grapefruit Juice Spritzer
For a refreshing nonalcoholic drink that's perfect before lunch or brunch, combine equal parts of grapefruit juice and soda water. Serve over ice cubes and garnish with thin slices of lime.

Asparagus with Poached Eggs
In spring, substitute cooked drained asparagus for the spinach in Eggs Florentine. Arrange hot asparagus spears on warmed individual plates or serving dish; sprinkle with lemon juice, salt and pepper. Top with a poached egg and grated Parmesan cheese or Yogurt Hollandaise. If desired, place under broiler for a minute to brown.

OMELET À LA JARDINIÈRE

This is delicious for a quick dinner, lunch or breakfast. Serve with toasted whole-wheat bread and a spinach salad.

1 tsp	vegetable oil	5 mL
1	small onion, finely chopped	1
1	clove garlic, minced	1
$\frac{1}{3}$ cup	grated carrot	75 mL
$\frac{1}{4}$ cup	chopped green pepper	50 mL
	Salt and freshly ground pepper	
4	eggs	4
1 tbsp	water	15 mL
1 tsp	butter	5 mL
$\frac{1}{2}$ cup	alfalfa sprouts	125 mL

A 2-egg omelet is easier to make than a 4-egg or larger omelet. Also, it's important to use the correct size of pan. For a 2- to 3-egg omelet, use an omelet pan 7 inches/18 cm in diameter at the bottom; for a 4-egg omelet, use an 8- to 9-inch/20 to 23 cm pan.

Egg yolks are high in cholesterol—limit your diet to about 5 eggs per week.

In skillet, heat oil; sauté onion and garlic over medium heat, stirring, until tender. Stir in carrot and green pepper and stir-fry for about 3 minutes or until carrot has wilted. Season with salt and pepper to taste.

Beat eggs with water and a large pinch of salt and pepper until whites and yolks are thoroughly blended. Heat an 8- to 9-inch/20 to 23 cm nonstick omelet pan or skillet over very high heat until pan is hot. Add butter to pan. When it sizzles but just before it starts to brown, pour in beaten eggs. Continuously shake the pan back and forth and at the same time stir eggs quickly with a fork to spread them evenly over bottom of pan as they thicken. When eggs have thickened and are almost set, spoon carrot mixture and alfalfa sprouts over eggs.

Tilt pan and roll up edges of omelet, or simply fold omelet in half. Slide onto serving plate. (This whole procedure should take about 1 minute.) Serve immediately. Makes 2 servings.

Calories per serving: 221
Grams fat per serving: 16
Vitamin A: Excellent
Iron, riboflavin, phosphorus and niacin: Good

BULGUR WHEAT, TOFU AND SWEET PEPPERS

This main-course vegetarian dish is a good source of protein and fiber. If possible, use bulgur instead of cracked wheat; it has a nuttier, richer flavor and takes less time to cook.

1 cup	coarse or medium bulgur or cracked wheat*	250 mL
2 tbsp	butter	25 mL
3	cloves, garlic, minced	3
2 tsp	ground cumin	10 mL
2	sweet red peppers, seeded and cut in strips	2
3 tbsp	vinegar	45 mL
$\frac{1}{3}$ cup	water	75 mL
1	pkg (10 oz/284 g) fresh spinach, washed, stemmed and cut in strips	1
1 tsp	salt	5 mL
	Freshly ground pepper	
$\frac{3}{4}$ lb	firm-style tofu or bean curd, cut in cubes	350 g

Rinse bulgur under cold water. Place in bowl and add enough cold water to cover by 2 inches/5 cm; soak for 1 hour. Drain thoroughly in sieve.

In large skillet, melt butter over medium heat, add garlic and cook for a few seconds. Stir in cumin, then peppers. Cover and cook for 5 minutes.

Add bulgur, vinegar and water; cook, uncovered, for 5 minutes or until bulgur is nearly tender, stirring often (cracked wheat will take about 15 minutes longer; add more water as necessary). Add spinach; stir until mixed and spinach is slightly wilted. Season with salt and pepper to taste. Add tofu; cover and simmer for 5 minutes or until heated through and flavors are blended. Makes 6 main-course servings.

Calories per serving: 252
Grams fat per serving: 7
Fiber: Excellent
Vitamins A and C and iron: Excellent
Niacin and phosphorus: Good

Tofu

It's cheap, nutritious, low in calories and fat. Tofu or soybean curd is one of the best sources of nonanimal protein you can find, as well as being rich in calcium, phosphorus and iron.

Tofu is usually sold in a custardlike cake form, covered in water, packed either in 1 lb/500 g plastic tubs or vacuum-packs. Check the "best before" date to make sure it is fresh.

Store tofu in the refrigerator and change the water it is packaged in every day. It will stay fresh for up to 7 days.

Tofu has a mild taste and can be used in everything from appetizers to desserts. Cut it into cubes and add it to soups or salads. Mash it and season with fresh herbs or spices, mustard or garlic; add a little yogurt or sour cream and serve as a dip or sauce.

*See page 64 for information on bulgur wheat.

FETTUCCINE WITH FRESH TOMATOES AND BASIL

This is a delightful supper in late summer or fall when tomatoes are at their best. For the most fiber, try to buy whole-wheat noodles.

6 oz	fettuccine noodles or 2 cups/500 mL dried medium egg noodles	175 g
2 tbsp	olive oil	25 mL
2	cloves garlic, minced	2
4	tomatoes, diced	4
½ tsp	dried basil or 2 tbsp/25 mL chopped fresh	2 mL
Pinch	granulated sugar	Pinch
¼ cup	chopped fresh parsley	50 mL
	Salt and freshly ground pepper	
2 tbsp	grated Parmesan cheese	25 mL

Easy Summer Supper
Fettuccine with Fresh Tomatoes and Basil (page 137)
Tossed Green Salad with Blue Cheese Dressing (page 84)
Sliced fresh peaches

In large pot of boiling salted water, cook noodles until al dente (tender but firm). Meanwhile, in heavy skillet, heat oil over medium heat; stir in garlic, tomatoes, basil and sugar and cook for 5 minutes, stirring occasionally. Add parsley, and salt and pepper to taste.

Drain noodles. Toss with tomato mixture and Parmesan. (If sauce is too thick, add a few spoonfuls of pasta cooking liquid.) Pass extra Parmesan. Makes 2 main-course servings, 4 appetizer or side-dish servings.

Calories per main-course serving: 425
Grams fat per main-course serving: 14
Fiber: Good
Vitamins A and C, thiamine and niacin: Excellent
Calcium, riboflavin, phosphorus and iron: Good

CREAMY PASTA WITH BROCCOLI, CAULIFLOWER AND MUSHROOMS

Here's a hearty pasta dish your family will love. The variety of vegetables you can use is limitless—try adding carrots, snow peas, celery or green beans.

1	small head cauliflower, trimmed and cut in florets	1
1	small bunch broccoli, trimmed and cut in florets	1
	Salt	
2 tbsp	olive oil or vegetable oil	25 mL
3	cloves garlic, minced	3
2½ cups	thickly sliced mushrooms	625 mL
2½ cups	whole-wheat noodles (or egg noodles or spaghettini) (about 4 oz/425 g)	625 mL
1 cup	small-curd cottage cheese	250 mL
½ cup	milk	125 mL
¼ cup	sour cream	50 mL
¼ cup	grated Parmesan cheese	50 mL
	Salt and cayenne pepper	

Calories per serving: 301
Grams fat per serving: 5
Fiber: Excellent
Vitamins A and C: Excellent
Thiamine, niacin, phosphorus and iron: Good

In large pot of boiling salted water, cook cauliflower and broccoli until tender-crisp, about 5 minutes. With slotted spoon, remove vegetables and save the liquid for cooking the pasta.

In large skillet, heat oil; sauté garlic for 2 minutes over medium heat; add mushrooms and sauté for about 5 minutes. Stir in broccoli and cauliflower; sauté for 2 to 3 minutes longer. Set aside.

Meanwhile, in reserved boiling vegetable liquid, cook pasta, adding water if necessary, until al dente (tender but firm), about 8 to 10 minutes; drain.

In food processor, combine cottage cheese, milk, sour cream and Parmesan. Pour over broccoli mixture; add drained pasta and toss until mixed. Season with salt and cayenne pepper to taste. Serve immediately. Makes about 8 servings.

DEEP-DISH VEGETABLE PIZZA

This scrumptious pizza is very filling. Two slices are plenty for dinner along with a salad.

	Whole-Wheat Pizza Dough (page 178)	
1 cup	tomato sauce	250 mL
1 tbsp	finely chopped fresh garlic	15 mL
1 tsp	each oregano and basil	5 mL
1 tsp	oil	5 mL
3	onions, sliced	3
2 cups	sliced mushrooms	500 mL
	Salt and freshly ground pepper	
6 cups	broccoli, 1-inch/2.5 cm pieces	1500 mL
3 cups	grated partly skimmed mozzarella cheese (1 lb/500 g)	750 mL

Prepare pizza dough. Divide dough into 2 pieces.* Roll out each piece to fit an 8- to 9-inch/20 to 23 cm round quiche or cake pan that's at least 1½ inches/ 4 cm deep.

In small bowl, combine tomato sauce, garlic, oregano and basil; stir to mix.

In heavy skillet, heat oil over medium heat; add onions and cook over medium to low heat, stirring until tender, 5 to 10 minutes.

Add mushrooms and cook over medium heat, stirring or shaking pan until mushrooms are lightly browned and liquid has evaporated. Sprinkle with salt and pepper to taste and set aside.

In large pot of boiling water, cook broccoli for 2 minutes or until bright green; drain and cool under cold running water to prevent any further cooking. Drain again and set aside.

Spread tomato mixture over dough in pans. Cover with broccoli, then with mushroom-onion mixture. Sprinkle with grated cheese. Bake in 425°F/220°C oven for 30 to 40 minutes or until crust is browned and top is bubbly. Makes 2 pizzas.

Children's Party
Deep-Dish Vegetable Pizza (page 139)
Crudités with Creamy Fresh Dill Dip (page 30)
Date Squares (page 183)
Coconut-Oatmeal Cookies (page 185)
Chocolate milk

*This method makes a thick crust. If you want a thin crust, divide dough into three portions and use the extra dough to make another pizza base. Dough can be frozen.

Calories per ¼ pizza: 293
Grams fat per ¼ pizza: 14
Fiber: Excellent
Vitamins A and C, riboflavin, niacin, phosphorus, thiamine and calcium: Excellent
Iron: Good

TRIPLE-CHEESE LASAGNE

If making this for a special occasion, add sliced mushrooms and chopped sweet green or red pepper to the tomato sauce. No one will notice it doesn't have meat.

1	can (19 oz/540 mL) tomatoes, undrained	1
1	can (14 oz/398 mL) tomato sauce	1
2	onions, chopped	2
2	cloves garlic, minced	2
1 tbsp	chopped parsley	15 mL
2 tsp	granulated sugar	10 mL
1 tsp	basil leaves	5 mL
1 tsp	thyme	5 mL
2 tsp	Salt	10 mL
	Freshly ground pepper	
$\frac{1}{2}$ lb	lasagne noodles	250 g
$\frac{2}{3}$ cup	grated Parmesan cheese	150 mL
2 cups	cottage cheese	500 mL
1	egg, lightly beaten	1
1 tsp	oregano	5 mL
2 cups	grated low-fat mozzarella cheese ($\frac{1}{2}$ lb/250 g)	500 mL

In saucepan, combine tomatoes, tomato sauce, onions, garlic, parsley, sugar, basil, thyme, 1 tsp/5 mL of the salt, and pepper to taste. Bring to a boil. Reduce heat and simmer, uncovered, stirring occasionally, for 30 minutes or until mixture has a spaghetti-sauce consistency.

In large pot of boiling water, cook lasagne noodles until al dente (tender but firm). Drain and rinse under cold running water; drain well.

Reserve 3 tbsp/45 mL of the Parmesan cheese for topping. In bowl, combine remaining Parmesan cheese, cottage cheese, egg, oregano, 1 tsp/5 mL salt, and pepper to taste. Mix well and set aside.

Reserve $\frac{1}{2}$ cup/125 mL of the tomato sauce for topping. In 13 × 9-inch/3.5 L baking dish, spoon just enough of the tomato sauce to cover bottom sparingly; top with a layer of lasagne noodles. Cover with $\frac{1}{3}$ of the cottage cheese mixture, then $\frac{1}{3}$ of the mozzarella cheese. Repeat with remaining sauce, noodles and cheeses to make 3 layers of each.

Top with reserved tomato sauce and sprinkle with reserved Parmesan cheese. Bake, uncovered, in 350°F/180°C oven for 45 minutes or until hot and bubbly. Remove from oven and let cool slightly before serving. Makes 8 servings.

Calories per serving: 210
Grams fat per serving: 6
Niacin: Excellent
Vitamins A and C, calcium and phosphorus: Good

WINTER VEGETABLE STEW

Other vegetables can be added to or substituted for the vegetables suggested here. Broccoli, green beans, asparagus in season, snow peas or other quick-cooking vegetables can be added to the stew when you add the zucchini.

2 tbsp	vegetable oil	25 mL
4	onions, coarsely chopped	4
4	large cloves garlic, minced	4
1	bunch leeks (3 or 4)	1
4	potatoes	4
4	carrots	4
$\frac{1}{2}$	small rutabaga (yellow turnip)	$\frac{1}{2}$
1	sweet potato or small acorn squash (optional)	1
5 cups	water (preferably vegetable cooking water) or chicken stock	1.25 L
2 tsp	crumbled oregano leaves	10 mL
2 tsp	crumbled thyme leaves	10 mL
2	small unpeeled zucchini, cut in chunks	2
	Salt and freshly ground pepper	
	Chopped fresh parsley	
	Grated Parmesan cheese	

In large heavy saucepan or Dutch oven, heat oil over medium heat. Add onions and garlic; cook until tender.

Discard tough green parts of leeks; cut leeks in half lengthwise and wash under cold running water. Cut into $\frac{3}{4}$-inch/2 cm pieces. Peel potatoes, carrots, rutabaga and sweet potato; cut into 1-inch/2.5 cm cubes.

Add vegetables to saucepan as they are prepared. Stir in water, oregano and thyme; bring to a boil. Cover and simmer until vegetables are tender, about 30 minutes. Stir in zucchini, and salt and pepper to taste; simmer for 5 minutes or until all vegetables are tender, adding more water if desired.

Ladle stew into bowls and sprinkle with parsley. Pass Parmesan cheese separately to sprinkle over stew. Makes 6 main-course servings.

Calories per serving without Parmesan: 205
Grams fat per serving without Parmesan: 4.8
Calories including 1 tbsp / 15 mL Parmesan per serving: 237
Grams fat including 1 tbsp / 15 mL Parmesan per serving: 6.3
Fiber: Excellent
Vitamins A and C, and niacin: Excellent
Phosphorus: Good

BAKED ZUCCHINI OMELET

Similar to a crustless zucchini and spinach quiche or a frittata, this is ideal with toast and salad or sliced tomatoes for brunch, lunch or dinner.

1 tsp	butter	5 mL
1	onion, chopped	1
1	clove garlic, minced	1
2 cups	thinly sliced unpeeled zucchini	500 mL
$\frac{1}{2}$ cup	grated skim-milk cheese	125 mL
2 tbsp	chopped fresh parsley	25 mL
5	eggs, lightly beaten	5
1	pkg (10 oz/300 g) frozen chopped spinach, thawed and drained	1
1 tsp	salt	5 mL
	Freshly ground pepper	

In heavy skillet, melt butter over medium heat; cook onion and garlic until onion is tender. Add zucchini and cook, stirring for 5 minutes.

In bowl, combine parsley, cheese, eggs, spinach, salt, and pepper to taste; mix well. Stir in zucchini mixture. Spoon into lightly oiled 9-inch/23 cm pie plate. Bake in 325°F/160°C oven for 35 to 45 minutes or until set but still moist. Serve hot or cold. Makes 4 main-course servings.

Calories per serving: 154
Grams fat per serving: 9
Fiber: Excellent
Vitamins A and C: Excellent
Iron and niacin: Good

TUSCAN WHITE KIDNEY BEAN AND TOMATO CASSEROLE

You'll want to have a little of this left over—it's delicious cold. Good as a main course with a green salad and whole-wheat pita bread, it's a high-fiber dinner that's easy to make.

Tomato Consommé
In large saucepan, combine $1\frac{1}{2}$ cups/375 mL tomato juice, 1 10 oz/284 mL can consommé or beef bouillon, 1 cup/250 mL water, $\frac{1}{2}$ tsp/2 mL basil and 1 tbsp/15 mL lemon juice. Bring to a boil. Reduce heat and simmer 1 to 2 minutes. Remove from heat and add 2 tbsp/25 mL sherry or white wine (or to taste) and some freshly ground pepper. Ladle into mugs and garnish with thinly sliced lemon. Serve hot. Makes 5 servings ($\frac{3}{4}$ cup/ 175 mL each).

1 tbsp	vegetable oil	15 mL
1	onion, thinly sliced	1
1	clove garlic, minced	1
1	large tomato, seeded and coarsely chopped	1
1	small sweet green pepper, diced	1
$\frac{1}{4}$ tsp	basil	1 mL
Pinch	oregano	Pinch
1	can (19 oz/540 mL) white kidney beans, drained	1
	Salt and freshly ground pepper	
$\frac{1}{2}$ cup	chopped fresh parsley	125 mL

In small heavy saucepan or flameproof casserole, heat oil over medium heat. Add onion and cook until tender. Stir in garlic, tomato and green pepper; cook for 1 minute. Stir in basil, oregano, kidney beans, and salt and pepper to taste. Simmer over low heat for 5 minutes or until heated through and flavors are blended. Stir in parsley. Makes 2 main-course servings.

Calories per serving: 243
Grams fat per serving: 7
Fiber: Excellent
Iron and vitamins A and C: Excellent
Phosphorus, thiamine and niacin: Good

SAUCES

For two years I was a national judge for Wiser's Deluxe Culinary Competition in Montreal. Most of the other judges were very experienced, award-winning chefs. It was here that I learned that the real test of a chef is his or her sauces. The judges would quickly decide how well meat was cooked, arranged and garnished, but the sauce for the meat would be tasted and discussed at great length. It had to be silky smooth, full of flavor but not overpowering, not too thick but not watery either. The sauces we tasted were exquisite, made from long-simmering stocks and enriched with butter and cream.

Now health-conscious diners are demanding lower-calorie sauces, and, as a result, a whole new collection of sauces is in vogue. Spa, light-lean or alternative cuisines are part of expense-account-trade restaurant menus with exciting, innovative dishes. Red peppers are slowly roasted, then puréed, to blanket a plate for tender, juicy chicken breasts. Sun-ripened mangoes, puréed with lemon or lime juice, complement perfectly cooked fish.

Most home cooks don't have wonderful homemade stock bases on hand. We want tasty sauces we can make in five to ten minutes. We want light sauces that are not loaded with calories, cholesterol and fat. Here is a selection of sauces that will fool even the most serious diners. They're full of flavor, yet low in fat, especially when compared to traditional sauces. And most are very quick to prepare.

Diet Hint: Reducing fat content in sauces

- To remove fat from pan juices, skim surface fat or throw in ice cubes. Fat will adhere to the ice and can be easily removed. Or, pour juices into a container and put in freezer. Remove solid fat from the surface. To thicken cold juices, add 2 tbsp/25 mL flour per cup/250 mL of juice and heat, stirring until thickened and smooth.

- Boil down pan juices if they're too thin.
- If using canned beef or chicken stock, refrigerate or freeze just before using. The fat will solidify on top and lift off easily.
- Use yogurt or puréed cottage cheese as a base for cold, cream-type sauces, instead of cream or mayonnaise.
- Instead of whipped cream, use fruits such as strawberries or raspberries puréed in a

food processor or blender. These make delicious sauces to serve with other fruits, ice creams, sherbets or cakes, and they are low in fat and calories.
- Many desserts are too sweet and need whipped cream or crème fraîche to tone down the sweetness. You won't need the whipped cream if you reduce the amount of sugar in puddings, pies and fruit desserts instead.

BLACKBERRY SAUCE

This sauce is delicious with turkey, chicken and ham. Conventional gravy is much higher in fat than this sweet, yet tart, sauce. Currant jelly can be used instead of blackberry.

1 cup	blackberry jelly	250 mL
$\frac{1}{3}$ cup	frozen orange juice concentrate	75 mL
$\frac{1}{3}$ cup	brandy	75 mL
$\frac{1}{4}$ cup	red wine vinegar or balsamic vinegar	50 mL

In small saucepan, combine jelly, orange juice, brandy and vinegar. Heat over low heat until jelly is melted; stir well. Makes 2 cups/500 mL sauce.

Calories per 1 tbsp / 15 mL: 30
Grams fat per 1 tbsp / 15 mL: 0

Holiday Turkey Dinner
Roast turkey with Blackberry Sauce (page 147)
Glazed Brussels Sprouts with Pecans (page 154)
Baked Squash with Ginger (pages 164-5) or Turnips Paysanne (page 169)
Orange Sponge Cake (page 213) with Sherry Orange Sauce (page 201) and Fruit Sorbets (pages 192-4)

DILL MUSTARD SAUCE

Serve with hot or cold fish dishes and seafood, as a dressing for salads, or with chicken or turkey, or toss with cold cooked pasta.

$\frac{1}{3}$ cup	plain yogurt	75 mL
$\frac{1}{3}$ cup	cottage cheese	75 mL
2 tbsp	chopped fresh dill*	25 mL
$1\frac{1}{2}$ tsp	Dijon mustard	7 mL

In food processor or blender, combine yogurt, cottage cheese, dill and mustard; process until smooth. Alternatively, pass cottage cheese through a sieve, then mix with remaining ingredients. Makes $\frac{2}{3}$ cup/150 mL sauce.

Calories per 1 tbsp / 15 mL: 11
Grams fat per 1 tbsp / 15 mL: 0.1

*Fresh dill gives this sauce excellent flavor; if not available, substitute 2 tbsp/25 mL chopped fresh parsley and 1 tsp/5 mL dried dillweed. You can also make this sauce using all yogurt or all cottage cheese.

CREAMY HERB SAUCE

Fresh herbs add wonderful flavor to sauces. Creamy Fresh Dill Dip (page 30) is delicious as a sauce and low in fat as well. Instead of fresh dill, substitute 1 to 2 tbsp/15 to 25 mL of chopped fresh tarragon, basil, or a combination of whatever fresh herbs you have on hand.

Calories per 1 tbsp / 15 mL: 12
Grams fat per 1 tbsp / 15 mL: 0.3

Ways To Cut Fat

SAUCE FOR	INSTEAD OF	Grams fat per 2 tbsp/25 mL	CHOOSE	Grams fat per 2 tbsp/25
Asparagus, broccoli Fish and eggs Benedict	Conventional Hollandaise	7.8+	Yogurt Hollandaise (pages 150-1)	1.8
Pork	Homemade gravy	5.9	Cinnamon Applesauce (page 219)	0.2
			Red Pepper Purée (pages 154-5)	1.5
Beef	Homemade gravy	5.9	Pan juices (fat removed)	0.15
Steak	Béarnaise sauce	7.2+	Tarragon and Mushroom Sauce (page 150)	1.4
Chicken and turkey	Homemade gravy	5.9	Pan juices (fat removed)	0.15
			Cranberry sauce or Blackberry Sauce (page 147)	0.5
Hot or cold poached salmon and other fish	Cream sauces: thick (white sauce) medium thin	3.6 3.1 2.6	Creamy Herb Sauce (page 148)	0.5
	Mayonnaise	24	Dill Mustard Sauce (page 147)	0.2
Pasta	Butter- and cream-based sauces	10 +	Tomato-Basil Sauce (page 149)	0
	Conventional pesto recipe	7	Pesto (page 46)	3

TOMATO-BASIL SAUCE

Use this sauce over spaghetti, macaroni or other pasta, as a base for pizza or with cooked vegetables such as zucchini or green beans. Use the dried leaf form of basil and oregano, not ground; crush the herbs by rubbing them between the palms of your hands before adding to the sauce.

2	cans (each 28 oz/796 mL) plum tomatoes, undrained	2
1	can (5½ oz/156 mL) tomato paste	1
2	onions, finely chopped	2
2	cloves garlic, minced	2
1	large bay leaf	1
2 tbsp	crumbled basil	25 mL
2 tsp	crumbled leaf oregano	10 mL
1 tsp	salt	5 mL
	Freshly ground pepper, sugar	

In food processor, purée tomatoes. Pour into large, heavy saucepan and add tomato paste, onions, garlic, bay leaf, basil and oregano. Simmer, uncovered, for 20 to 30 minutes or until sauce has thickened slightly and onions are tender. (If sauce thickens too quickly, cover for remaining cooking time.) Add salt, and pepper and sugar to taste. Makes about 6 cups/1.5 L sauce.

Calories per ½ cup / 125 mL: 38
Grams fat per ½ cup / 125 mL: 0.3
Vitamins A and C: Excellent

TARRAGON AND MUSHROOM SAUCE

Similar in taste to a Béarnaise sauce but with much less butter, this is delicious served warm with steak, meatballs, lentil burgers and other meats.

1 tbsp	butter	15 mL
1 cup	chopped fresh mushrooms (about $\frac{1}{4}$ lb/125 g)	250 mL
2 tbsp	chopped green onions	25 mL
4 tsp	all-purpose flour	20 mL
$\frac{1}{2}$ tsp	dried tarragon	2 mL
2 cups	beef stock	500 mL

In small saucepan, melt butter over medium heat. Add mushrooms and onion and cook, stirring occasionally, until tender and most of the liquid has evaporated. Sprinkle with flour and tarragon; cook, stirring, for 2 minutes.

Bring stock to a boil; gradually pour into mushroom mixture while whisking constantly. Cook, stirring constantly, until mixture thickens slightly and boils. Simmer, uncovered, for 10 to 20 minutes or until sauce is reduced to about 1 cup/250 mL. Serve hot. Makes 1 cup/250 mL.

Calories per 1 tbsp / 15 mL: 10
Grams fat per 1 tbsp / 15 mL: 0.7

YOGURT HOLLANDAISE

Use this sauce with vegetables or fish. It is like a Hollandaise in taste but is made with yogurt instead of butter.

1 cup	plain yogurt	250 mL
2 tsp	lemon juice	10 mL
3	egg yolks	3
$\frac{1}{2}$ tsp	salt	2 mL
$\frac{1}{2}$ tsp	Dijon mustard	2 mL
Pinch	freshly ground pepper	Pinch
1 tbsp	chopped fresh dill or parsley (optional)	15 mL

*Egg-yolk mixtures cooked in an aluminum pan will discolor.

For other sauce recipes, see:
Red Pepper Purée (pages 154-5)
Curry Sauce (page 171)
Pesto (pages 46-7)

For dessert sauces, see pages 219-21.

In top of nonaluminum double boiler or saucepan,* beat yogurt, lemon juice and egg yolks. Heat over simmering water, stirring frequently, until sauce has thickened, about 15 minutes. (Sauce will become thinner after about 10 minutes of cooking, then will thicken again.) Remove from heat and stir in salt, mustard, pepper and dill (if using). Serve warm. (Sauce can be prepared in advance, refrigerated for up to 1 week, then reheated over hot, not simmering, water.) Makes about $1\frac{1}{4}$ cups/300 mL.

Calories per 1 tbsp / 15 mL: 17
Grams fat per 1 tbsp / 15 mL: 0.9

TOMATO SALSA

Serve this Mexican staple on lettuce, or as a topping for tacos or tostados, over cottage cheese, as a dip with Belgian endive wedges, as a filling for pita bread or as an accompaniment to meats.

4	large tomatoes, peeled, seeded and diced	4
1	large sweet green pepper, seeded and diced	1
1	fresh hot chili pepper, 1 pickled jalapeño pepper, or 1 or 2 canned green chili peppers, seeded and diced	1
1 tbsp	grated onion	15 mL
1	small clove garlic, crushed	1
2 tbsp	chopped cilantro leaves (also called fresh coriander or Chinese parsley)	25 mL
1 tsp	crumbled leaf oregano	5 mL
	Salt and freshly ground pepper	

In bowl, combine tomatoes, green pepper, chili pepper, onion, garlic, cilantro and oregano; mix well. Season with salt and pepper to taste. Cover and refrigerate until needed. Makes 8 servings ($\frac{1}{2}$ cup/125 mL each).

Calories per serving: 27
Grams fat per serving: 0.2
Vitamins A and C: Excellent

VEGETABLES

I always look forward to the change in seasons, not because of the weather, but for the new vegetables it brings to the table. What could possibly taste better than the first bite of June's tender asparagus, July's juicy tomatoes full of sun-sweetened flavor or your first feed of locally grown, sweet and juicy corn-on-the-cob in August? I enjoy the vegetables as much as, if not more than, the meat portion of a meal.

Not only are vegetables delicious, they also play an important role in a healthy diet. Many vegetables are good sources of fiber, vitamins (especially A and C) and minerals, as well as being low in fat and calories. It's the butter, oil and cream you serve with vegetables that add the fat and calories, not the vegetables themselves.

Eating three or more servings a day of a variety of vegetables will help you meet the Canadian Cancer Society's Diet Guidelines. A daily intake of at least three vegetables will help you meet their recommendations for fiber, vitamin C and carotene (which is converted to vitamin A in the body). At the same time, as long as you don't add extra butter or other fats, vegetables will help you maintain your ideal weight and restrict your total fat intake to no more than 30 percent of your daily calorie intake.

When planning meals, include both fresh and raw vegetables. (Raw contain more fiber.) Make sure you have a pleasing combination of colors, flavors and textures. For instance, don't serve turnip, cauliflower and parsnip at the same meal. They're all strongly flavored, similar in texture and lacking in color contrast. Include bright green, deep-yellow and orange vegetables as much as possible, not only for their visual appeal but for their nutrients.

For the most fiber and vitamins:
- Don't peel vegetables if the skins are edible (e.g., potatoes, zucchini, cucumber). They contain fiber as well as nutrients.
- Don't discard the seeds if they're edible (e.g., those in tomatoes and cucumbers). They are excellent sources of fiber.
- Don't overcook vegetables.
- Eat vegetables raw as often as possible.
- Refer to Table G (page 237) to see which vegetables have the most fiber.

Photo:

Scallops and Shrimp in Wine Bouillon with Julienne Vegetables (page 124)

TOMATOES FLORENTINE

These are an attractive make-ahead addition to a buffet table or dinner.

6	tomatoes	6
2 tsp	butter	10 mL
1	small onion, finely chopped	1
1	clove garlic, minced	1
1	pkg (12 oz/340 g) frozen chopped spinach, thawed and drained	1
$\frac{1}{3}$ cup	milk	75 mL
	Salt and freshly ground pepper	
Topping:		
2 tbsp	fine dry bread crumbs	25 mL
2 tbsp	chopped fresh parsley	25 mL
2 tsp	grated Parmesan cheese	10 mL

Cut a slice from top of each tomato. Scoop out pulp to halfway down tomato and save for sauce or soup.

In skillet, melt butter. Stir in onion and garlic; cook over medium heat until tender. Stir in spinach, milk, and salt and pepper to taste. Spoon mixture into tomatoes and arrange in ovenproof serving dish or on baking sheet.

Topping: Combine bread crumbs, parsley and cheese; sprinkle over top of tomatoes. Bake in 400°F/200°C oven for 20 minutes or until heated through. Makes 6 servings.

Calories per serving: 70
Grams fat per serving: 2
Fiber: Excellent
Vitamins A and C: Excellent
Folacin: Good

Variation:
Tomatoes Provençal: Cut 6 tomatoes in half crosswise. Combine $\frac{1}{2}$ cup/125 mL fine bread crumbs, 1 large clove minced garlic, $\frac{1}{4}$ cup/50 mL chopped parsley and 1 tbsp/15 mL olive oil. Sprinkle crumb mixture over tomato halves and place on baking sheet. Bake in 400°F/200°C oven for 15 minutes or until heated through. Makes 6 servings.

Photo:

Deep-Dish Vegetable Pizza (page 139)

Brussels sprouts belong to the brassica genus of the cruciferous family of vegetables. People whose diets frequently include these vegetables have a lower risk of colon cancer.

Spring Dinner Party Menu
Asparagus with Red Pepper Purée (pages 154-5)
Marinated Leg of Lamb with Coriander (pages 114-15)
Cracked Wheat and Basil Pilaf (page 173)
Steamed cherry tomatoes and snow peas or Sautéed Zucchini with Yogurt and Herbs (page 163) or Stir-fried Vegetables with Ginger and Garlic (pages 166-7)
Fresh Strawberry Sorbet (page 193)

Roasted red peppers have a wonderful rich flavor. They're usually quickly roasted under a broiler, over a flame or on the barbecue until they char and blacken. We recommend roasting them slowly just until they blister, not until they char, since charred or barbecued food may contain carcinogenic substances.

GLAZED BRUSSELS SPROUTS WITH PECANS

Traditional with a turkey dinner, this recipe can be easily doubled or tripled. Walnuts can be used instead of pecans. Just make sure they are fresh.

2 cups	small Brussels sprouts	500 mL
1 tbsp	butter	15 mL
2 tsp	granulated sugar	10 mL
2 tbsp	coarsely chopped pecans	25 mL
	Salt and freshly ground pepper	

Trim base of sprouts and outside leaves. Steam sprouts over boiling water for about 10 minutes or until tender. Drain thoroughly.

In skillet, melt butter over medium heat; add sugar and stir until melted. Add sprouts and pecans; stir to coat well and cook for 1 to 2 minutes. Season with salt and pepper to taste. Makes 4 servings.

Calories per serving: 81
Grams fat per serving: 5
Fiber: Good
Vitamin C: Excellent

ASPARAGUS WITH RED PEPPER PURÉE

Serve this colorful dish as a first course in asparagus season.

2	large sweet red peppers	2
2 tsp	olive oil	10 mL
$\frac{1}{4}$ tsp	dried thyme	1 mL
	Freshly ground pepper	
2 lb	asparagus	1 kg

Roast peppers on a baking sheet in 375°F/190°C oven for 18 minutes. Turn and roast on other side for 18 minutes longer or until peppers are blistered and soft. Remove from oven and place hot peppers in a heavy paper or plastic bag. Close bag and let peppers steam for 10 to 15 minutes. Using fingers and a small knife, peel skin from peppers (it should come off easily); seed peppers and cut into strips.

In skillet, heat oil over medium heat; when hot, add roasted peppers and thyme. Sauté for 2 minutes; season with pepper to taste. Purée in food processor. (Purée can be prepared in advance, covered and refrigerated for up to 1 week; reheat gently over low heat before continuing with recipe.)

Wash and break tough ends off asparagus; cook in large pot of boiling water for 5 to 8 minutes or until tender; drain thoroughly.

Spoon hot pepper purée over individual plates. Arrange hot asparagus on top. Makes 6 servings.

Calories per serving: 56
Grams fat per serving: 2.6
Fiber: Good
Vitamins A and C: Excellent

Lemon-Ginger Carrots
Combine 1 tbsp/15 mL each butter, granulated sugar and lemon juice with 1 tsp/5 mL each of grated lemon rind and grated fresh ginger root; cook until sugar dissolves. Toss with 2 to 3 cups/500 to 700 mL of hot cooked carrots.

Add butter at the end of the cooking of vegetables to get maximum flavor with minimum fat.

TARRAGON CARROTS

Onion and tarragon add extra flavor and color to carrots. Cook them in the oven or microwave to retain the vitamins, and save time by slicing the carrots and onions in the food processor.

4	large carrots, thinly sliced (2 cups/500 mL)	4
2	small onions, thinly sliced	2
1 tsp	tarragon	5 mL
2 tbsp	water	25 mL
	Salt and freshly ground pepper	
2 tsp	butter	10 mL

Lightly oil a large sheet of foil or a 6-cup/1.5 L microwave dish. On foil or in dish, place carrots and onion; sprinkle with tarragon, water, and salt and pepper to taste. Wrap tightly or cover. Cook in 350°F/180°C oven for 30 minutes, or microwave on High for 10 to 12 minutes, or until tender. Stir in butter. Makes 4 servings.

Calories per serving: 37
Grams fat per serving: 2
Fiber: Good
Vitamin A: Excellent

BROCCOLI AND SWEET PEPPER STIR-FRY

This colorful red, yellow and green vegetable dish tastes as good as it looks.

1	bunch broccoli (about 1 lb/500 g)	1
1	sweet red pepper	1
1	sweet yellow pepper	1
1 tbsp	vegetable oil	15 mL
1	onion, chopped	1
1 tsp	grated fresh ginger root	5 mL
$\frac{1}{4}$ cup	chicken stock	50 mL
2 tsp	soy sauce	10 mL

Peel tough broccoli stems. Cut stems and florets into pieces about $1\frac{1}{2}$ inches/4 cm long. Blanch in large pot of boiling water for 2 to 3 minutes or until bright green and tender-crisp; drain, cool under cold running water and dry on paper towels. Seed peppers and cut into thin strips. (This can be done in advance.)

In large heavy skillet or wok, heat oil over medium heat. Add onion and ginger; stir-fry for 1 minute. Add peppers and stir-fry for 2 to 3 minutes, adding chicken stock when necessary to prevent sticking or scorching. Add broccoli; stir-fry until heated through; sprinkle with soy sauce. Serve immediately. Makes 8 servings.

Calories per serving: 40
Grams fat per serving: 2
Fiber: **Good**
Vitamins A and C: Excellent

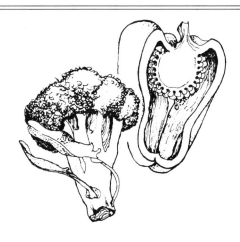

BRAISED RED CABBAGE

Here's a colorful and flavorful vegetable that's especially good with pork or poultry. You can make this a day or two in advance and reheat it. To retain a bright red color when cooking red cabbage, include an acid such as vinegar or lemon juice in the cooking liquid.

$\frac{1}{2}$	medium red cabbage	$\frac{1}{2}$
1	cooking apple	1
$\frac{1}{3}$ cup	water	75 mL
$\frac{1}{4}$ cup	white wine vinegar	50 mL
	Salt and freshly ground pepper	
2 tbsp	(approx) honey or granulated sugar	25 mL

Remove outer leaves and center core of cabbage. Slice thinly. Peel, core and slice apple. In large skillet or heavy pan, combine cabbage, apple, water and vinegar. Stir and bring to a boil. Reduce heat and simmer, covered, stirring occasionally, for 1 hour or until cabbage is very tender.

Stir in salt, pepper and honey to taste. The flavor should be sweet and sour. Adjust seasonings if necessary. Makes 4 servings.

Calories per serving: 55
Grams fat per serving: 0.3
Fiber: Good
Vitamin C: Excellent

Eating cabbage and other brassica vegetables may reduce the risk of cancer of the colon.

Excellent Sources of Fiber (more than 4 grams of fiber per serving)
$\frac{1}{2}$ cup/125 mL kidney beans
$\frac{1}{2}$ cup/125 mL green peas
1 cup/250 mL white beans
$\frac{1}{2}$ cup/125 mL pinto beans
$\frac{2}{3}$ cup/150 mL broccoli
$\frac{1}{2}$ cup/125 mL spinach

Good Sources of Fiber (2 to 3.9 grams fiber per serving)
2 beets
4 Brussels sprouts
$\frac{3}{4}$ cup/175 mL raw cabbage
$\frac{1}{2}$ cup/125 mL parsnips
1 carrot
$\frac{1}{2}$ cup/125 mL lentils
$\frac{1}{2}$ cup/125 mL turnip
$\frac{1}{2}$ cup/125 mL lima beans
(Measurements are for cooked vegetables except cabbage.)

The Mysterious Ingredient
Several studies have indicated that vegetables from the cabbage family, or brassica genus (of the cruciferous family), may reduce the risk of cancer of the colon. Something in these vegetables may help block formation of this cancer in the body.

The brassica vegetables include: cabbage, broccoli, cauliflower, Brussels spouts, rutabaga, kale, turnip, kohlrabi and collard.

SCALLOPED CABBAGE AU GRATIN

Here's a good way to serve cabbage. It's a delicious dish that adds some protein to a meatless meal, and also goes well with hot or cold beef, pork and lamb. The dish may be prepared in advance and baked just before serving.

4 cups	coarsely shredded cabbage	1 L
1	can (14 oz/398 mL) tomatoes, undrained	1
2 tsp	granulated sugar	10 mL
$\frac{1}{4}$ tsp	paprika	1 mL
1 tsp	salt	5 mL
1 tsp	oregano	5 mL
	Salt and freshly ground pepper	
$\frac{1}{2}$ cup	grated Cheddar cheese	125 mL
1 cup	fine fresh bread crumbs	250 mL

Cook cabbage in boiling salted water until wilted, about 6 minutes; drain well. Combine tomatoes, sugar, paprika, salt and oregano, breaking up tomatoes with back of spoon. In greased 6-cup/1.5 L baking dish, place cabbage. Sprinkle with salt and pepper to taste. Cover with tomato mixture, then cheese. Top with crumbs. Bake, uncovered, in 350°F/180°C oven for 30 minutes or until heated through. Makes 6 servings.

Calories per serving: 133
Grams fat per serving: 7
Fiber: Good
Vitamin C: Excellent
Calcium and vitamin A: Good

TWO-CABBAGE STIR-FRY

Red and green cabbage stir-fried with ginger and onion is a delicious, colorful vegetable dish that's especially good with pork and turkey. Rice vinegar is a mild, sweet vinegar, available in the Chinese food section of many supermarkets. (Recipe can be doubled.)

1 tbsp	rice vinegar	15 mL
1 tbsp	water	15 mL
1 tsp	soy sauce	5 mL
1 tsp	cornstarch	5 mL
1 tbsp	vegetable oil	15 mL
1 tsp	chopped fresh ginger root	5 mL
1	small onion, chopped	1
1 cup	thinly sliced red cabbage	250 mL
1 cup	thinly sliced green cabbage	250 mL

Fall Dinner Menu:
Pork Tenderloin with Rosemary and Thyme (page 111)
Two-Cabbage Stir-Fry
(page 159)
Mashed Potatoes with Onions
(page 170) and/or green peas
Peach Blueberry Crisp
(page 208)

In small dish, mix together vinegar, water, soy sauce and cornstarch; set aside.

In wok or heavy skillet, heat oil over medium heat. Add ginger and onion; stir-fry for 1 minute. Add both kinds of cabbage and stir-fry until tender, 3 to 5 minutes.

Pour in soy sauce mixture and stir-fry until liquid comes to a boil, about 1 minute. Serve hot. Makes 3 servings.

Calories per serving: 75
Grams fat per serving: 5
Fiber: Good
Vitamin C: Excellent

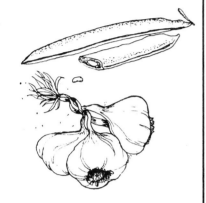

HERBED GREEN BEANS WITH GARLIC

Herbs, onion and garlic enhance the flavor of beans without adding calories or fat.

1 lb	green beans	500 g
2 tsp	butter or oil	10 mL
1	small onion, thinly sliced	1
1	clove garlic, minced	1
1 tbsp	chopped fresh thyme or oregano (or $\frac{1}{2}$ tsp/2 mL dried)	15 mL
	Salt and freshly ground pepper	

Trim beans and cook in rapidly boiling water for 4 to 5 minutes or until tender-crisp; drain.

In heavy skillet or saucepan, melt butter; add onion and garlic and cook over medium-low heat, stirring occasionally, until onion is tender. Stir in beans, thyme, and salt and pepper to taste. Cook until heated. Makes 4 servings.

Calories per serving: 42
Grams fat per serving: 2
Fiber: Good

October-November Friday Night Dinner Menu
Lemon Chicken Schnitzel (page 90)
Baked Leeks au Gratin (pages 160-1)
Baked Squash with Ginger (pages 164-5)
Tossed green salad
Deep-Dish Plum Pie (page 218)

BAKED LEEKS AU GRATIN

Though leeks are available nearly all year round, they're in season and most reasonably priced during the fall. They're delicious with any cut of meat or poultry, or as part of an all-vegetable dinner.

4	large leeks	4
2 tsp	butter	10 mL
	Salt and freshly ground pepper	
4 tsp	grated Parmesan cheese	20 mL
1 tsp	water	5 mL

Trim base and tough green leaves from leeks, leaving

tender green and white parts. Cut leeks in half lengthwise; wash under cold running water and drain. Place leeks, cut side up, in single layer in microwave dish or on lightly oiled foil. Dot with butter and season with salt and pepper to taste. Sprinkle cheese on top. Add 1 tsp/5 mL water to side of leeks. Cover dish or wrap in foil. Microwave on High for 5 to 7 minutes, or bake in 350°F/180°C oven for 25 minutes, or until tender. Makes 4 servings.

Calories per serving: 53
Grams fat per serving: 2.6
Fiber: Good
Vitamin C: Good

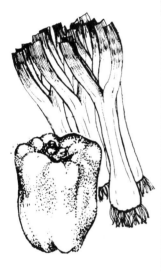

BRAISED RED PEPPER AND LEEKS

This dish goes well with lamb, pork or beef, but don't use more red pepper than called for—it could overpower the subtle flavor of the leeks.

6	leeks	6
1	large sweet red pepper	1
½ cup	water or chicken stock	125 mL
1 tbsp	butter	15 mL
	Salt and freshly ground pepper	

Cut dark green part and base from leeks and discard. Cut leeks in half lengthwise and wash thoroughly under cold running water. Cut leeks into ½-inch/1 cm thick slices. (You should have about 4 cups/1 L.) Remove core and seeds from red pepper; cut into thin 1-inch/2.5 cm long strips.

In saucepan, combine chicken stock and leeks; cover and simmer for 5 to 10 minutes or until leeks are almost tender. Add red pepper strips, cover and simmer for another 5 to 10 minutes, or until tender. If too much liquid, uncover and cook for 1 to 2 minutes. Add butter, and salt and pepper to taste. Makes 4 servings.

Calories per serving: 84
Grams fat per serving: 3
Fiber: Good
Vitamins A and C: Excellent

Steam Cooking

To steam food means to cook over, not in, boiling water or other liquid. Foods wrapped in foil, then baked or barbecued, steam in their own liquids. Herbs, salt, sugar or spices can be added to the foods or to the liquid before steaming. The advantage of steaming is that vegetables retain their flavor, color and vitamins; and fish is moist and flavorful. Food can be steamed in the oven, on top of the stove or on the barbecue.

Equipment for steaming

There are a number of steamers on the market, but you don't have to have special equipment.

- Wrap foods in foil, then cook in the oven or on the barbecue.
- In top-of-stove cooking, you can use a deep pot with a tight-fitting lid and something to keep the food above the liquid. This could be a steamer with perforated petals and short legs, a flat-bottomed metal colander or one with feet, or a metal strainer. Large foods such as chicken or pudding can be placed on an inverted heat-proof plate or bowl, or on custard cups or a wire rack. A wok with a rack inside, and covered with a lid (or foil if the lid isn't tight-fitting), can also be used.
- To oven-steam, use a roasting pan with a trivet, wire rack or anything that is heat-proof to keep the food above the liquid.
- Steam-cook in a deep-frier with basket set over water instead of oil.
- Use a clay baker.

FOIL-STEAMED SPRING VEGETABLES

These vegetables are delicious with fish or chicken. In winter, use parsnips, snow peas or beans instead of asparagus and cut the carrots into $\frac{1}{2}$-inch / 1 cm pieces. White pearl onions, which are the size of small grapes, are sold in pint boxes. They keep for a month or two in a cool, dry place.

$\frac{1}{2}$ lb	fresh pearl onions	250 g
$\frac{3}{4}$ lb	fresh baby carrots	375 g
$\frac{1}{2}$ lb	asparagus	250 g
2 tbsp	water	25 mL
1 tbsp	butter	15 mL
1	bay leaf	1
$\frac{1}{2}$ tsp	salt	2 mL
Pinch	white pepper	Pinch

In large pot of boiling water, blanch pearl onions for 2 minutes; drain. Cut off root end and gently squeeze to remove skin. In another large pot of boiling water, blanch carrots for 2 minutes; drain, and rinse under cold running water; drain again. Snap tough ends from asparagus.

On large piece of heavy-duty foil, arrange vegetables in a single layer. Sprinkle with water, dot with butter and add bay leaf, salt and pepper. Fold foil over vegetables and seal. Bake in 375°F/190°C oven for 20-30 minutes or until vegetables are tender. Makes 6 servings.

Calories per serving: 65
Grams fat per serving: 3
Fiber: Good
Vitamin A: Excellent
Vitamin C: Good

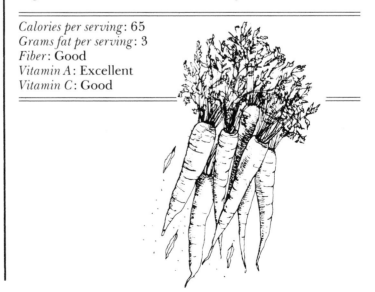

SAUTÉED ZUCCHINI WITH YOGURT AND HERBS

Sautéed zucchini dressed with yogurt or sour cream is one of my favorite quick-vegetable recipes; because sour cream is higher in fat content, it is healthier to substitute yogurt.

1 lb	zucchini (about 3 small)	500 g
2 tsp	butter	10 mL
1	small onion, sliced and separated into rings	1
6 tbsp	plain yogurt or sour cream	90 mL
2 tbsp	chopped fresh parsley	25 mL
$\frac{1}{2}$ tsp	crumbled leaf oregano or 2 tsp/10 mL chopped fresh	2 mL
	Salt and freshly ground pepper	

Trim ends from zucchini. In food processor or by hand, slice zucchini thinly.

In heavy skillet, melt butter over medium heat; add onion and cook, stirring, until tender. Add zucchini and cook, stirring often, just until barely tender, about 5 minutes.

Remove from heat and stir in yogurt, parsley, oregano, and salt and pepper to taste. Stir to coat well and serve immediately. Makes 6 servings.

Calories per serving: 34
Grams fat per serving: 1.4
Vitamin C: **Good**

30-Minute Summer Dinner
Sole Fillets with Lemon and Parsley (page 119)
Sautéed Zucchini with Yogurt and Herbs (page 163)
Tomatoes Provençal (page 153)
Tiny boiled potatoes in skins
Fresh strawberries or cantaloupe

PARSNIP PURÉE

You can use carrots, turnips or squash instead of parsnips in this recipe. When buying parsnips, remember the small ones are more tender and sweet than the older fat ones.

2 lb	parsnips	1 kg
1 tbsp	butter	15 mL
$\frac{1}{4}$ cup	milk	50 mL
1 tbsp	sherry (optional)	15 mL
$\frac{1}{4}$ tsp	freshly ground nutmeg	1 mL
	Salt and freshly ground pepper	

Peel parsnips and cut into chunks. Cook in boiling salted water until tender; drain and purée in a food processor, blender or food mill. Add butter, milk, sherry (if using), nutmeg, and salt and pepper to taste; process or stir until mixed. Return to saucepan to reheat or spoon into serving dish; cover and keep warm. (Purée can be prepared in advance and gently reheated before serving.) Makes 8 servings.

Calories per serving: 93
Grams fat per serving: 2
Fiber: Good
Vitamin C: Good

Puréed vegetables, because of their creamy texture, can be served instead of a vegetable with a cream sauce. Puréed parsnips team well with green beans, broccoli or other green vegetables that have been steamed or boiled. Serve with any meats or poultry. For a slightly milder flavor, combine puréed parsnips or turnips with mashed potatoes.

BAKED SQUASH WITH GINGER

Ginger goes particularly well with squash. Grated orange rind also heightens the flavor and can be used instead of ginger.

$2\frac{1}{4}$ lb	squash (Hubbard, butternut or acorn)	1 kg
2 tbsp	butter	25 mL
2 tbsp	brown sugar	25 mL
1 tsp	ground ginger	5 mL
	Salt, freshly ground pepper and freshly grated nutmeg	

Cut squash in half; scoop out seeds. Cover squash with foil and place on baking sheet. Bake in 400°F/200°C oven for 40 minutes or until tender. Alternatively, place in microwave dish, partially cover and cook in microwave on High for 7 to 10 minutes.

Drain squash and scoop out pulp; mash or purée with 2 or 3 on-off turns in food processor. Stir in butter, brown sugar, ginger, and salt, pepper and nutmeg to taste. (Squash can be prepared ahead to this point; transfer to baking dish and reheat, covered, in 350°F/180°C oven or microwave until hot.) Makes 6 servings.

Calories per serving: 93
Grams fat per serving: 4
Vitamin A: Excellent
Vitamin C: Good

BARLEY AND PARSLEY PILAF

Red onion adds crunch and flavor to this intriguing rice dish.

¾ cup	pearl barley	175 mL
¾ cup	brown rice	175 mL
½ cup	hot chicken stock	125 mL
½ cup	chopped red or green onion	125 mL
1 cup	chopped fresh parsley	250 mL
	Salt and freshly ground pepper	

Cook barley in 3 cups/750 mL boiling water for 30 minutes or until tender; drain.

In another saucepan, bring 2 cups/500 mL water to a boil; add rice, cover and simmer for 30 minutes or until rice is tender and water has been absorbed.

In 6-cup/1.5 L casserole, combine rice, barley, chicken stock, onion, parsley, and salt and pepper to taste. (May be prepared in advance to this point.) Bake in 350°F/180°C oven for 20 minutes or until heated through. Makes 8 servings.

Calories per serving: 116
Grams fat per serving: 0.6
Fiber: Good
Vitamins A and C: Good

STIR-FRIED VEGETABLES WITH GINGER AND GARLIC

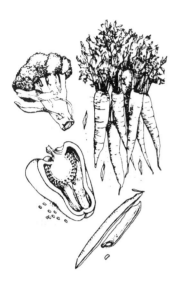

The wonderful colors and flavor combinations in this dish comple-ment any meat from chicken and lamb to beef. You need only add rice to complete the main course. For a one-dish meal, add chicken, turkey, shellfish or ham to the stir-fry and serve over hot pasta.

$\frac{1}{4}$ lb	green beans	125 g
1	small zucchini	1
2	carrots	2
$\frac{1}{2}$	small cauliflower	$\frac{1}{2}$
1	large stalk broccoli	1
1	sweet red or yellow pepper (or combination)	1
$\frac{1}{4}$ lb	snow peas	125 g
2 tbsp	vegetable oil	25 mL
1	red onion, thinly sliced	1
3	cloves garlic, minced	3
2 tbsp	minced fresh ginger root	25 mL
2 tbsp	soy sauce	25 mL
	Salt and freshly ground pepper	

Because of its high sodium content, use soy sauce sparingly. Naturally brewed and sodium-reduced soy sauces are lower in sodium than chemically brewed ones.

Cut beans on the diagonal into $1\frac{1}{2}$-inch/4 cm lengths. Thinly slice zucchini and carrots on the diagonal. Cut cauli-flower and broccoli into florets. Slice broccoli stem cross-wise on the diagonal. Seed peppers and cut into 1-inch/2.5 cm squares. Remove flower ends from snow peas.

In large pot of boiling water, blanch beans, carrots, cauli-flower and broccoli separately just until tender-crisp. Drain, and immediately rinse under cold running water to prevent further cooking; drain thoroughly. (Vegetables can be prepared in advance to this point.)

Twenty minutes before serving, heat about 2 tsp/10 mL of the oil in heavy skillet over medium heat. Add onion and 1 clove garlic; stir-fry for 3 to 4 minutes. Add zucchini and some ginger and more garlic; stir-fry for 3 minutes longer, adding more oil if necessary. If pan is full, transfer vege-tables to baking dish and keep warm in 250°F/130°C oven. Add as many of the blanched vegetables as you can stir-fry at one time, plus some of the garlic and ginger, and cook, stirring, for 2 to 3 minutes or until hot; transfer to baking dish in oven to keep warm and continue stir-frying remaining vegetables, adding a small amount of oil as necessary. Finish with peppers and snow peas, cooking until tender-crisp. Combine all vegetables; toss with soy sauce, and salt and pepper to taste. Makes 8 servings.

Calories per serving: 67
Grams fat per serving: 3
Fiber: Good
Vitamins A and C: Excellent

ORANGE SHERRIED SWEET POTATOES

These sweet potatoes can be prepared a day in advance, then reheated just before serving. They go well with turkey, goose or ham. Instead of sherry, you can substitute ginger, maple syrup or crushed pineapple (adjust amount to taste).

4	large sweet potatoes	4
1 tbsp	butter	15 mL
	Grated rind of $\frac{1}{2}$ orange	
$\frac{1}{4}$ cup	orange juice	50 mL
2 tbsp	(approx) sherry	25 mL
2 tbsp	brown sugar	25 mL
Pinch	freshly grated nutmeg	Pinch
	Salt and freshly ground pepper	

In pot of boiling water, cook unpeeled potatoes until tender, 30 to 40 minutes. Drain, let cool slightly, then peel. While still warm, mash potatoes with butter, orange rind, orange juice, sherry, sugar, nutmeg, and salt and pepper to taste. Return to saucepan and reheat over medium heat, or refrigerate until 1 hour before serving, then reheat, covered, in 350°F/180°C oven for about 25 minutes or until hot. Makes 5 servings.

Calories per serving: 208
Grams fat per serving: 3
Fiber: Good
Vitamins A and C: Excellent

MASHED TURNIPS WITH CARROTS AND ORANGE

Adding mashed carrots to turnips, along with a pinch of brown sugar and a dollop of butter, mellows the turnip and at the same time adds flavor to the carrots.

1	small yellow turnip (rutabaga)	1
4	carrots	4
2 tbsp	brown sugar	25 mL
2 tbsp	frozen orange juice concentrate (undiluted)	25 mL
1 tbsp	butter	15 mL
Pinch	nutmeg	Pinch
	Salt and freshly ground pepper	
	Chopped parsley (optional)	

Peel turnip and carrots. Cut into ¾-inch/2 cm chunks. Cook in separate pots of simmering water until very tender; drain. Mash each, either with potato masher or in food processor.

Combine turnip, carrots, sugar, orange juice, butter, nutmeg, and salt and pepper to taste. Sprinkle with parsley (if using). Serve immediately or cover and reheat before serving. Makes 8 servings.

Calories per serving: 31
Grams fat per serving: 2
Vitamin A:Excellent

TURNIPS PAYSANNE

Either white turnips or a yellow rutabaga can be used in this recipe but the rutabaga will take longer to cook. To save time use the food processor to slice the vegetables.

1	small rutabaga or 4-6 white turnips (about 2 lb/1 kg)	1
1 cup	sliced celery	250 mL
1 cup	sliced carrots	250 mL
1	large clove garlic, minced	1
1	onion, chopped	1
1 cup	chicken stock	1
$\frac{1}{4}$ cup	chopped fresh parsley	50 mL
1 tbsp	butter	15 mL
	Salt and freshly ground pepper	

Peel and dice turnips (or slice in a food processor). In heavy saucepan, combine turnip, celery, carrots, garlic, onion and stock. Bring to a boil; cover, and simmer until vegetables are tender, about 20 minutes.

Uncover and cook until liquid has reduced to a glaze. Sprinkle with parsley, butter, and salt and pepper to taste. Makes 6 servings.

Calories per serving: 54
Grams fat per serving: 2.4
Fiber: Good
Vitamins A and C: Excellent

Many studies have associated frequent use of vegetables from the cabbage family or brassica family with reduced risk of cancer of the colon. The brassica vegetables include rutabaga, turnip, cabbage, broccoli, cauliflower and Brussels sprouts.

MASHED POTATOES WITH ONIONS

These everyday vegetables are delicious when mixed. The onions add such flavor to the potatoes, you won't notice the absence of butter. Remember this recipe when you have baked potatoes. Scoop out the center of the potatoes and mix with the rest of the ingredients. Spoon it back into the potato skins and reheat in 350°F / 180°C oven for about 10 minutes. Or, if you are using another filling for the potato skins, use the scooped-out potatoes for this recipe.

6	potatoes	6
2 tsp	butter	10 mL
2	onions, finely chopped	2
1 tbsp	water	15 mL
$\frac{1}{2}$ cup	milk	125 mL
	Salt and pepper	

Peel potatoes and cut into quarters. Cook potatoes in boiling water until tender, about 20 minutes.

Meanwhile, in heavy skillet, melt butter; add onions and water and cook over medium-low heat, stirring occasionally, until onions are tender, 10 to 15 minutes, reducing the heat if necessary so onions don't brown.

Drain potatoes and return pan to stove; heat over low heat for 1 to 2 minutes, shaking pan to dry potatoes. Mash potatoes with half of the milk, adding remaining milk to taste (amount of milk needed will vary depending on size and kind of potatoes). Stir in onions, add salt and pepper to taste. Makes 6 servings.

Calories per serving: 123
Grams fat per serving: 2
Fiber: Good
Vitamin C: Excellent
Baked potato stuffed with Mashed Potatoes with Onions:
Fiber: Excellent for large potato

Compare:
For maximum fiber, don't peel potatoes.

	Grams dietary fiber
1 large baked or boiled potato with skin	4
1 large potato, peeled then boiled	2

CURRIED FRUIT WITH RICE

Light and juicy fruits plus curry make a fresh, pleasing flavor-and-texture combination. Along with rice, they go well with lamb or baked ham.

New Year's Day or Easter Dinner
Sherry-Braised Ham with Curried Fruit with rice (page 112)
Steamed broccoli
Green salad with Parsley Dressing (page 85)
Poached Pears with Chocolate Sauce (pages 190-1)

* To toast almonds, place on baking sheet and roast in 350°F/180°C oven for 5 minutes or until lightly golden in color.

2 cups	cantaloupe or honeydew melon balls	500 mL
1 cup	diced fresh pineapple	250 mL
1	banana, sliced	1
1 cup	sliced peaches, strawberries, grapes or mandarin oranges (or combination)	250 mL
1 cup	chicken stock	250 mL
$1\frac{1}{2}$ tsp	cornstarch	22 mL
2 tsp	curry powder	10 mL
$\frac{1}{2}$ cup	finely chopped chutney	125 mL
$\frac{1}{4}$ cup	raisins	50 mL
2 tbsp	butter	25 mL
5 cups	hot cooked rice	1.25 L
$\frac{1}{4}$ cup	slivered toasted almonds*	50 mL

Combine fruits in bowl; set aside.

In saucepan, combine stock, cornstarch and curry; mix well. Bring to a boil over medium heat, stirring constantly. (Sauce can be prepared ahead to this point; reheat before continuing with recipe.)

Just before serving, combine chutney, fruits, and raisins; stir to mix. Add to hot curry sauce. Add butter; stir until melted.

To serve: transfer to serving bowl and sprinkle nuts on top. Place rice in a separate serving dish. Spoon some curried fruit over some of the rice on each person's plate. Or, spoon hot rice around edge of shallow serving dish; spoon curry mixture into center. Makes 8 servings.

Calories per serving (including rice): 268
Grams fat per serving: 6
Fiber: Good
Iron, and vitamin C: Good
This curry sauce is mildly flavored so as not to overpower the fruit. Add more curry powder for a spicier dish.

BROWN RICE WITH CURRANTS

This flavorful rice dish goes well with chicken, turkey, pork, lamb and fish.

½ cup	currants	125 mL
2 tbsp	sherry	25 mL
1 tsp	butter	5 mL
1	onion, chopped	1
2 cups	brown rice	500 mL
4 cups	chicken broth	1 L
1 tsp	dried basil leaves	5 mL
	Salt and freshly ground pepper	

Soak currants in sherry and set aside until needed.

In heavy saucepan, melt butter over medium heat; stir in onion and cook, stirring, until tender. Add rice and stir to mix well.

Bring stock to a boil. Pour over rice; stir in basil, and salt and pepper to taste. Simmer, covered, until water has been absorbed, about 40 minutes. Stir in currants and sherry. Makes 8 servings.

Calories per serving: 112
Grams fat per serving: 2.5

CRACKED WHEAT AND BASIL PILAF

Keep this flavorful dish in mind for an all-vegetable dinner or serve with meats or poultry.

$\frac{3}{4}$ cup	cracked wheat or bulgur	175 mL
1 tbsp	oil	15 mL
1	large onion, finely chopped	1
2	cloves garlic, minced	2
1 cup	thinly sliced mushrooms	250 mL
1	large tomato, seeded and diced, or 1 tbsp/15 mL each tomato paste and water	1
$\frac{1}{2}$ cup	chopped fresh basil*	125 mL
$\frac{1}{4}$ cup	slivered almonds	50 mL
$\frac{1}{2}$ tsp	salt	2 mL
	Freshly ground pepper	

*If fresh basil is not available, use $\frac{1}{2}$ cup/125 mL chopped fresh parsley and 1 tbsp/15 mL dried basil.

Rinse cracked wheat under cold running water; place in bowl and add water to cover by at least 2 inches/5 cm. Soak for 1 hour or until tender. Drain thoroughly.

In heavy skillet, heat oil. Add onion and cook, stirring, over medium heat until tender. Stir in garlic and mushrooms and cook until mushrooms are tender, about 2 minutes.

Stir in tomato, cracked wheat, basil, almonds, salt, and pepper to taste; stir until mixed and heated through. Makes 6 servings ($\frac{1}{2}$ cup/125 mL each).

Calories per serving: 172
Grams fat per serving without almonds: 3
Grams fat per serving with almonds: 6
Fiber: Excellent
Phosphorus, vitamins A and C and niacin: Good

MUFFINS, BREADS AND COOKIES

Nothing smells better than freshly baked breads, muffins and cookies. And nothing tastes better either. Low in fat (if you don't spread on extra butter) and a good source of fiber and carbohydrates, the following muffins, breads and cookies make excellent snacks and are an important part of every balanced meal. They also give you a chance to have sweet treats without all the fats, sugars and refined flours that lurk in most store-bought baked goods.

Moderation is the key to all good eating habits, and this applies to sweets as well. Enjoy them, but eat them in reasonable amounts.

BANANA-APRICOT BRAN MUFFINS

A good way to start the day. With a glass of milk and fresh fruit, it'll take you through to lunchtime.

*Natural bran is sold in the grain sections of supermarkets. Because it has some fat, store it in the refrigerator or freezer to prevent it from becoming rancid. Use in muffins, biscuits, bread and cookies. It is an excellent source of fiber.

1½ cups	natural bran*	375 mL
1 cup	whole-wheat flour	250 mL
1 tsp	baking powder	5 mL
1 tsp	baking soda	5 mL
½ tsp	salt	2 mL
½ cup	chopped dried apricots	125 mL
⅓ cup	vegetable oil	75 mL
⅓ cup	packed brown sugar	75 mL
1	egg, slightly beaten	1
2	ripe bananas, mashed	2
1 cup	plain yogurt	250 mL

Combine bran, flour, baking powder, baking soda, salt and apricots; mix lightly.

In large mixing bowl, combine oil, brown sugar, egg, bananas and yogurt; mix well. Add dry ingredients and mix just until combined.

Spoon batter into paper-lined or nonstick muffin tins. Bake in 400°F/200°C oven for 25 to 30 minutes or until firm to the touch. Remove from pan and let cool on wire rack. Makes 12 muffins.

Calories per muffin: 173
Grams fat per muffin: 7
Fiber: Excellent
Iron, vitamin A and niacin: Good

PUMPKIN MUFFINS

My daughter Susie has been making these muffins since she was seven years old. She makes them the night before we go on a car trip so we can have them for a very quick breakfast before leaving or in the car. Her only problem is keeping us from eating them that evening, so she hides them until the next morning.

¾ cup	natural bran	175 mL
¾ cup	whole-wheat flour	175 mL
¾ cup	granulated sugar	175 mL
1½ tsp	cinnamon	7 mL
1 tsp	baking powder	5 mL
1 tsp	baking soda	5 mL
½ tsp	salt	2 mL
1 cup	raisins	250 mL
1 cup	mashed or canned cooked pumpkin	250 mL
2	eggs (unbeaten)	2
½ cup	vegetable oil	125 mL
½ cup	plain yogurt or buttermilk	125 mL

In bowl, combine bran, flour, sugar, cinnamon, baking powder, baking soda, salt and raisins; toss to mix. Add pumpkin, eggs, oil and yogurt; stir just until combined.

Spoon batter into paper-lined or nonstick muffin tins. Bake in 400°F/200°C oven for 25 minutes or until firm to the touch. Makes 12 muffins.

Calories per muffin: 185
Grams fat per muffin: 8
Fiber: Good
Vitamin A: Good

Substituting Whole-Wheat Flour for All-Purpose Flour in Baking

Whole-wheat flour contains 11.4 grams of fiber per 1 cup/250 mL, while the same amount of all-purpose contains 4.7 grams.

Whole-wheat flour is made from the whole grain of wheat. Along with fiber, it also contains some fat. All-purpose flour has had the bran and germ removed from the wheat. It is enriched with the same nutrients naturally present in bran and germ, but it doesn't have the fiber or fat that whole-wheat flour does.

Because of the fat content, whole-wheat flour doesn't have the same shelf life as all-purpose flour, which will keep for up to two years. Whole-wheat flour will keep 6 weeks to 6 months, depending on the milling method, before it turns rancid. For this reason, buy whole-wheat flour in small amounts unless you use it regularly.

As a general rule, you can substitute whole-wheat flour for half of the all-purpose flour called for in a recipe. For example, if a recipe calls for 1 cup/250 mL of all-purpose flour, you can use ½ cup/125 mL all-purpose flour and ½ cup/125 mL whole-wheat flour.

Using all whole-wheat flour results in a heavier product. In some cases, such as oatmeal cookies, this is fine; in others such as cakes, it may be undesirable. Experiment with your favorite recipes to see how much whole-wheat flour you can substitute.

REFRIGERATOR BRAN MUFFINS

You can mix up this muffin batter and keep it in the refrigerator to have on hand to make delicious hot muffins for breakfast. If you wish, use reconstituted skim milk powder in place of milk. This recipe has less sugar and more fiber than any other bran muffin recipe I know.

1 cup	vegetable oil	250 mL
1 cup	granulated sugar	250 mL
6	eggs	6
⅓ cup	molasses	75 mL
3 cups	milk	750 mL
5 cups	natural bran	1.25 L
3 cups	whole-wheat flour	750 mL
2 tsp	baking powder	10 mL
2 tsp	baking soda	10 mL
1 tsp	salt	5 mL
1 cup	raisins or dates	250 mL

In large bowl, beat together oil, sugar and eggs until well mixed. Add remaining ingredients and stir until combined. Cover, and refrigerate overnight or for up to 6 weeks.

Spoon batter into paper-lined or nonstick muffin tins and bake in 425°F/220°C oven for 15 to 20 minutes or until firm to the touch. Makes 24 large muffins or 48 medium muffins.

	Large	Medium
Calories per muffin:	231	116
Grams fat per muffin:	11	5.5
Fiber:	Excellent	Good
Phosphorus, niacin and iron:	Good	Good

OATMEAL RAISIN MUFFINS

Serve these extra-moist muffins with fruit and yogurt or milk for a great quick breakfast. They are also delicious in a packed lunch.

1 cup	rolled oats	250 mL
1 cup	buttermilk (or 1 cup milk mixed with 2 tsp/10 mL vinegar)	250 mL
1 cup	all-purpose flour (or half whole-wheat flour and half all-purpose flour)	250 mL
1 tbsp	natural bran	15 mL
1 tsp	cinnamon	5 mL
1 tsp	baking powder	5 mL
½ tsp	baking soda	2 mL
½ tsp	salt	2 mL
½ cup	raisins or chopped apricots	125 mL
½ cup	vegetable oil	125 mL
½ cup	packed brown sugar	125 mL
1	egg, lightly beaten	1

Stir rolled oats into buttermilk and let stand for 10 minutes.

Mix together flour, bran, cinnamon, baking powder, baking soda, salt and raisins. Stir oil, sugar and egg into buttermilk mixture; blend well. Stir dry ingredients into buttermilk mixture, stirring just until combined.

Spoon batter into paper-lined or nonstick muffin tins. Bake in 375°F/180°C oven for 20 to 25 minutes or until firm to the touch. Makes 12 muffins.

Calories per muffin: 160
Grams fat per muffin: 9

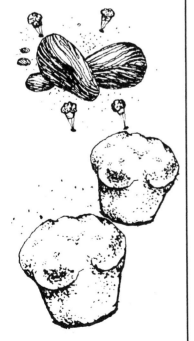

You can use this dough in our Deep-Dish Vegetable Pizza (page 139).

Food Processor Variation:
In measuring cup, combine sugar and warm water; add yeast and let stand until bubbly. In food processor bowl combine whole-wheat flour and 1 cup/250 mL of all-purpose flour and salt. Add oil to yeast mixture. While processing, pour yeast mixture down feed tube. Process 30 seconds. Turn onto floured board and knead in enough remaining flour to prevent dough from sticking to board. Roll out as in Whole-Wheat Pizza Dough.

All-Dressed Pizza
Spread pizza dough with tomato sauce seasoned with oregano and basil. Then finish with your favorite toppings. Try
• chopped red, yellow, green or purple peppers
• blanched broccoli florets
• sliced mushrooms
• sliced regular cherry or sun-dried tomatoes
• artichoke halves
• grated partly skimmed mozzarella cheese
Bake in lower half of 450°F/230°C oven for 16 to 18 minutes or until crust is golden brown and cheese is bubbly.

WHOLE-WHEAT PIZZA DOUGH

Use this basic dough for any type of pizza. Whole-wheat flour adds color, flavor and fiber.

1 tsp	granulated sugar	5 mL
1 cup	warm water	250 mL
1	pkg active dry yeast or 1 tbsp/15 mL	1
$1\frac{1}{2}$ cups	all-purpose flour	375 mL
$1\frac{1}{2}$ cups	whole-wheat flour	375 mL
1 tsp	salt	5 mL
2 tbsp	vegetable oil	25 mL

In large mixing bowl, dissolve sugar in warm water. Sprinkle yeast over water and let stand for 10 minutes or until foamy. Meanwhile, combine flours and salt.

Stir oil into foamy yeast mixture. Stir in about half the flour mixture. Add more flour, mixing until dough can be gathered into a slightly sticky ball (you may need a little more or less than 3 cups/750 mL of flour).

On lightly floured surface, knead dough for about 5 minutes or until smooth and elastic, adding more flour as necessary to prevent dough from sticking to counter. Cut dough in half; cover with waxed paper and let rest for 10 minutes.

On lightly floured surface, use a rolling pin to roll each piece of dough into a 12-inch/30 cm circle, about $\frac{1}{4}$ inch/5 mm thick.

Transfer rounds to 2 lightly oiled pizza pans or baking sheets. Carefully, using fingers, stretch dough into large circles.

Let dough rise for about 15 minutes before adding toppings. For a thicker crust, let dough rise for 30 minutes. Add toppings just before baking. Makes two 12-inch/30 cm pizza rounds.

ALMOND MERINGUES

It's hard to find good-tasting cookies that are low in fat. These are both.

$\frac{1}{4}$ cup	slivered almonds	50 mL
3	egg whites	3
$\frac{1}{2}$ cup	granulated sugar	125 mL
1 tbsp	cornstarch	15 mL
$\frac{1}{2}$ tsp	almond extract	2 mL

Place almonds on baking sheet and toast in 325°F/ 160°C oven for 3 minutes or until golden. Let cool. Reduce oven temperature to 225°F/110°C.

In large bowl, beat egg whites until soft peaks form. Continue beating, gradually adding sugar, then cornstarch and almond extract; beat until mixture forms stiff peaks. Fold in almonds.

Line baking sheet with foil, shiny side down. Drop batter by small spoonfuls onto prepared pan. Bake in 225°F/ 110°C oven for $1\frac{1}{2}$ hours or until cookies can be easily removed from foil. When cool, store in airtight container. Makes 30 cookies.

Calories per cookie: 22
Grams fat per cookie: 5
A low-calorie cookie.

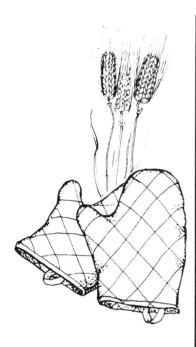

OLD-FASHIONED MOLASSES BREAD

Moist and full of flavor, this bread keeps well. Serve for brunch or lunch with salad or soup.

1 cup	all-purpose flour	250 mL
1 cup	whole-wheat flour	250 mL
$\frac{1}{2}$ tsp	salt	2 mL
$\frac{1}{2}$ tsp	baking soda	2 mL
2 tsp	baking powder	10 mL
$\frac{2}{3}$ cup	skim milk powder	150 mL
$\frac{1}{3}$ cup	wheat germ	75 mL
$\frac{1}{2}$ cup	packed brown sugar	50 mL
$\frac{1}{4}$ cup	chopped nuts	60 mL
$\frac{1}{2}$ cup	raisins	125 mL
$\frac{1}{3}$ cup	finely chopped dried apricots	75 mL
3	eggs	3
$\frac{3}{4}$ cup	orange juice	175 mL
$\frac{1}{2}$ cup	vegetable oil	125 mL
$\frac{1}{2}$ cup	molasses	125 mL
2	bananas	2

In a large bowl, combine flours, salt, baking soda, baking powder, skim milk powder, wheat germ, brown sugar, nuts, raisins and apricots. In food processor with metal blade, in blender, or using electric mixer, whirl eggs until foamy. Add orange juice, oil, molasses and bananas; process until mixed.

Pour into dry ingredients and stir just until moistened. Pour into two 8 × 4-inch/1.5 L greased pans. Bake in 325°F/160°C oven for 1 hour or until firm. Let cool on wire rack, then remove from pan to cool completely. Makes 2 loaves (18 slices per loaf).

Calories per slice: 101
Grams fat per slice: 3.7
Two slices are a good source of fiber.

WHOLE-WHEAT IRISH SODA BREAD

Variation:
Raisin Whole-Wheat Soda
Bread: Add 1 cup/250 mL
raisins along with flour.

After-Theatre Supper
Nova Scotia Seafood Chowder
(page 48)
Arugula and Radicchio Salad
with Balsamic Vinaigrette
(page 66)
Whole-Wheat Irish Soda Bread
(page 181)
Lemon Sorbet (page 197)
Coconut-Oatmeal Cookies
(page 185)

Quick and easy to prepare, this bread dough can be mixed in a few minutes, then popped into the oven. Serve with any meal from breakfast to dinner.

3 cups	whole-wheat flour	750 mL
1 cup	all-purpose flour	250 mL
2 tbsp	granulated sugar	25 mL
2 tsp	baking powder	10 mL
$1\frac{1}{2}$ tsp	baking soda	7 mL
1 tsp	salt	5 mL
2 tbsp	butter	25 mL
$1\frac{3}{4}$ cups	buttermilk (or $1\frac{3}{4}$ cups/425 mL milk, plus 2 tbsp/25 mL vinegar)	425 mL

Combine flours, sugar, baking powder, baking soda and salt. With pastry blender or 2 knives, cut in butter until crumbly. Add buttermilk and stir to make a soft dough. Turn out onto lightly floured counter and knead about 10 times until smooth.

Place dough on greased baking sheet; flatten into circle about $2\frac{1}{2}$ inches/6 cm thick. Cut a large "+" about $\frac{1}{4}$ inch/5 mm deep on top. Bake in 350°F/180°C oven for 1 hour or until toothpick inserted in center comes out clean. Makes 1 loaf (about 16 slices).

Calories per slice: 143
Grams fat per slice: 1.7
Fiber: Good

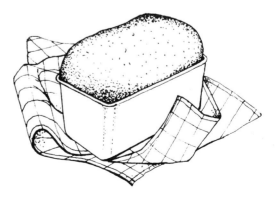

WHOLE-WHEAT RAISIN SCONES

Make these for a late Sunday morning breakfast or to serve with salad or soup for a light supper.

3 tbsp	granulated sugar	45 mL
1 cup	all-purpose flour	250 mL
1 cup	whole-wheat flour	250 mL
1 tbsp	baking powder	15 mL
1½ tsp	cinnamon	7 mL
½ tsp	nutmeg	2 mL
½ tsp	salt	2 mL
⅓ cup	butter or margarine	75 mL
2	eggs, lightly beaten	2
⅓ cup	milk	75 mL
½ cup	raisins	125 mL

Reserve 1 tsp/5 mL of the sugar. In mixing bowl, combine remaining sugar, both flours, baking powder, cinnamon, nutmeg and salt. With pastry blender or 2 knives, cut in butter until mixture resembles coarse crumbs.

Reserve 1 tbsp/15 mL of the beaten eggs. Stir remaining eggs, milk and raisins into flour mixture and mix lightly. Turn out onto lightly floured counter and knead about 5 times. Pat into a circle about ¾ inch/2 cm thick. Cut into 8 wedges and place slightly apart on greased baking sheet.

Brush reserved beaten egg over each wedge; sprinkle with reserved sugar. Bake in 425°F/220°C oven for 18 to 20 minutes or until browned. Serve warm. Makes 8 scones.

Calories per serving: 220
Grams fat per serving: 8
Fiber: Good

DATE SQUARES

Called matrimonial cake in British Columbia, these squares are very flavorful. If possible, use fresh pitted dates.

Date Filling:		
2 cups	packed chopped pitted dates ($\frac{2}{3}$ lb/350g)	500 mL
1 cup	cold coffee	250 mL
2 tbsp	brown sugar	25 mL
	Grated rind and juice of $\frac{1}{2}$ orange	
1 tbsp	lemon juice	15 mL
Crumb Mixture:		
1$\frac{1}{4}$ cups	all-purpose flour	300 mL
1 tsp	baking powder	5 mL
$\frac{1}{2}$ tsp	baking soda	2 mL
$\frac{1}{2}$ tsp	salt	2 mL
$\frac{3}{4}$ cup	butter	175 mL
1$\frac{1}{4}$ cups	rolled oats	300 mL
$\frac{3}{4}$ cup	lightly packed brown sugar	175 mL

Date Filling: In small saucepan, combine dates, coffee, brown sugar and orange rind; bring to a boil. Reduce heat and simmer, uncovered, until mixture is soft enough to mash and has the consistency of jam (runny but easy to spread), about 10 minutes. Remove from heat; stir in orange and lemon juices. Let cool.

Crumb Mixture: Sift together flour, baking powder, baking soda and salt. With pastry blender or 2 knives, cut in butter until mixture is the size of small peas. Stir in rolled oats and sugar. Press half of the crumb mixture firmly into 9-inch/2 L square baking pan. Spread date mixture evenly over crumb mixture and top with remaining crumbs, pressing lightly. Bake in 325°F/160°C oven for 25 minutes or until lightly browned. Makes about 25 squares.

Calories per square: 140
Grams fat per square: 5.6
Three squares are an excellent source of fiber.

ALMOND-APRICOT SQUARES

Apricots add extra flavor to these tasty low-calorie squares.

$\frac{3}{4}$ cup	packed dried apricots	175 mL
$\frac{1}{2}$ cup	butter	125 mL
$1\frac{1}{4}$ cups	whole-wheat flour	300 mL
$\frac{3}{4}$ cup	chopped almonds	175 mL
$\frac{3}{4}$ cup	granulated sugar	175 mL
$\frac{1}{4}$ cup	natural bran or wheat germ	50 mL
$\frac{1}{2}$ tsp	cinnamon	2 mL
2	eggs	2
$\frac{1}{2}$ tsp	almond extract	2 mL
$\frac{1}{2}$ tsp	baking powder	2 mL
$\frac{1}{2}$ tsp	salt	2 mL

In small saucepan, combine apricots with enough water to cover. Cover and bring to boil; reduce heat and simmer for 20 minutes. Drain, let cool and chop apricots finely; set aside.

In mixing bowl, cut butter into 1 cup/250 mL flour. Mix in $\frac{1}{4}$ cup/50 mL of the almonds, $\frac{1}{4}$ cup/50 mL of the sugar, bran and cinnamon. Press half of this mixture into greased 8-inch/2 L square baking pan.

In another mixing bowl, beat remaining $\frac{1}{2}$ cup/125 mL sugar with eggs and almond extract. Beat in baking powder, salt, apricots, remaining $\frac{1}{4}$ cup/50 mL flour and remaining $\frac{1}{2}$ cup/125 mL almonds. Pour over pressed layer in pan. Sprinkle with remaining flour-bran mixture. Bake in 350°F/180°C oven for 40 minutes. Let cool, then cut into squares. Makes about 18 squares.

Calories per square: 77
Grams fat per square: 4
Two squares are a good source of fiber.

Photo:

**Omelet à la Jardinière
(page 135)**

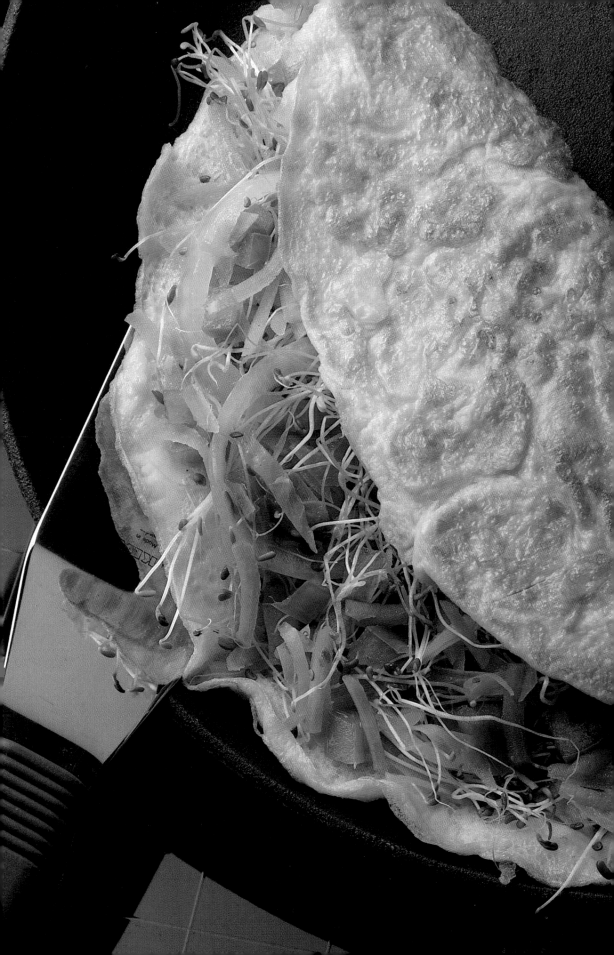

COCONUT-OATMEAL COOKIES

These cookies are a family favorite, especially of my son Jeff's, but don't eat too many. Coconut is an excellent source of fiber, but it is high in fat.

$\frac{3}{4}$ cup	butter or margarine	175 mL
$\frac{3}{4}$ cup	granulated sugar	175 mL
$\frac{1}{2}$ cup	lightly packed brown sugar	125 mL
1	egg	1
1 cup	whole-wheat flour	250 mL
1 cup	rolled oats	250 mL
$\frac{3}{4}$ cup	coconut	175 mL
$\frac{1}{4}$ cup	wheat germ	50 mL
1 tsp	baking powder	5 mL
1 tsp	baking soda	5 mL
$1\frac{1}{2}$ cups	raisins	375 mL

Cream butter, sugars and egg together thoroughly. Add flour, oats, coconut, wheat germ, baking powder and baking soda; mix well. Stir in raisins. Drop by spoonfuls onto lightly greased baking sheets. Flatten slightly with floured fork. Bake in 350°F/180°C oven for 12 to 15 minutes or until light golden. Makes about 36 cookies.

Calories per cookie: 118
Grams fat per cookie: 5.6
Three cookies are an excellent source of fiber.

Variation:
Raisin Oatmeal Cookies: Omit coconut
Calories per cookie: 96
Grams fat per cookie: 4

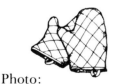

Photo:

Pumpkin Muffins (page 175)
Coconut-Oatmeal Cookies (page 185)
Breakfast Bran-and-Fruit Mix (pages 222-3)

WHEAT GERM CRISPY COOKIES

Packed with whole grains, these low-fat, low-calorie cookies are good for packed lunches, after-school snacks and desserts.

$1\frac{1}{4}$ cups	whole-wheat flour	300 mL
1 cup	wheat germ	250 mL
1 tsp	cinnamon	5 mL
$\frac{1}{4}$ tsp	ground cloves	1 mL
$\frac{1}{4}$ tsp	salt	1 mL
$\frac{1}{2}$ cup	butter or margarine	125 mL
$\frac{1}{2}$ cup	packed brown sugar	125 mL
1	egg	1
1 tsp	vanilla	5 mL
2 tbsp	granulated sugar	25 mL

In bowl, combine flour, wheat germ, cinnamon, cloves and salt; mix well. In another large bowl, cream butter and brown sugar thoroughly; beat in egg and vanilla. Add mixed dry ingredients to creamed mixture and mix well.

Divide dough in half. On lightly floured counter, roll each half $\frac{1}{8}$ inch/2.5 mm thick. Cut with $2\frac{1}{2}$-inch/6 cm round cutter. Place on ungreased baking sheets. Sprinkle with granulated sugar. Bake in 350°F/180°C oven for 8 to 10 minutes or until lightly browned. Let cool until firm, then remove from baking sheets. Makes 36 cookies.

Calories per cookie: 57
Grams fat per cookie: 3

DATE MERINGUE SQUARES

One of my mother's recipes, these go well with frozen desserts such as Grapefruit Ice (page 196) or other fruit sorbets.

$1\frac{3}{4}$ cups	chopped dates	425 mL
$\frac{3}{4}$ cup	water	175 mL
$\frac{1}{3}$ cup	shortening	75 mL
$\frac{1}{3}$ cup	granulated sugar	75 mL
2	eggs, separated	2
1 tsp	vanilla	5 mL
$\frac{3}{4}$ cup	all-purpose flour	175 mL
$\frac{3}{4}$ cup	whole-wheat flour	175 mL
1 tsp	baking powder	5 mL
$\frac{1}{2}$ cup	packed brown sugar	125 mL
$\frac{1}{4}$ cup	slivered almonds (optional)	50 mL

In saucepan, simmer dates and water until mixture is thick and soft, about 4 minutes.

In mixing bowl, cream shortening; beat in granulated sugar and mix well. Add egg yolks and vanilla; beat until well mixed. Beat in flours and baking powder until mixed. Pat into lightly greased 9-inch/2 L square baking pan. Spread date paste on top.

Beat egg whites until stiff peaks form. Continue beating, gradually adding brown sugar; beat until stiff. Spread over date mixture. Sprinkle with nuts (if using). Bake in 350°F/180°C oven for 35 to 40 minutes or until golden. Makes about 25 squares.

Calories per square: 125
Grams fat per square: 3.8
Fiber: **Good**

DESSERTS

Desserts are where we can really go astray when it comes to reducing the fat content in our diet. Most cookies are deadly, and mousses, chocolate desserts and lovely whipped-cream confections are filled with fat. However, don't despair. This doesn't mean you have to deprive yourself forever of these delicious desserts. Just be aware of their high fat content and savor them in moderation. Save them for special occasions, enjoy small servings and select low-fat dishes for the rest of the meal.

This section of the cookbook has many delicious desserts that are not high in fat. Remember that fresh strawberries, juicy peaches and sweet cherries are among the delights of summer. And what tastes better after a two- or three-course dinner than a homemade fruit sorbet?

Many of the dessert recipes in this book are fruit desserts. They are low in fat, yet full of flavor. They are also high in vitamins, minerals and fiber. You will find them a delight to both the eye and the palate!

BLACKBERRIES WITH ORANGE CREAM SAUCE

In Vancouver, where I grew up, blackberries grow wild, and it wasn't until I moved to Toronto that I realized what a high-priced treat they were. One of my favorite traditions was the annual Elliott family's blackberry expedition to Lulu Island (now Delta). In just a few hours, we would fill large baskets with huge, juicy Himalayan blackberries—lots to eat raw, some for pies and the rest to make into jelly.

2½ cups	fresh blackberries	625 mL
1 cup	Orange Cream Sauce (pages 220-1)	250 mL

Wash blackberries. Remove any stems. Spoon sauce into individual dessert plates and top with blackberries. Alternatively, spoon blackberries into stemmed glasses and pour sauce over them. Makes 4 servings.

Calories per serving: 126
Grams fat per serving: 0.7
Fiber: Excellent
Vitamin C: Excellent

Compare: strawberries served with $\frac{1}{4}$ cup/50 mL whipped cream instead of with Raspberry-Rhubarb Sauce.
Calories per serving: 146
Grams fat per serving: 10
Fiber: Good
Vitamin C: Excellent

STRAWBERRIES WITH RASPBERRY-RHUBARB SAUCE

Dress up strawberries, cherries, plums, blackberries or other fresh seasonal fruit with a delicious fruit sauce for a low-fat dessert.

4 cups	strawberries	1 L
$1\frac{1}{2}$ cups	Raspberry-Rhubarb Sauce (page 220)	375 mL

Wash, then hull strawberries. Serve them in stemmed glasses and pour Raspberry-Rhubarb Sauce over them. Makes 6 servings.

Calories per serving: 97
Grams fat per serving: 0.7
Fiber: Excellent
Calcium and vitamin C: Excellent

DESSERT TOPPINGS

Apple pie with Cheddar cheese, blueberry pie with vanilla ice cream, pumpkin pie with whipped cream—these innocent toppings can add disastrous amounts of fats and calories.

Ice cream varies considerably in the amount of fat it contains. Do read labels and choose ones with lower fat content.

Compare:
Fat Content of Dessert Toppings

	Grams fat per $\frac{1}{4}$ cup/50 mL
Whipping cream (unwhipped)	24
Whipped cream	12
Dream Whip	7
Sour cream (12% fat)	4
Whipped cream (pressurized)	3

	Grams fat per $\frac{1}{2}$ cup/125 mL
Ice cream (vanilla, 16% fat)	12
Ice cream (vanilla, 10% fat)	8
Yogurt (partially skim milk)	3

1 oz/28g Cheddar cheese has 8 grams fat.

Fat Content of Our Dessert Sauces	Grams fat per $\frac{1}{4}$ cup/50 mL
Custard Sauce (page 212)	2
Orange Cream Sauce (pages 220-1)	0.1
Raspberry or Strawberry Coulis (page 193)	0.1
Raspberry-Rhubarb Sauce (page 220)	trace
Easy Chocolate Sauce (page 221)	0.1
Sherry Orange Sauce (page 201)	trace

PEACHES WITH RASPBERRY-YOGURT SAUCE

You can use fresh or frozen raspberries or strawberries in this sauce. It's good over any fresh fruit.

4	fresh ripe peaches	4
Raspberry-Yogurt Sauce:		
1 cup	frozen unsweetened raspberries	250 mL
$\frac{1}{2}$ cup	plain yogurt	125 mL
1 tbsp	granulated sugar or honey	15 mL
Garnish:		
	Fresh raspberries or mint	

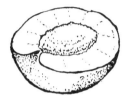

Peaches are a good source, and raspberries an excellent source, of fiber.

Peel peaches (blanch in boiling water to make peeling easier) and slice.

Raspberry-Yogurt Sauce: In food processor or blender, process raspberries, yogurt and sugar until smooth. Refrigerate until needed.

Spoon peaches into individual dishes and spoon sauce over peaches. Alternatively, spread sauce on plates and arrange peaches on top. Garnish with fresh raspberries or mint. Makes 4 servings.

Calories per serving: 141
Grams fat per serving: 0.3
Fiber: Excellent
Vitamins A and C: Excellent

POACHED PEARS WITH CHOCOLATE SAUCE

Poached fruit can be served in the poaching liquid. Remove cooled fruit from liquid and strain liquid. Boil poaching liquid until reduced to 1 cup/250 mL; let cool, then serve over poached fruit.

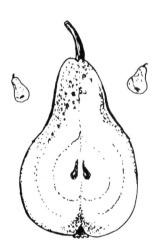

Many other fruits, such as peaches, plums, apricots and apples, can also be poached. Serve them with Easy Chocolate Sauce or one of the other fruit dessert sauces in this book, such as Raspberry Coulis (page 193).

3 cups	water	750 mL
½ cup	granulated sugar	125 mL
	Grated rind and juice of 1 lemon	
1	vanilla bean and/or cinnamon stick	1
4	pears	4
¼ cup	Easy Chocolate Sauce (page 221)	50 mL

In large saucepan, combine water, sugar, lemon rind, lemon juice, vanilla bean and/or cinnamon stick. Bring to a boil, stirring until sugar is dissolved.

Peel, halve and core pears. Add pears to boiling syrup. (Pears should be covered in liquid; if not, double the amount of poaching liquid or poach in batches.) Reduce heat to medium-low and simmer gently for 15 to 20 minutes or until pears are almost tender (time will vary depending on ripeness and type of pear; remember, pears will continue to cook while cooling). Remove from heat and let cool in liquid.

Drain pears thoroughly and pat dry on paper towels. Arrange pear halves on individual plates. Drizzle with Chocolate Sauce. Serve at room temperature. Makes 4 large servings or 8 small.

Calories per small serving: 168
Grams fat per small serving: 0.8
Fiber: Good
Vitamin C: Good

RASPBERRY SORBET WITH STRAWBERRY COULIS

Don't strain the raspberry mixture; the seeds are an excellent source of fiber. Coulis is a purée of fruits or vegetables and is used as a sauce.

2	pkg (9 oz/225 g each) frozen sweetened raspberries, thawed	2
1 cup	water	250 mL
1 tbsp	lemon juice	15 mL
1 cup	Strawberry Coulis (page 193)	250 mL

In food processor, purée raspberries. Stir in water and lemon juice.

Freezing Instructions:

Method 1 — Ice-Cream Machine: Follow manufacturer's instructions.

Method 2 — Food Processor: Freeze in metal pan or bowl until hard. Process in food processor until mixture is a hard slush. Return to freezer until needed.

Method 3 — Hand Method: Freeze in metal pan or bowl until barely firm. Beat by hand or electric mixer until slushy. Return to freezer until needed.

To Serve: Sorbet should not be rock-hard. If necessary, transfer to refrigerator 15 minutes before serving or process in food processor. To serve, spoon sorbet into individual dishes or stemmed glasses and pour sauce over it. Alternatively, spoon some sauce onto dessert plates and spoon a scoop or two of sorbet on top of each plate. (This looks very attractive when different kinds of sorbets are served on each plate and are garnished with fresh raspberries or other fresh fruits.) Makes 8 servings.

	Without coulis	With $\frac{1}{4}$ cup/ 50 mL coulis
Calories per serving:	56	116
Grams fat per serving:	0.1	0.2
Fiber:	Excellent	Excellent
Vitamin C:	Good	Good

FRESH STRAWBERRY SORBET

Fresh, ripe strawberries make a delicious easy-to-make sorbet. Serve with other fruit ices or sorbets and fresh fruit, or with Orange Cream Sauce (pages 220-1).

1 cup	water	250 mL
1 cup	granulated sugar	250 mL
4 cups	ripe strawberries, washed, and hulled	1 L
	Juice of 2 oranges	
	Juice of 1 lemon	
	Fresh strawberries for garnishing	

Bring water and sugar to a boil, stirring, to dissolve sugar; boil for 2 minutes and let cool. In food processor or blender, purée strawberries. Combine strawberries, syrup, orange juice and lemon juice; mix well.

Freeze and serve according to instructions in Raspberry Sorbet recipe (page 192). Garnish each serving with fresh strawberry. Makes 8 servings.

Calories per serving: 142
Grams fat per serving: 0.4
Vitamin C: Excellent

RASPBERRY OR STRAWBERRY COULIS

In blender or food processor, purée 1 package (9 oz / 255 g) frozen raspberries or strawberries. If using unsweetened berries, add icing sugar to taste. Makes about 1 cup / 250 mL sauce.

Calories per $\frac{1}{4}$ cup / 50 mL: 60
Grams fat per $\frac{1}{4}$ cup / 50 mL: 0.1
Fiber: Excellent (when made with raspberries)

APPLE CINNAMON SORBET WITH RASPBERRY COULIS

A light, colorful year-round dessert. This sorbet is full of flavor, and is very good by itself, or with Applesauce Whole-Wheat Cake (page 215), Pumpkin Muffins (page 175) or the Raspberry Coulis.

1 cup	finely grated, peeled and cored apple	250 mL
2 tbsp	lemon juice	25 mL
2 tbsp	Calvados or apple brandy (optional)	25 mL
$\frac{1}{2}$ tsp	cinnamon	2 mL
$2\frac{1}{2}$ cups	water	625 mL
1 cup	granulated sugar	250 mL
$2\frac{1}{2}$ cups	apple juice	625 mL
1 cup	Raspberry Coulis (page 193)	250 mL

In skillet, combine grated apple, lemon juice, Calvados (if using) and cinnamon; cook over medium heat, stirring, until apple is tender, about 3 minutes. In saucepan, bring water and sugar to a boil and cook until sugar dissolved. Remove from heat; stir in apple mixture and apple juice.

Freeze and serve according to instructions in Raspberry Sorbet recipe (page 192). Serve it with fresh fruit such as grapes, sliced kiwi or strawberries, plus a fresh mint leaf, or drizzle with Raspberry Coulis. Makes 8 servings.

Calories per serving: 158
Grams fat per serving: 0.2
Fiber: **Good**
Vitamin C: **Excellent**

FROZEN LEMON CREAM

It's hard to tell the base of this creamy dessert is yogurt. It's also delicious with a topping of fresh fruit such as strawberries, blueberries, peaches, bananas, papaya or kiwi.

3 cups	plain yogurt	750 mL
2 tsp	vanilla	10 mL
4 tsp	grated lemon rind	20 mL
$\frac{1}{4}$ cup	lemon juice	50 mL
$\frac{1}{2}$ cup	granulated sugar	125 mL

Combine all ingredients and mix well. Freeze and serve according to instructions in Raspberry Sorbet recipe (page 192). Makes 8 servings.

Calories per serving: 106
Grams fat per serving: 0.2
Calcium and phosphorus: Good

For a festive frozen dessert, use Frozen Lemon Cream as a filling between layers of Orange Sponge Cake (page 213) or sandwiched between Meringues (page 206), and freeze.

GRAPEFRUIT ICE

Fresh-squeezed grapefruit juice made into an ice is a delicious, refreshing dessert at any time of year. Arrange scoops of ice on individual plates with fresh grapefruit sections or other fresh fruit, or serve with cookies or squares.

2 cups	granulated sugar	500 mL
2 cups	water	500 mL
6	grapefruit	6
$\frac{1}{4}$ cup	lemon juice	50 mL

In saucepan, combine sugar and water, stirring to dissolve sugar. Bring to a boil and boil for 5 minutes. Remove from heat. Grate rind from 1 grapefruit (be careful to grate only yellow part—white part of rind is too bitter). Stir rind into syrup and let cool.

Squeeze juice from the 6 grapefruit to measure 4 cups/ 1 L. Stir grapefruit juice and lemon juice into cool syrup.

Freeze and serve according to instructions in Raspberry Sorbet recipe (page 192). Makes 12 servings.

Calories per serving: 171
Grams fat per serving: trace
Vitamin C: Excellent

LEMON SORBET

A light, refreshing dessert. Compare the fat content of a serving of Lemon Sorbet with that of ice cream: 0.04 versus 8 grams.

	Grated rind and juice of 3 lemons	
2 cups	water	500 mL
1 cup	granulated sugar	250 mL
1	egg white	1

In saucepan, combine lemon rind, lemon juice, water and sugar; bring to a boil. Reduce heat and simmer for 5 minutes; let cool. Pour into metal pan and freeze until firm—at least 4 hours. Break frozen mixture into chunks, place in food processor and process until smooth. Add egg white and process for a few seconds longer. Spoon into freezer container; cover, and return to freezer until firm, about 1 to 2 hours. Place in refrigerator for 15 minutes, or until slightly softened, before serving. (To make without using a food processor, omit egg white and freeze according to instructions in Raspberry Sorbet recipe, page 192.

Calories per serving: 152
Grams fat per serving: trace
Vitamin C: Excellent

YOGURT FRUIT FREEZE

This is a pleasure for dieters who are dessert lovers. It's also the perfect year-round treat for children.

2½ cups	plain low-fat yogurt	625 mL
2	small bananas	2
⅔ cup	frozen orange juice concentrate (undiluted)	150 mL

In food processor or blender, process yogurt, bananas and orange juice concentrate until smooth. Alternatively, mash bananas and beat in remaining ingredients with electric mixer until smooth. Freeze and serve according to instructions in Raspberry Sorbet recipe (page 192). For kids, freeze in Popsicle containers after processing. Makes 8 servings.

Calories per serving: 100
Grams fat per serving: 0.2
Vitamin C: Excellent
Calcium: Good

PRUNE CAKE

This easy-to-make cake is ideal for packed lunches or for feeding a crowd of kids. Sprinkle it with icing sugar or ice with Lemon Icing (page 215).

1½ cups	prunes	375 mL
1½ cups	water	375 mL
¾ cup	packed brown sugar	175 mL
⅓ cup	granulated sugar	75 mL
1 cup	plain yogurt	250 mL
2	eggs	2
1½ cups	all-purpose flour	375 mL
1 cup	whole-wheat flour	250 mL
2 tsp	baking powder	10 mL
½ tsp	baking soda	2 mL
1 tsp	cinnamon	5 mL
½ tsp	salt	2 mL

In saucepan, combine prunes and water; bring to a boil and simmer for 1 minute. Cover and let stand until cool; drain. Remove pits and chop prunes (you should have about 1½ cups/375 mL); set aside.

In mixing bowl, combine sugars and yogurt; beat until smooth. Add eggs and beat until well mixed. Add flours, baking powder, baking soda, cinnamon and salt; beat well. Stir in prunes.

Pour into lightly greased and floured 12×8-inch/3 L baking pan. Bake in 375°F/190°C oven for 30 minutes or until toothpick inserted in center comes out clean.

When cool, ice with Lemon Icing (page 215) if desired. Makes 18 servings.

	With icing	Without icing
Calories per serving:	182	140
Grams fat per serving:	1.25	1.22
Fiber: **Good**		

MELON WITH BLUEBERRIES

A quick-to-make, refreshing dessert. Or try it as a first course or breakfast treat. Peaches, grapes, kiwi or other fresh fruit in season can be used instead of blueberries. If serving as a first course, omit the honey; arrange wedges of melon on individual salad plates, drizzle with lemon juice mixed with liqueur or lime juice, and garnish with blueberries.

$\frac{1}{2}$	cantaloupe	$\frac{1}{2}$
$\frac{1}{2}$	honeydew melon	$\frac{1}{2}$
2 cups	watermelon cubes	500 mL
1 cup	blueberries	250 mL
2 tbsp	honey	25 mL
2 tbsp	lemon juice	25 mL
2 tbsp	melon or orange liqueur or sherry (optional)	25 mL
	Fresh mint leaves	

Cut cantaloupe and honeydew melon into cubes or balls. In glass serving bowl, combine cantaloupe, honeydew, watermelon and blueberries.

In small dish, combine honey and lemon juice; stir until mixed. Blend in liqueur (if using). Pour over melons; toss to mix. Cover and refrigerate until serving time.

Serve in stemmed glasses and garnish with mint. Serve at room temperature. Makes 6 servings.

Calories per serving: 122
Grams fat per serving: 0.9
Fiber: Excellent
Vitamins A and C: Excellent

CANTALOUPE, PEAR AND GRAPES WITH SHERRY ORANGE SAUCE

This sauce is easy to make and keeps well in the refrigerator for at least a week. Use any fresh fruit in season. Japanese pears, which look more like apples than pears, are available in the winter; they are very crisp and juicy and add a lot of crunch. Top this dessert with yogurt and brown sugar, or spoon over sherbet for another variation.

1	cantaloupe	1
1	pear (Japanese or domestic), mango or papaya	1
1 cup	red, green, or black grapes	250 mL
Sherry Orange Sauce:		
½ cup	granulated sugar	125 mL
1 tbsp	cornstarch	15 mL
1 tbsp	grated orange rind	15 mL
½ cup	orange juice	125 mL
½ cup	medium to dry sherry	125 mL
1 tbsp	lemon juice	15 mL

Cut cantaloupe in half; discard seeds. Cut flesh into cubes or balls. Cut unpeeled pear into cubes (if using mango or papaya, peel and cut flesh into cubes). Cut grapes in half if large, and remove any seeds. Spoon into stemmed wine or sherbet glasses.

Sherry Orange Sauce: In small saucepan, blend sugar and cornstarch; stir in orange rind, orange juice, sherry and lemon juice. Cook, stirring, over medium heat until sauce thickens, bubbles and becomes clear. Cook for 2 to 3 minutes, stirring constantly. Remove from heat and let cool.

At serving time, spoon sauce over fruit. Makes 6 servings.

Calories per serving: 166
Grams fat per serving: 0.4
Vitamins A and C: Excellent

LEMON CHARLOTTE WITH STRAWBERRIES

Top this light, frothy dessert with your favorite kind of fresh fruit. Choose whatever is available—kiwi, raspberries, blueberries, or a combination.

7	eggs, separated	7
1½ cups	granulated sugar	375 mL
¾ cup	lemon juice	175 mL
1	pkg unflavored gelatin	1
½ cup	water	125 mL
28	(approx) ladyfingers*	28
2 cups	strawberries, blueberries, raspberries or sliced peaches	500 mL

*Soft ladyfingers are available in bread sections of some supermarkets, bakeries and specialty food stores.

In mixing bowl, beat together egg yolks and ¾ cup/175 mL of the sugar until well mixed; beat in lemon juice. Transfer to top of nonaluminum double boiler. Place over simmering water and cook, stirring, until mixture is thick enough to coat back of metal spoon, 8 to 10 minutes.

Meanwhile, sprinkle gelatin over water and let stand for 5 minutes to soften. Stir into hot yolk mixture; let cool, stirring occasionally.

Beat egg whites until frothy; gradually beat in remaining sugar, beating until stiff peaks form. Stir one-third of the whites into yolk mixture to lighten, then fold into remaining whites.

Split ladyfingers in half. Line bottom, then sides, of 10-inch/25 cm springform pan with ladyfingers, cut side in. Spoon in custard mixture. Refrigerate until firm, about 3 hours or overnight. (Cake can be frozen for up to 3 weeks; remove from freezer at least 1 hour before serving.)

Just before serving, place pan on serving platter and remove sides. Arrange fruit on top. Makes 10 servings.

Calories per serving: 326
Grams fat per serving: 6.6
Fiber: Good (Excellent if made with blackberries or raspberries)

LEMON CLOUD

This light, frothy lemon dessert looks like a mousse but contains no cream. This one is easy to make but should be served the day you make it; it can separate slightly if it stands longer than a day.

2	lemons	2
$\frac{1}{2}$	orange	$\frac{1}{2}$
3 tbsp	cornstarch	45 mL
$\frac{1}{2}$ cup	granulated sugar	125 mL
$1\frac{1}{2}$ cups	hot water	375 mL
2	eggs, separated	2

Variations:
Lemon Sauce: Use as a dessert sauce over fresh fruits such as strawberries, peaches.

Grate rind from 1 of the lemons and orange half. Squeeze juice from orange and lemons (you should have about $\frac{1}{2}$ cup/125 mL lemon juice).

In nonaluminum saucepan, combine cornstarch and half the sugar. Stir in water and bring to a boil, stirring constantly. Reduce heat and boil gently for 3 minutes. Beat egg yolks slightly; stir a little hot mixture into yolks; then slowly pour yolk mixture back into saucepan. Cook, stirring, over medium-low heat for 2 minutes. Remove from heat and stir in juices and rinds. Transfer to mixing bowl and refrigerate to cool slightly.

Beat egg whites until soft peaks form; continue beating, slowly adding remaining sugar and beating until stiff peaks form. Fold egg whites into lemon mixture. Spoon into stemmed glasses or serving bowl. Refrigerate until serving time. Makes 6 servings.

Calories per serving: 125
Grams fat per serving: 2
Vitamin C: Excellent

LEMON AND FRESH BLUEBERRY TART

Meringue on the bottom, lemon filling in the center and blueberries on the top make a luscious, low-fat dessert that's lower in calories than a pie with traditional pastry.

Meringue Crust:		
2	egg whites	2
Pinch	cream of tartar	Pinch
$\frac{1}{2}$ cup	granulated sugar	125 mL
$\frac{1}{4}$ tsp	cornstarch	1 mL
$\frac{1}{2}$ tsp	vanilla	2 mL
Lemon Filling:		
$\frac{1}{2}$ cup	granulated sugar	125 mL
5 tbsp	cornstarch	75 mL
$1\frac{1}{2}$ cups	hot water	375 mL
2	egg yolks	2
	Grated rind and juice of 1 large lemon	
	Grated rind of $\frac{1}{2}$ orange	
Blueberry Topping:		
$\frac{1}{4}$ cup	granulated sugar	50 mL
2 tsp	cornstarch	10 mL
$\frac{1}{3}$ cup	water	75 mL
1 tsp	fresh lemon juice	5 mL
2 cups	fresh blueberries	500 mL

Meringue Crust: Line an 8- or 9-inch/20 or 23 cm pie plate with foil; butter foil lightly, sprinkle with flour and shake off excess flour.

In medium bowl, beat egg whites with cream of tartar until soft peaks form. Beat in sugar, 1 tbsp/15 mL at a time, until stiff glossy peaks form. Beat in cornstarch and vanilla. Spread mixture into foil-lined pie plate; bring sides about $\frac{1}{2}$ inch/1 cm higher than pan. Bake in 300°F/150°C oven for 90 minutes or until firm and dry; let cool slightly on rack. While still warm, remove meringue from pie plate and peel off foil. Return meringue shell to pie plate.

Lemon Filling: Grate rind from lemon and $\frac{1}{2}$ orange. Squeeze juice from lemon (you should have about $\frac{1}{3}$ cup/ 75 mL). In nonaluminum heavy saucepan, mix sugar and cornstarch. Stir in water and bring to a boil over medium heat, stirring constantly. Reduce heat and boil gently for 3 minutes, stirring constantly.

In small bowl, beat egg yolks lightly. Whisk a little hot mixture into egg yolks, then slowly pour yolk mixture back into saucepan, stirring constantly. Cook over medium-low heat, stirring constantly, for 2 minutes. Remove from heat. Stir in lemon juice and grated rinds. Let cool slightly; pour into prepared pie shell.

Blueberry Topping: In heavy saucepan, combine sugar and cornstarch. Stir in water and lemon juice. Cook, stirring, over medium heat until mixture thickens, comes to a boil and becomes clear. Remove from heat and add blueberries, stirring to coat well. Spoon blueberries over lemon filling. Refrigerate for at least 30 minutes before serving. Makes 8 servings.

Calories per serving: 190
Grams fat per serving: 1.5
Fiber: Excellent
Vitamin C: Good

RASPBERRY MERINGUE TORTE

Individually frozen raspberries are available in most supermarkets, making this torte a year-round treat. It's not as complicated as it looks. The meringues can be made well in advance, and the custard sauce early in the day, or even a day in advance; neither procedure takes very long. Use strawberries or other berries when they are in season instead of raspberries.

Make-Ahead Summer Dinner
Chilled Melon and Yogurt
Soup (page 37)
Cold chicken
Pasta Salad with Sweet Peppers
and Fresh Dill (pages 80-1)
Sliced tomatoes with basil
Whole-wheat buns
Raspberry Meringue Torte
(page 206)

Meringues:		
6	egg whites	6
1 $\frac{1}{2}$ cups	granulated sugar	375 mL
1 tsp	cornstarch	5 mL
1 tsp	vanilla	5 mL
Custard Filling:		
$\frac{1}{4}$ cup	granulated sugar	50 mL
2 tbsp	cornstarch	25 mL
Pinch	salt	Pinch
2 cups	milk	500 mL
4	egg yolks	4
2 tsp	vanilla	10 mL
Pinch	freshly grated nutmeg	Pinch
2 tbsp	orange or almond liqueur (optional)	25 mL
Fruit Layers:		
2 cups	blueberries or 3 cups/750 mL sliced peaches, bananas, kiwi, mangoes or other fresh fruit	500 mL
2 cups	raspberries or strawberries	500 mL

Meringues: Line 2 baking sheets with foil; oil foil lightly.

In large bowl, beat egg whites until soft peaks form. Combine sugar and cornstarch. Continuing to beat egg whites, gradually add sugar mixture, beating until stiff peaks form. Stir in vanilla.

Spread meringue mixture over foil-lined baking sheet to form 2 circles about 11 inches/28 cm in diameter. Bake in 275°F/140°C oven for 2 hours or until meringues are firm. Remove from oven; while warm, carefully remove foil. (If foil is difficult to remove, meringues may not be cooked enough or foil wasn't oiled enough.)

Custard Filling: In nonaluminum saucepan or top of double-boiler, combine sugar, cornstarch and salt. Stir in milk. Cook, stirring, over medium-low heat or simmering water until mixture thickens and comes to a simmer; cook for 5 minutes, stirring constantly.

Beat egg yolks until mixed; gradually whisk a small amount of hot milk mixture into yolks. While stirring, pour warmed yolk mixture into hot milk mixture. Stir over low heat for about 2 minutes or until thickened slightly. Remove from heat; stir in vanilla, nutmeg and liqueur (if using); let cool.

A few hours before serving, place one meringue on serving platter; spread custard over meringue. Arrange blueberries over custard. Place second meringue on top. Arrange raspberries on top. To serve, cut into wedges. Makes 10 servings.

Calories per serving: 240
Grams fat per serving: 3.7
Fiber: Excellent
Vitamin C: Good

PEACH BLUEBERRY CRISP

It's hard to find a better-tasting fall fruit dessert than this one. If you cook it in a microwave, it takes only 10 minutes.

6 cups	peeled, sliced fresh peaches	1.5 L
2 cups	blueberries	500 mL
$\frac{1}{3}$ cup	brown sugar, packed	75 mL
2 tbsp	all-purpose flour	25 mL
2 tsp	cinnamon	10 mL
Topping:		
1 cup	quick-cooking rolled oats	250 mL
1 tsp	cinnamon	5 mL
$\frac{1}{4}$ cup	brown sugar, packed	50 mL
3 tbsp	soft butter	45 mL

In 8-cup/2 L baking dish, combine peaches and blueberries. In small bowl, combine sugar, flour and cinnamon; add to fruit and toss to mix.

Topping: Combine rolled oats, sugar and cinnamon; with pastry blender or 2 knives, cut in butter until crumbly. Sprinkle over top of fruit mixture. Bake in 350°F/180°C oven for 25 minutes or microwave on High for 10 minutes or until mixture is bubbling and fruit is barely tender. Serve warm or cold. Makes 8 servings.

Calories per serving: 255
Grams fat per serving: 5
Fiber: Excellent
Vitamin A: Excellent
Vitamin C: Good

PEAR CRISP WITH ROLLED OATS TOPPING

You'll enjoy the lemon and ginger flavors of the sauce in this fall or winter dessert. The amount of juice will vary depending on the kind and size of pears used.

8	pears, cored and sliced	8
2 tbsp	lemon juice	25 mL
1 tsp	grated lemon rind	5 mL
1 tbsp	grated fresh ginger root or 1 tsp/5 mL ground ginger	15 mL
$\frac{1}{2}$ cup	granulated sugar	125 mL
$\frac{1}{4}$ cup	all-purpose flour	50 mL
Topping:		
$\frac{1}{2}$ cup	packed brown sugar	125 mL
$\frac{1}{3}$ cup	whole-wheat flour	75 mL
$\frac{2}{3}$ cup	rolled oats	150 mL
$\frac{1}{4}$ cup	powdered skim milk	50 mL
1 tsp	cinnamon	5 mL
3 tbsp	butter	45 mL

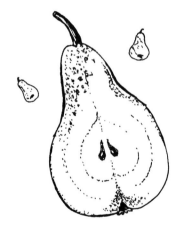

Adding powdered skim milk to crumb toppings is an easy way to add calcium and extra protein as well as flavor.

In mixing bowl, toss pears with lemon juice, lemon rind and ginger. Mix together sugar and flour; sprinkle over pears and toss to mix. Spoon into lightly buttered 8-cup/2 L soufflé or baking dish.

Topping: Mix together sugar, flour, oats, powdered milk, sugar and cinnamon; with pastry blender or 2 knives, cut in butter until mixture resembles fine crumbs. Sprinkle over pear mixture.

Bake in 375°F/190°C oven for 30 to 45 minutes or until pears are tender and mixture is bubbling. Serve hot or warm. Makes 8 servings.

Calories per serving: 271
Grams fat per serving: 5
Fiber: Good
Vitamin C: Excellent

APRICOT CLAFOUTI

Clafouti is a French baked-fruit custard dessert. It's easy to make and can be made with almost any kind of fruit besides apricots— cherries, plums, peaches, or whatever is available.

4 cups	fresh apricots	1 L
1 tbsp	butter	15 mL
6 tbsp	granulated sugar	90 mL
3	eggs	3
1⅓ cups	milk	325 mL
⅔ cup	all-purpose flour	150 mL
1 tsp	grated lemon rind	5 mL
½ tsp	cinnamon	2 mL
2 tsp	vanilla	10 mL
Pinch	salt	Pinch
	Icing sugar	

Halve apricots, then pit them. Grease an 11-inch/27 cm glass pie plate or large quiche dish with the butter. Sprinkle with 1 tbsp/15 mL of the granulated sugar. Arrange apricots, cut side down, in dish and sprinkle with 2 tbsp/25 mL of the granulated sugar.

In blender or food processor, combine remaining sugar, eggs, milk, flour, lemon rind, cinnamon, vanilla and salt; process until smooth. Alternatively, beat remaining sugar with eggs; add remaining ingredients and beat until smooth. Pour mixture evenly over fruit.

Bake in 375°F/190°C oven for 50 to 60 minutes or until top is browned and filling is set. Just before serving, sift icing sugar over top. Serve warm or cold. Makes 6 to 8 servings.

	6 servings	8 servings
Calories per serving:	213	162
Grams fat per serving:	5.8	4.4
Fiber: Good	2.7 g	2.1 g
Vitamin A:	Excellent	Excellent
Vitamin C:	Good	Good
Niacin:	Good	

OLD-FASHIONED PEACH COBBLER

Make this old-fashioned comforting dessert in the summertime when peaches are juicy and plentiful.

½ cup	packed brown sugar	125 mL
½ tsp	cinnamon	2 mL
1 tsp	grated lemon or orange rind	5 mL
1 tbsp	lemon juice	15 mL
4 cups	sliced, peeled peaches	1 L
¾ cup	all-purpose flour	175 mL
½ cup	whole-wheat flour	125 mL
1 tbsp	baking powder	15 mL
¼ cup	butter or margarine	50 mL
¼ cup	granulated sugar	50 mL
1	egg, lightly beaten	1
½ cup	milk	125 mL
½ tsp	vanilla	2 mL

Lightly butter an 8-cup/2 L baking dish. In large bowl, combine brown sugar, cinnamon, grated lemon rind and lemon juice; mix well. Add peaches and toss to mix; transfer to baking dish.

Combine flours and baking powder. In mixing bowl, cream butter and granulated sugar until light and fluffy; beat in egg. Add dry ingredients alternately with milk. Add vanilla, mixing just until combined. Drop batter by spoonfuls over peach mixture. Bake in 375°F/190°C oven for 25 to 35 minutes or until peaches are tender and top is golden brown. Serve warm. Makes 8 servings.

Calories per serving: 212
Grams fat per serving: 5.6
Fiber: Good
Vitamin A: Excellent
Niacin and vitamin C: Good

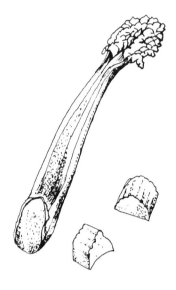

RHUBARB PUDDING WITH CUSTARD SAUCE

Tart rhubarb is a delicious contrast to this light sauce. The tart-ness will vary, depending on whether you use frozen, hothouse or home-grown rhubarb, so add more sugar if necessary.

2 lb	fresh or frozen rhubarb	1 kg
1¼ cups	(approx) granulated sugar	300 mL
1 tsp	grated orange rind	5 mL
2 cups	water	500 mL
2 tbsp	cornstarch	25 mL
¼ cup	cold water	50 mL
1½ tsp	vanilla	7 mL
Custard Sauce:		
2 tbsp	granulated sugar	25 mL
2 tsp	cornstarch	10 mL
Pinch	salt	Pinch
1 cup	milk	250 mL
1	egg yolk	1
1 tsp	vanilla	5 mL
	Freshly grated nutmeg	

Cut fresh rhubarb into ¾-inch/2 cm pieces. In sauce-pan, combine rhubarb, sugar, orange rind and water. Bring to a boil; reduce heat and simmer, uncovered, until rhu-barb is tender, about 10 minutes for fresh, 3 minutes for frozen. Taste, and add more sugar if necessary.

Mix cornstarch with ¼ cup/50 mL cold water; stir into rhubarb. Cook, stirring, over medium heat until mixture thickens and becomes clear. Boil gently for about 3 minutes. Remove from heat and stir in vanilla. Transfer to serving bowl. Let cool, cover and refrigerate.

Custard Sauce: In heavy nonaluminum saucepan or top of double-boiler, combine sugar, cornstarch and salt. Stir in milk. Stir over medium heat; bring to a simmer and cook for 5 minutes or until sauce is thickened slightly. Whisk egg yolk; whisk about ½ cup/125 mL of hot mixture into yolk. Whisk yolk mixture back into hot milk mixture. Cook, stirring, over low heat for about 2 minutes or until sauce is thickened. Remove from heat; stir in vanilla, and freshly grated nutmeg to taste. Cover, and refrigerate until needed. Makes about 1 cup/250 mL.

To serve, pour custard sauce over individual servings of rhubarb. Makes 8 servings.

Calories per serving (including 2 tbsp / 25 mL custard sauce): 183
Grams fat per serving (including 2 tbsp / 25 mL custard sauce): 1.4
Fiber: Good
Vitamin C: Good

Angel food cake is very low in fat because it is made from egg whites only. However, you then have a lot of egg yolks to use up. For this reason, you may want to use a cake mix for making angel food cakes.

Serve wedges of sponge cake topped with Sherry Orange Sauce (page 201) and sections of fresh oranges.

ORANGE SPONGE CAKE

This cake is delicious on its own or with fresh fruit, dessert sauces or sherbets. Make sure you use large eggs at room temperature.

¾ cup	granulated sugar	175 mL
4	eggs, separated	4
1 tbsp	grated orange rind	15 mL
½ cup	fresh orange juice	125 mL
1 cup	all-purpose flour	250 mL
1 tsp	baking powder	5 mL
Pinch	salt	Pinch
2 tsp	icing sugar	10 mL

In mixing bowl, combine granulated sugar, egg yolks, orange rind and orange juice; beat until very light in color. Add flour and baking powder; beat until combined.

In separate bowl, combine egg whites with a pinch of salt and beat until stiff peaks form. Mix a small amount of whites into yolk mixture, then fold yolk mixture into whites.

Pour mixture into ungreased 10-inch/1.5 L tube pan with removable bottom. Bake in 325°F/160°C oven for 50 to 55 minutes or until cake is golden brown and springs back when lightly touched. Invert and let cool completely before removing from pan.

Sift icing sugar over top, or ice with Orange Icing (page 215), or serve with sherbet or Raspberry Coulis (page 193). Makes 12 servings.

Calories per serving: 96
Grams fat per serving: 1.9

CINNAMON COFFEE CAKE

Serve this easy-to-make, moist cake with fresh fruit or sorbet for any meal any time of day.

1 cup	plain yogurt	250 mL
1 tsp	baking soda	5 mL
$\frac{1}{4}$ cup	butter or margarine	50 mL
1 cup	lightly packed brown sugar	250 mL
1	egg	1
1 tsp	vanilla	5 mL
1 $\frac{1}{2}$ cups	all-purpose flour	375 mL
2 tsp	baking powder	10 mL
Topping:		
$\frac{1}{2}$ cup	lightly packed brown sugar	125 mL
1 tbsp	cinnamon	15 mL

Grease and flour a bundt pan or 9-inch/2 L square baking pan.

In small bowl, combine yogurt and baking soda; mix well and set aside. (Yogurt mixture will increase in volume.)

In large mixing bowl, beat butter with sugar until well mixed. Add egg and vanilla; beat well, about 2 minutes. Sift together flour and baking powder; add to butter mixture alternately with yogurt mixture.

Topping: Combine sugar and cinnamon; mix well.

Spread half the batter in prepared pan. Sprinkle with half the topping. Cover with remaining batter and sprinkle with remaining topping. Bake in 350°F/180°C oven for 45 minutes or until toothpick inserted in center comes out clean. Let cool for 10 to 15 minutes in pan, then invert onto wire rack. Makes 12 servings.

Calories per serving: 172
Grams fat per serving: 3.8

APPLESAUCE WHOLE-WHEAT CAKE

Full of flavor, this delicious moist cake looks attractive when made in a bundt or tube pan. It's easy to make and keeps well.

1¾ cups	granulated sugar	425 mL
¼ cup	butter, at room temperature	50 mL
1	egg	1
½ cup	plain yogurt	125 mL
2 cups	applesauce	500 mL
1 tsp	grated orange rind	5 mL
1 tsp	vanilla	5 mL
1½ cups	all-purpose flour	375 mL
1¼ cups	whole-wheat flour	300 mL
3 tbsp	natural bran	45 mL
2 tsp	cinnamon	10 mL
2 tsp	baking soda	10 mL
1 cup	raisins	250 mL

Serve cake with fresh fruit desserts, poached pears or sorbets.

Lemon Icing
Using yogurt instead of butter makes a creamy low-fat icing. In mixing bowl, combine 1½ cups/375 mL icing sugar (sifted), 2 tbsp/25 mL plain yogurt, 1 tsp/5 mL each grated lemon rind and lemon juice; mix until smooth.

Orange Icing
Substitute 1 tsp/5 mL each of grated orange rind and juice for lemon rind and juice.

Butter and flour a 10-inch/25 cm bundt pan. In mixing bowl, combine sugar and butter; beat until mixed. Add egg and beat until light in color. Add yogurt and beat until mixed. Beat in applesauce, orange rind and vanilla.

In another bowl, combine flours, bran, cinnamon, baking soda and raisins; stir to mix. Pour dry ingredients over applesauce mixture and stir just until combined.

Pour into prepared pan and bake in 325°F/160°C oven for 70 to 80 minutes or until toothpick inserted in center comes out clean. Remove from oven. Let cool on rack for 20 minutes, then remove from pan and place on wire rack to finish cooling. Makes 16 slices.

Calories per slice: 224
Grams fat per slice: 3.8
Fiber: Good
Vitamin C: Good

RHUBARB CRUMB PIE

Welcome spring with this pie. A crumb topping reduces the amount of pastry needed. If you are using frozen rhubarb, be sure to thaw the rhubarb first so there won't be too much liquid.

Pastry:		
¾ cup	all-purpose flour	175 mL
½ cup	whole-wheat flour	125 mL
½ tsp	salt	2 mL
3 tbsp	butter or margarine	45 mL
3 tbsp	ice water	45 mL
Filling:		
1 cup	granulated sugar	250 mL
¼ cup	all-purpose flour	50 mL
1 tsp	grated orange or lemon rind	5 mL
1	egg, well beaten	1
5 cups	sliced fresh or frozen (thawed) rhubarb, cut into ½-inch/1 cm pieces	1.25 L
Topping:		
⅓ cup	packed brown sugar	75 mL
3 tbsp	quick-cooking rolled oats	45 mL
3 tbsp	powdered milk (optional)	45 mL
3 tbsp	whole-wheat flour	45 mL
1 tsp	cinnamon	5 mL
2 tbsp	butter	25 mL

Variation:
Rhubarb Crisp with Oatmeal Topping: Follow Rhubarb Crumb Pie but omit the pastry and reduce flour in filling to 2 tbsp/25 mL and omit egg. Combine filling ingredients and spoon into lightly greased 6-cup/1.5 L baking dish. Prepare topping as above and sprinkle over rhubarb. Bake in 375°F/190°C oven for 40 to 50 minutes or until filling is bubbly and top is brown. Makes 6 servings.

Calories per serving: 234
Grams fat per serving: 3.6
Fiber: Good
Vitamin C: Good

Pastry: In mixing bowl, combine flours and salt. With pastry blender or 2 knives, cut in butter until mixture is crumbly. Sprinkle water over mixture and toss with a fork to mix. Press onto bottom and up sides of a 9-inch/23 cm pie plate.

Filling: Combine sugar, flour and grated orange rind; mix well. In another bowl, mix egg and rhubarb; add sugar mixture and stir to mix.

Topping: In bowl, combine sugar, rolled oats, powdered milk (if using), flour and cinnamon. Cut in butter until mixture is crumbly.

Spoon rhubarb filling into pie shell. Sprinkle topping over filling. Bake in 400°F/200°C oven for 50 to 60 minutes or until top is golden brown and rhubarb is tender.

Photo:

Lemon Charlotte with Raspberries (page 202)

Photo:

Peach Blueberry Crisp (page 208)

To prevent top from becoming too brown, cover lightly with foil after 30 minutes of baking. Makes 8 servings.

Calories per serving: 285
Grams fat per serving: 8
Fiber: Good
Calcium: Good

Should I Use Butter or Margarine?

Total fat consumption is the important risk factor in cancer: results from various studies don't identify one particular kind of fat, either saturated or unsaturated. However, since saturated fats and cholesterol may also be factors in coronary heart disease, it might be prudent to use a moderate amount of butter, solid vegetable shortening and lard; they are saturated fats high in cholesterol.

Saturated fats are mainly of animal origin, unsaturated fats of vegetable origin. However, it isn't that simple—some vegetable oils are hydrogenated to make them solid, and highly hydrogenated vegetable oils tend to raise blood cholesterol levels. When shopping, look for oils and margarines made from corn, sunflower, soybean or safflower with as little hydrogenated oil as possible. When buying margarines, choose the ones with the highest polyunsaturated level.

The answer to what kind of fats to use in cooking is to use a variety but to keep the amounts as low as possible. Try cutting down the fat in your favorite recipes by a tablespoon/15 mL at a time to determine the minimum amount of fat necessary to produce a good-tasting result. I think you'll be surprised at how good many foods taste with less fat. By cutting out just one tablespoon/15 mL of butter, you reduce the fat content by 11 grams; cut out a tablespoon/15 mL of oil and you avoid 14 grams of fat.

I like the taste of butter, so I use it wherever I will actually taste it, e.g. on steamed or boiled vegetables, or on toast when I'm not using jam (if using jam, omit butter or margarine—it's not necessary). This is a matter of personal taste and everyone should make his or her own choice as to what to "butter", as long as it is in moderation. I use margarine in baking or cooking where other ingredients overpower the taste of butter; for example, in gingersnaps I use margarine; in shortbread, butter; in muffins I use oil, because it is much quicker to incorporate. When frying or sautéing foods, use half butter and half oil, or all oil. Be conscious of where you are using butter and margarine— often they aren't necessary. Peanut butter sandwiches don't need buttering, for instance, and butter is lost on hot-dog buns smothered with mustard and relish.

DEEP-DISH PLUM PIE

Make this tasty fruit dessert in summer or fall when plums are plentiful. The easy-to-make yogurt pastry is lower in fat and calories than a traditional pastry and is very easy to roll out.

Pastry:		
3 tbsp	margarine or butter	45 mL
1 cup	all-purpose flour	250 mL
6 tbsp	plain yogurt	90 mL
Filling:		
1 cup	granulated sugar	250 mL
$\frac{1}{4}$ cup	instant tapioca	50 mL
1 tsp	cinnamon	5 mL
	Grated rind and juice of 1 lemon	
6 cups	pitted and quartered fresh plums	1.5 L

To reduce calories and fat content, make single-crust or deep-dish pies rather than double-crust pies. Or make a lattice top instead of a full top crust.

Pastry: In bowl, use 2 knives or pastry blender to cut butter into flour until mixture is crumbly. Add yogurt and mix thoroughly. Form dough into ball, wrap in plastic and refrigerate for at least 1 hour. On lightly floured board, roll out dough into circle slightly larger than circumference of baking dish.

Filling: In large bowl, combine sugar, tapioca, cinnamon and grated rind; mix well. Add lemon juice and plums; toss to mix. Transfer to lightly oiled 6-cup/1.5 L soufflé or deep baking dish. Place dough over filling and press firmly against sides of dish. Cut slits in pastry to vent steam. Place on baking sheet and bake in 400°F/200°C oven for 50 to 60 minutes or until top is golden brown and filling is bubbly. If top browns too quickly, cover with foil. Makes 6 servings.

Calories per serving: 288
Grams fat per serving: 6
Fiber: Good
Vitamin C: Excellent
Vitamin A: Good

CINNAMON APPLESAUCE

Applesauce is so easy and quick to make, it isn't necessary to follow a recipe. Treat this one merely as a guide. The amount of sugar and cooking time will vary depending on the kind of apples and how ripe they are. To save time, don't peel or core apples; instead, pass cooked mixture through a food mill or sieve. If you want to keep the skin for more fiber and a chunky sauce, core the apples and chop coarsely; cook until apples are tender, then add sugar to taste. Grated lemon or orange rind or raisins can be added.

6	apples (about 3 lb/1.5 kg)	6
$\frac{1}{4}$ cup	water	50 mL
1 tbsp	lemon juice	15 mL
3 tbsp	granulated sugar	45 mL
1 tsp	cinnamon	5 mL

Serve this sauce with meats (especially pork) instead of gravy or other high-fat sauces, or as a dessert or breakfast fruit.

When making applesauce, add the sugar after the apples are cooked. If you add the sugar at the beginning, the apples will take longer to cook.

Variation:
Pear and Ginger Sauce: Substitute pears for apples and ginger for cinnamon in Cinnamon Applesauce; increase water to 1 cup/250 mL; add sugar to taste. (Fiber: Good.) Serve over Old-Fashioned Molasses Bread (page 180).

Cut apples into quarters. In saucepan, combine apples, water and lemon juice. Bring to a boil; reduce heat and simmer gently, uncovered, until apples are tender, about 20 minutes; stir often.

Place food mill or sieve over mixing bowl. Pass apple mixture through food mill (skin and seeds will stay in top of mill). Add sugar and cinnamon to purée; stir to dissolve sugar. Taste and add more if needed. Amount will vary depending on type of apple. (If sauce is too thin, return to saucepan and cook, stirring, over medium heat until it thickens.) Serve alone or with Applesauce Whole-Wheat Cake (page 215). Makes 6 servings.

Calories per serving: 101
Grams fat per serving: 0.5
Vitamin C: Good

RASPBERRY-RHUBARB SAUCE

This sauce has a delightful sweet-tart taste that's perfect over ice cream, fresh or frozen yogurt and sliced peaches or other fresh fruit.

$2\frac{1}{2}$ cups	sliced rhubarb, $\frac{1}{2}$-inch/1 cm slices (fresh or frozen)	625 mL
$\frac{3}{4}$ cup	water	175 mL
$\frac{1}{2}$ cup	granulated sugar	125 mL
	Grated rind and juice of 1 lemon	
$\frac{1}{4}$ tsp	cinnamon	1 mL
2 cups	fresh raspberries or 1 cup/250 mL previously frozen unsweetened raspberries*	500 mL

In saucepan, combine rhubarb, water, sugar and lemon rind; bring to a boil over medium heat. Reduce heat and simmer until rhubarb is tender, 10 to 15 minutes. Remove from heat; stir in lemon juice, cinnamon and raspberries. Let cool. Serve warm or cool over vanilla ice cream. Makes about 3 cups/750 mL sauce.

Calories per $\frac{1}{2}$ cup / 125 mL sauce: 110
Grams fat per $\frac{1}{2}$ cup / 125 mL sauce: 0.3
Fiber: Excellent
Vitamin C: Good

ORANGE CREAM SAUCE

Delicious over Lemon Sorbet (page 197) or with cake, this sauce also makes a creamy base for fresh fruit. For a nouvelle dessert, spread sauce over rimmed individual dessert plates and arrange three kinds of fresh fruit—strawberries, kiwi, sliced peaches, grapes or blackberries—artistically over the top.

$\frac{1}{4}$ cup	granulated sugar	50 mL
1 tbsp	frozen orange juice concentrate	15 mL
	Grated rind of 1 orange	
$\frac{3}{4}$ cup	plain yogurt	175 mL

Compare:
This is a creamy, low-fat dessert sauce; 1 tbsp/15 mL whipping cream has 5 grams of fat.

Variation:
Orange Cream Dressing: Reduce sugar in Orange Cream Sauce to 2 tbsp/25 mL. Use with fruit salads.

Variation:
Frozen Lemon Cream with Raspberry-Rhubarb Sauce: Spoon Frozen Lemon Cream (page 195) in layers into parfait glasses, alternating with Raspberry-Rhubarb Sauce (page 220), or pour the sauce over Frozen Lemon Cream. Use about $\frac{1}{4}$ cup/50 mL sauce per person.

*If measuring raspberries while frozen, use 2 cups/ 500 mL; if thawed, about 1 cup/250 mL.

Cocoa powder is made from solid chocolate with the cocoa butter removed; therefore, it is much lower in fat than chocolate.

Choose chocolate recipes using cocoa powder instead of chocolate if other fat ingredients, such as butter or oil, are in comparatively similar amounts.

Chocolate Milk
Combine 2 tbsp/25 mL Easy Chocolate Sauce with ¾ cup/175 mL milk. Serve hot or cold.

In small mixing bowl, combine sugar, orange juice concentrate and orange rind; stir to mix. Stir in yogurt and mix well. Makes 1 cup/250 mL sauce.

Calories per 1 tbsp / 15 mL: 21
Grams fat per 1 tbsp / 15 mL: trace

EASY CHOCOLATE SAUCE

Spoon this on ice cream, drizzle over bananas, pears or chocolate cake, or use as a dipping sauce for fresh fruit.

1 cup	cocoa	250 mL
¾ cup	granulated sugar	175 mL
¾ cup	water	175 mL
½ cup	corn syrup	125 mL
1 tsp	vanilla	5 mL

In saucepan, combine cocoa and sugar. Whisk in water and corn syrup. Bring to a full boil over medium heat; boil for 2 minutes, stirring constantly. Remove from heat and stir in vanilla. Let cool (sauce will thicken upon cooling). Cover and store in refrigerator. Makes 2 cups/500 mL sauce.

Calories per 1 tbsp / 15 mL: 38
Grams fat per 1 tbsp / 15 mL: 0.3

BREAKFASTS

The Breakfast Debate: To eat or not to eat

Food experts have long been telling us about the importance of starting the day with a good breakfast. In the '70s we were bombarded with the evils of a high-cholesterol, high-fat breakfast of sausages and eggs. Now some researchers claim the studies on the merits of eating breakfast are not conclusive and adults who don't want to eat breakfast shouldn't worry about it. Here are some reasons why we should eat breakfast.

Research has shown that the lack of morning fuel for children can affect their mental ability. Children who don't eat breakfast concentrate less than those who do. Children learn from example, so if you want them to eat breakfast, you should eat one yourself. Dieters often skip breakfast, yet studies show that it is easier to lose weight if you consume some of your daily calories in the morning. You will be more likely to burn these calories off, and you will be less likely to eat fattening, empty-calorie snacks between meals. The Canadian Cancer Society recommends weight control as one way to reduce cancer risk. It also wants us to eat more fiber-containing foods.

Breakfast provides an easy way to consume some of the body's needs for fiber, vitamins and minerals in the form of cereals and fruits; if you don't eat breakfast, it is harder to meet these requirements. On the other hand, breakfast-skippers can pick up nutrients at a morning coffee break if they choose the right foods—fresh fruit, bran muffins, whole-wheat bagels, yogurt, cottage cheese or low-fat cream cheese. Avoid energy-only calories and high-fat items such as Danish pastries, doughnuts, and too much butter. Spread cheese or peanut butter over a bagel rather than butter; these spreads have protein as well as fat.

Because we need fiber from grains as well as from fruits and vegetables, include both grains and fruit for breakfast.

BREAKFAST BRAN-AND-FRUIT MIX

With this mixture on your kitchen shelf, breakfast can be ready in a jiffy—just add sliced apples, peaches, grapefruit sections, strawberries or banana, and top with yogurt or milk.

2 cups	bran flakes	500 mL
1 cup	All-Bran	250 mL
½ cup	sliced or chopped nuts (almonds, walnuts or pecans)	125 mL
½ cup	chopped dried apricots	125 mL
½ cup	chopped prunes	125 mL
½ cup	raisins	125 mL

Combine bran flakes, All-Bran, nuts, apricots, prunes and raisins; mix well. Store, covered, in an airtight container. Serve with sliced fresh fruit and either milk or yogurt. Makes 10 servings (½ cup/125 mL each).

Calories per ½ cup / 125 mL with ½ cup / 125 mL (2%) milk: 219
Grams fat per serving with ½ cup / 125 mL (2%) milk: 7
Fiber: Excellent
Vitamin A and phosphorus: Excellent
Calcium, riboflavin, thiamine, niacin and iron: Good

BLENDER BREAKFAST

Keep this in mind for days when you want breakfast on the run; it takes only a minute to make and is packed with nutrients.

1	banana, peach or nectarine, peeled and cut in chunks	1
½ cup	milk or plain yogurt	125 mL
1 tsp	honey, sugar or maple syrup	5 mL
1 tbsp	natural bran	15 mL
1	egg (optional)	1

In blender or food processor, combine banana, milk, honey, bran and egg (if using); process until smooth. Pour into tall glass. Makes 1 serving.

	With Egg	Without Egg
Calories per serving:	296	217
Grams fat per serving:	9	3
Fiber:	Excellent	Excellent
Iron, phosphorus and niacin:	Excellent	Excellent
Calcium, vitamins A and C and riboflavin:	Good	Good
Thiamine:	Good	

Diet Hint: Reducing fat content of breakfasts
- Don't smother toast with butter.
- If using jam, omit butter altogether.
- Boil or poach eggs rather than frying them.
- Avoid bacon, Danish pastries and croissants.
- Don't limit yourself to traditional breakfast foods—leftover salads, rice, pasta or vegetable dishes, soups and sandwiches can taste just as delicious in the morning as at noon or dinnertime.

Fall Brunch Menu
Honeydew, cantaloupe and watermelon wedges with Honey-Lime Dip (page 34)
Eggs Florentine with Yogurt Hollandaise (page 134)
Tomatoes Provençal (page 153)
Old-Fashioned Molasses Bread (page 180), or Whole-Wheat Raisin Scones (page 182)
Fresh berries and sliced peaches with Raspberry Coulis (page 193)

For other breakfast and brunch dishes, see:
Eggs Florentine (page 134)
Omelet à la Jardinière (page 135)
Baked Zucchini Omelet (page 144)
Broccoli Frittata (pages 132-3)
Breads and Muffins (pages 174 to 187)
Cinnamon Coffee Cake (page 214)
Applesauce Whole-Wheat Cake (page 215)

GRANOLA

This delicious, easy-to-make granola is one of the few granola recipes that doesn't use oil. Serve with yogurt and fresh fruit.

4 cups	quick-cooking rolled oats	1 L
1½ cups	whole-wheat flour	375 mL
1 cup	natural bran	250 mL
¼ cup	toasted wheat germ	50 mL
¼ cup	chopped walnuts or almonds	50 mL
¼ cup	sesame seeds	50 mL
¼ cup	sunflower seeds	50 mL
½ tsp	salt	2 mL
1 cup	hot water	250 mL
½ cup	honey	125 mL
1 tsp	vanilla	5 mL
1 cup	raisins	250 mL

In large bowl, combine oatmeal, flour, bran, wheat germ, nuts, sesame seeds, sunflower seeds and salt; mix well. In small bowl, mix together water, honey and vanilla; pour into dry ingredients and stir to mix. Spread on 2 lightly oiled baking sheets and squeeze mixture together to form small clumps. Bake in 325°F/160°C oven for 30 minutes or until golden brown, stirring occasionally, so granola will brown evenly. Stir in raisins and bake for 5 minutes longer. Let cool completely. Store in airtight containers. Makes 8 cups/2 L granola.

Calories per ½ cup / 125 mL: 250
Grams fat per ½ cup / 125 mL: 5.3
Fiber: **Excellent**
Niacin and thiamine: **Good**
Calcium: **Excellent,** when eaten with ½ cup/125 mL milk.

WHOLE-WHEAT PANCAKES WITH BLUEBERRIES AND YOGURT

Use any fresh fruit in season as a topping. Peaches, strawberries and raspberries are delicious alternatives.

$\frac{3}{4}$ cup	whole-wheat flour	175 mL
$\frac{1}{2}$ cup	all-purpose flour	125 mL
1 tbsp	baking powder	15 mL
2 tbsp	granulated sugar	25 mL
$\frac{1}{2}$ tsp	salt	2 mL
1	egg, beaten	1
$1\frac{1}{4}$ cups	skim milk	300 mL
2 tbsp	vegetable oil	25 mL
Topping:		
$\frac{1}{2}$ cup	yogurt	125 mL
2 tbsp	maple syrup	25 mL
2 cups	blueberries	500 mL

In mixing bowl, combine flours, baking powder, sugar and salt; stir to mix. Pour in egg, milk and oil; stir until dry ingredients are wet. (Don't worry about a few lumps.)

Heat nonstick skillet over medium heat until hot (a drop of water will sizzle or dance). Lightly grease pan if desired. Drop batter into skillet from large spoon to form rounds. Cook until surface is full of bubbles that start to pop and underside is golden brown; turn and brown other side.

Topping: Combine yogurt and maple syrup; mix well. Spoon yogurt mixture over each pancake and top with blueberries. Makes about 12 4-inch/10 cm pancakes (2 pancakes per serving).

Calories per serving: 300
Grams fat per serving: 7.5
Fiber: Excellent
Calcium: Excellent
Riboflavin, niacin and iron: Good

SWISS FRUIT MUESLI

This Swiss breakfast is a complete meal in one dish. Soft wheat kernels add extra body and texture. Keep a mixture of the dried ingredients on hand and add the wheat berries, fresh fruit and yogurt just before serving.

$\frac{1}{2}$ cup	soft wheat kernels*	125 mL
$\frac{1}{2}$ cup	rolled oats	125 mL
$\frac{1}{2}$ cup	raisins, chopped apricots or prunes	125 mL
$\frac{1}{4}$ cup	chopped nuts (pecans, almonds, walnuts)	50 mL
	Fresh fruit (sliced peach, pear, strawberries, banana, apple or seedless red or green grapes)	
1 cup	plain yogurt	250 mL
	Honey or maple syrup (optional)	

Place wheat kernels in bowl; add enough water to cover by at least 2 inches/5 cm. Soak overnight; drain.

In bowl or jar, combine oats, raisins and nuts; mix well.

To serve, spoon some wheat berries and rolled-oat mixture into individual bowls. Top with fresh fruit, then with yogurt sweetened, if desired, with honey or maple syrup to taste. Makes 4 servings.

Calories per serving: 282 (will vary slightly depending on type of fruit used)
Grams fat per serving: 6
Fiber: Excellent
Calcium: Excellent
Niacin, riboflavin, thiamine, and iron: Good

Winter Brunch Menu
Grapefruit halves
Broccoli Frittata (pages 132-3)
Tossed green salad
Pumpkin Muffins (page 175)
Apple Cinnamon Sorbet (page 194) with Raspberry Coulis (page 193)

*Available at health food stores.

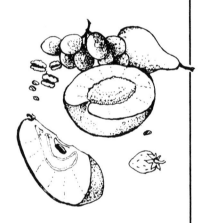

Breakfast Menus

Fresh fruit
Whole-grain cereal
Whole-wheat toast
Yogurt or thin slice of cheese
Milk

Cantaloupe wedges
Bran flakes
Whole-wheat toast
Yogurt

Fresh orange wedges
Whole-wheat English muffin
Poached egg
Milk
Coffee

Fresh fruit (melon, apple or berries) topped with yogurt, and sprinkled with cinnamon sugar and wheat germ
Milk

Whole-wheat pita bread filled with cottage cheese and raisins
Orange juice
Milk

Hot oatmeal with milk
Half grapefruit
Whole-wheat toast
Milk

Whole-wheat toast spread with low-fat cottage cheese and topped with freshly grated nutmeg and fresh blueberries or other fruit
Milk

Swiss Fruit Muesli (page 226)
Yogurt and sliced peaches or papaya

Quick Breakfast Menus

Orange juice
Granola (page 224) (made with bran) topped with yogurt and fresh strawberries
Milk

Honeydew melon with blueberries
Whole-wheat English muffin with melted mozzarella cheese
Milk

Orange or apple juice
Breakfast Bran-and-Fruit Mix (pages 222-3)
Milk

Refrigerator Bran Muffin (page 176)
Tomato juice
Blender Breakfast (page 223)
Milk

Weekend Breakfast Menus

Whole-Wheat Pancakes with Blueberries and Yogurt (page 225)
Sliced mango with grapefruit sections

Fresh fruit or stewed figs
Poached eggs on whole-wheat toast
English muffins
Tomatoes Provençal (page 153)
Coffee

Melon with Blueberries (page 200)
Whole-Wheat Raisin Scones (page 182) toasted and spread with cream cheese

APPENDIX

To find out the ideal amount of fat you should consume in a day or how many grams of fat you need to cut per day:

1. First estimate how many calories you need in a day. Turn to page 229, refer to Table A (Recommended Daily Dietary Allowances) and find your energy needs and the corresponding calorie (kcal/day) requirement per day. Note: these are averages only.

In the average Canadian diet, 40 percent of the calories come from fat. The Canadian Cancer Society guidelines recommend that no more than 30 percent of your calories should come from fat.

---

2. Turn to Table B (Daily Total Fat Intake), page 230; find your closest calorie level. Then look across to the next column at the 30 percent level; the corresponding grams of fat per day are the amount you can consume in order to have 30 percent of your calories from fat. The difference in grams of fat between a 40 percent level and a 30 percent level is the amount you need to cut per day.

   For example, if you are a man consuming about 3000 calories per day with 40 percent from fat, and you want to reduce to 30 percent fat, your desired intake of fat would be 100 grams of fat, or a cut of 33 (133–100) grams.

   If you are a woman consuming about 2200 calories per day with 40 percent from fat, and you want to reduce to 30 percent fat, your desired intake would be 73 grams of fat or a cut of 25 (98–73) grams.

3. The following is another way to find out how many grams of fat you should eat in a day to have 30 percent of your calories from fat:

$$\frac{\text{Daily calorie requirement}}{9} \times .30 = \text{Daily fat intake}$$

Table A
Recommended Daily Dietary Allowances
Mean Heights and Weights and Recommended Energy Intake

Category	Age (years)	Weight (kg)	(lb)	Height (cm)	(in)	Energy Needs (with range) (kcal)
Infants	0.0–0.5	6	13	60	24	kg × 115 (95–145)
	0.5–1.0	9	20	71	28	kg × 105(80–135)
Children	1–3	13	29	90	35	1300 (900–1800)
	4–6	20	44	112	44	1700 (1300–2300)
	7–10	28	62	132	52	2400 (1650–3300)
Males	11–14	45	99	157	62	2700 (2000–3700)
	15–18	66	145	176	69	2800(2100–3900)
	19–22	70	154	177	70	2900 (2500–3300)
	23–50	70	154	178	70	2700 (2300–3100)
	51–75	70	154	178	70	2400 (2000–2800)
	76+	70	154	178	70	2050 (1650–2450)
Females	11–14	46	101	157	62	2200 (1500–3000)
	15–18	55	120	163	64	2100 (1200–3000)
	19–22	55	120	163	64	2100 (1700–2500)
	23–50	55	120	163	64	2000 (1600–2400)
	51–75	55	120	163	64	1800 (1400–2200)
	76+	55	120	163	64	1600 (1200–2000)
Pregnancy						+ 300
Lactation						+ 500

Realistically assess the fat content in your diet. If you aren't overweight, rarely eat meat or rich desserts, use little butter, margarine, oils or mayonnaise and stay away from fried foods, you already probably consume 30 percent or fewer calories from fat in your diet and don't need to reduce it any further.

The energy allowances for the young adults are for men and women doing light work. The allowances for the two older age groups represent mean energy needs over these age spans, allowing for a 2% decrease in basal (resting) metabolic rate per decade and a reduction of activity of 200 kcal/day for men and women between 51 and 75 years, 500 kcal for men over 75 years and 400 kcal for women over 75 (see text). The customary range of daily energy output is shown for adults in parentheses, and is based on a variation in energy needs of 400 kcal at any one age (see text and Garrow, 1978), emphasizing the wide range of energy intakes appropriate for any group of people.

From: Recommended Dietary Allowances, Revised 1979. Food and Nutrition Board, National Academy of Sciences–National Research Council, Washington, D.C.

Table B
Daily Total Fat Intake According to Percentage of Total Calories

Calorie intake	% calories from fat	Grams fat / day
	20	27
1200	30	40
	40	53
	20	40
1800	30	60
	40	80
	20	49
2200	30	73
	40	98
	20	56
2500	30	83
	40	111
	20	67
3000	30	100
	40	133
	20	71
3200	30	107
	40	142

Table C
Fat and Calorie Content of Meat, Fish and Poultry

Type and / or cut	Portion 4 oz / 112 g Grams fat	Calories	Portion 8 oz / 224 g Grams fat	Calories
Beef				
Cross rib roast, lean only, braised	12	252	24	504
Cross rib roast, lean + fat, braised	33	418	67	835
Prime rib roast, lean only, roasted	11	241	23	482
Prime rib roast, lean + fat, roasted	41	467	81	934
Rump roast, lean only, roasted	8	213	16	426
Rump roast, lean + fat, roasted	26	355	52	710

Type and / or cut	Portion 4 oz / 112 g		Portion 8 oz / 224 g	
	Grams fat	Calories	Grams fat	Calories
Brisket, lean only, simmered	9	223	17	446
Brisket, lean + fat, simmered	42	484	83	968
Flank steak, braised	7	214	15	429
Club steak, lean only, broiled	11	243	21	486
Club steak, lean + fat, broiled	37	446	74	891
Porterhouse, lean only, broiled	8	221	16	441
Porterhouse, lean + fat, broiled	45	499	89	999
T-bone steak, lean only, broiled	8	223	16	446
T-bone steak, lean + fat, broiled	44	495	89	990
Round steak, lean only, broiled	7	212	14	423
Round steak, lean + fat, broiled	17	292	35	585
Sirloin steak, lean only, broiled	6	205	12	410
Sirloin steak, lean + fat, broiled	31	395	62	791
Ground beef, lean, cooked	13	245	25	491
Ground beef, regular, cooked	23	320	45	641
Veal, cutlet or chop (boneless)	14	262	28	524
Pork				
Ham, roasted, lean only	10	176	20	419
Ham, roasted, lean + fat	19	272	38	544
Pork loin chop, lean only, broiled	17	289	34	578
Pork loin chop, lean + fat, broiled	25	354	50	708
Pork loin roast, lean only	16	269	32	538
Pork loin roast, including fat	27	357	54	715
Spareribs	34	445	68	889
Bacon, back	21	309	42	618
Bacon, side	67	686	134	1372

Bacon, back, 4 slices (84 g), 16 g fat, 232 calories
Bacon, side, 4 slices (30 g), 18 g fat, 184 calories (fried crisp)

Type and/or cut	Portion 4 oz / 112 g		Portion 8 oz / 224 g	
	Grams fat	Calories	Grams fat	Calories
Lamb				
Lamb shoulder, lean only	11	230	22	459.
Lamb shoulder, including fat	30	379	60	757
Lamb leg, lean only	8	208	16	417
Lamb leg, including fat	21	312	42	625
Lamb loin chop, lean only	9	211	17	421
Lamb loin chop, including fat	33	402	66	804
Poultry				
Chicken breast with skin, fried	11	252	20	503
Chicken breast without skin, fried	5	212	11	424
Chicken breast with skin, roasted	9	223	18	446
Chicken breast without skin, roasted	4	187	8	374
Chicken, light meat with skin, roasted	12	252	25	503
Chicken, dark meat with skin, roasted	18	287	36	574
Chicken, light meat without skin, roasted	5	196	10	392
Chicken, dark meat without skin, roasted	11	232	22	465
Turkey, light meat without skin, roasted	5	186	10	372
Turkey, dark meat without skin, roasted	8	206	16	413
Duck, without skin, roasted	13	228	25	456
Goose, without skin, roasted	14	270	29	540
Processed Meats				
Hot dog (2 hot dogs)	20	248		
Bologna (8 slices, 3 inches/8 cm in diameter)	32	320		
Salami (4 slices, 4 inches/ 11 cm in diameter)	28	352		

Type and / or cut	Portion 4 oz / 112 g		Portion 8 oz / 224 g	
	Grams fat	Calories	Grams fat	Calories
Fish				
Sole fillets, cooked, steamed	2	72	4	145
Tuna in water	1	142	2	284
Tuna in oil	23	323	46	645
Trout	16	242	32	484
Shrimp	1	130	2.5	260
Salmon, fresh	8	204	16	408
Cod	6	190	12	381
Mackerel	18	264	35	529

4 oz/112 g portion = $3 \times 3 \times \frac{3}{4}$-inch chop ($6 \times 6 \times 2$ cm)

= $4 \times 2 \times \frac{1}{2}$-inch slice ($10 \times 5 \times 1$ cm)

= 2 pieces $4 \times 2 \times \frac{1}{4}$ inch ($10 \times 5 \times 0.5$ cm)

Table D
Fat and Calorie Content of Cheese

Type	Grams fat / 1 oz / 28 g	Calories / 1oz / 28 g
Cheese spread	5.9	81.2
Cheese spread (skim)	1.7	53.8
Blue cheese	8.1	98.9
Brick cheese	8.4	103.9
Brie	7.8	93.6
Camembert	6.7	84.0
Cheddar	9.2	112.9
Processed slices	8.7	105.0
Processed slices (skim)	1.7	53.5
Colby	8.9	110.4
Cottage cheese, 1% fat	.3	21.0
Cottage cheese, 2% fat	.6	25.2
Cottage cheese, creamed	1.4	28.9
Cream cheese	9.8	97.8
Edam cheese	7.8	100.0
Feta	6.2	76.1
Gouda	7.8	101.6
Gruyère	8.9	115.7
Monterey	8.4	104.5
Mozzarella	7.0	89.1
Mozzarella, part skim	4.8	78.4
Parmesan, grated	8.4	127.7
Ricotta, made with whole milk	3.6	48.7
Ricotta, partly skim	2.2	38.7
Roquefort	8.7	103.4
Swiss	7.6	105.3

28 g = 1 oz = $\frac{1}{4}$ cup/50 mL of grated or chopped or crumbled Cheddar or other hard cheese

= $\frac{1}{8}$ cup/25 mL of cottage or cream cheese

Canadian Nutrient File, 1985 Edition, Ottawa, Canada

Table E
Fat Content of Dairy Products, Fats and Oils*

	Grams fat / 1 tbsp / 15 mL
Butter	12
Margarine	12
Coffee cream	2.9
Half & half cream	1.7
Whipping cream	5.6
Sour cream	2.5
Yogurt (low fat)	trace
Yogurt (high fat, 8%)	.5
Oils (corn, safflower, olive)	14
Salad Dressings	
French	6
Blue/Roquefort	8
Mayonnaise	11
Miracle Whip	7
Oil & Vinegar (Kraft)	7.5
Oil & vinegar (homemade)	10
Low-calorie	2.0 (or less)
Miracle Whip, Light	4
Thousand Island	8

Milk, Ice Cream, Frozen Desserts	*Grams fat per 1 cup / 250 mL*
Homogenized milk (3.3% fat)	8
Milk (2% fat)	5
Skim milk (0.2% fat)	0.4
Ice milk (vanilla)	10.6
Ice milk (strawberry)	4
Ice cream (10% fat)	14
Ice cream (16% fat)	24
Fruit ice	0
Sherbet	0 to 4
Ice cream bar (vanilla, chocolate-coated)	11

*Cream % fat is under provincial legislation and varies between provinces.

Table F
Breakfast Cereals by Fiber Content

Excellent Source of Fiber
(over 4 g of fiber per 1 oz/30 g serving)

Cereal Name	Fiber / 1 oz = 1 serving
All-Bran	9.1
100% Bran	8.8
Bran Buds	7.3
Corn Bran	6.2
Fiber Crunch	4.5

Good Source of Fiber
(2 to 3.9 g of fiber per 1 oz/30 g serving)

Cereal Name	Fiber / 1 oz = 1 serving
Bran Crunchies	3.2
Bran Flakes, Kellogg's	3.0
Bran Flakes, Post	2.9
Frosted Mini Wheats (with brown sugar)	2.3
Fruit & Fiber with Date/ Raisin/Walnut	3.5
Grape Nuts	2.5
Harvest Crunch	2.5
Harvest Crunch with Bran/Raisins	2.7
Harvest Crunch with Raisins/Dates	2.1
Muffets	3.1
Raisin Bran	2.6
Shredded Wheat (spoon size)	2.9
Shredded Wheat (biscuit)	3.1
Total	2.1
Wheat germ (toasted/plain)	3.5
Wheaties	2.1

Under 2 g of Fiber per 1 oz/30 g serving

Cereal Name	Fiber / 1 oz = 1 serving
Alpen	1.3
Alpha Bits	0.5
Apple Jacks	0.2
Boo-Berry	0.5
Buckwheat and Maple	1.9
Captain Crunch	0.5
Cheerios	1.0
Cocoa Pebbles	0.1

Cereal Name	Fiber / 1 oz = 1 serving
Cocoa Puffs	0.3
Corn Flakes, Kellogg's	0.1
Count Chocula	0.4
Crispy Wheat 'n Raisin	1.4
Frankenberry	0.5
Froot Loops	0.3
Frosted Flakes	0.1
Frosted Mini Wheats (with frosting)	1.9
Frosted Rice	0.1
Golden Honeys	0.5
Grape-Nuts Flakes	1.9
Honey-Combs	0.2
Life (plain)	1.1
Lucky Charms	0.5
Pep	1.7
Pro Stars	1.5
Product 19	0.8
Puffed Rice	0.1
Raisin Crisp	1.8
Rice Crispies	0.2
Rice Flakes	0.0
Shreddies	1.9
Special K	0.2
Sugar Corn Pops	0.2
Sugar Crisp	0.6
Sugar Smacks	0.4
Team	0.2
Trix	0.2
Wheat, Puffed	1.3

Source: Canadian Nutrient File. Neutral detergent fiber analyzed in Bureau of Nutritional Sciences, Ottawa.

Table G
Vegetable Fiber Values*

Vegetable	Serving size[†]	Grams dietary fiber / serving	Dietary fiber / 100 grams
Beans, white, cooked	100 mL	6	7
green or yellow, cooked	125 mL	2	3
Beets, red, cooked	2	3	3
Broccoli, fresh or frozen, cooked	250 mL	4	4
Brussels sprouts, cooked	4	2	3
Cabbage, red or green, raw, chopped	100 mL	1	3
Carrots, sliced cooked	100 mL	2	3
raw	1	2	3
Cauliflower, raw, chopped	100 mL	1	2
Celery, raw, inner stalks	3	1	2
Chard, Swiss, cooked	100 mL	5	6
Corn kernels, frozen, cooked	125 mL	2	2
Cucumber (not pared) (8 × 2 inches/21 × 5 cm)	1		1
Lentils, cooked	125 mL	3	4
Lettuce (iceberg)	1 wedge	1	2
Parsnips, cooked, mashed	100 mL	2	3
Peas, green frozen, cooked	125 mL	3	5
Pepper, sweet, red or green, raw	1 large	2	1
cooked	1 large	1	1
Potatoes, boiled in skin	1 long	5	2
peeled, boiled	1 long	2	1
Spinach, fresh, frozen or canned, cooked, drained	125 mL	10	6
Squash, summer (zucchini and crookneck), cooked	100 mL	1	1
Squash, winter, all varieties, cooked, baked	100	2	2
Sweet potato, boiled in skin	1 large	4	2
Tomato, ripe, raw, unpeeled	1 6-cm	2	2
Turnip, boiled, mashed	100 mL	2	2

*Fiber values as of August 1985
[†]125 mL is about ½ cup; 100 mL is about 6 tbsp.

Source: Canadian Nutrient File Data Bank, 1985, Health and Welfare, Canada

Dishes Containing an Excellent Source of Vitamin C

(More than 15 mg per serving)

Soup Dishes
Chicken and Leek Chowder
Chilled Yogurt and Melon Soup
Corn and Tomato Chowder with Tarragon
Cream of Broccoli Soup
Fish Chowder, Family Style
Fresh Tomato and Basil Soup
Gazpacho
Portuguese Collard Soup
Potage Vert
Spa Vegetable Soup
Summer Garden Italian Soup with Pesto
Tomato-Bean Chowder

Salads
Artichoke-Tomato Salad
Arugula and Radicchio Salad with Balsamic
    Vinaigrette
Bermuda Bean Salad
Broccoli Buffet Salad
Chicken and Melon Salad
Chick-Pea Salad with Red Onion and
    Tomato
Coleslaw with Apple and Onion
Cracked Wheat with Peas and Onions
Greek Salad
Julienne Vegetable Salad with Lemon
    Vinaigrette
Melon and Bean Salad
Pasta Salad with Sweet Peppers and Dill
Red Potato Salad with Sour Cream and
    Chives
Spinach and Red Cabbage Salad with Blue
    Cheese Dressing
Spinach Supper Salad
Tabbouleh
Tomato Raita
White Kidney Bean Salad

Vegetables
Asparagus with Red Pepper Purée
Braised Red Cabbage
Braised Red Peppers and Leeks
Broccoli Frittata
Broccoli and Sweet Pepper Stir-Fry
Glazed Brussels Sprouts with Pecans
Mashed Potatoes with Onions
Orange Sherried Sweet Potatoes
Scalloped Cabbage au Gratin
Stir-Fried Vegetables with Ginger and Garlic
Tomatoes Florentine
Tomato Raita
Tomatoes Provençal
Two-Cabbage Stir-Fry
Turnips Paysanne

Dishes Containing an Excellent Source of Vitamin A

(More than 1,200 I.U. per serving)

Soups
Chicken and Leek Chowder
Chilled Melon and Yogurt Soup
Cream of Broccoli Soup
Fish Chowder, Family Style
Fresh Tomato and Basil Soup
Nova Scotia Seafood Chowder
Portuguese Collard Soup
Red Lentil Soup
Spa Vegetable Soup
Summer Garden Italian Soup with Pesto

Salads and Vegetables
Asparagus with Red Pepper Purée
Baked Squash with Ginger
Baked Zucchini Omelet
Bulgur Wheat, Tofu and Sweet Peppers
Chinese Pork and Vegetables
Creamy Pasta with Broccoli, Cauliflower and
    Mushrooms
Deep-Dish Vegetable Pizza
Eggs Florentine
Fettuccine with Fresh Tomatoes and Basil
Ginger-Apricot Stuffed Lamb with
    Kumquats
Microwave Fillets Provençal
Microwave Tarragon Chicken with Julienne
    Vegetables
Mexican Pork Stew
Mussels Sicilian Style
Navarin of Lamb

Braised Red Pepper and Leeks
Broccoli and Sweet Pepper Stir-Fry
Broccoli Frittata
Foil-Steamed Spring Vegetables
Lemon-Ginger Carrots
Mashed Turnips with Carrots and Orange
Orange Sherried Sweet Potatoes
Stir-Fried Vegetables with Ginger and Garlic
Tabbouleh
Tarragon Carrots
Tomatoes Provençal
Turnips Paysanne

Sauces
Tomato-Basil Sauce
Tomato Salsa

Main Courses
Almond Chicken
Beef and Vegetable Stew
Breast of Chicken Florentine

Omelet à la Jardinière
Pot au Feu
Scallops and Shrimp in Wine Bouillon with
   Julienne Vegetables
Sole Florentine
Souvlakia of Lamb
Tex-Mex Chili
Tomato Sauce Provençal with Veal on Pasta
Tuscan White Kidney Bean and Tomato
   Casserole
Winter Vegetable Stew

Desserts
Apricot Clafouti
Cantaloupe, Pear and Grapes with Sherry
   Orange Sauce
Deep-Dish Plum Pie
Melon with Blueberries
Old-Fashioned Peach Cobbler
Peach Blueberry Crisp
Peaches with Raspberry-Yogurt Sauce

Dishes Containing an Excellent Source of Fiber

(Over 4 g of fiber per serving)

Breakfast Dishes
Banana-Apricot Bran Muffins
Blender Breakfast
Breakfast Bran-and-Fruit Mix
Melon with Blueberries
Refrigerator Bran Muffins
Swiss Fruit Muesli

Lunch *
Chicken and Leek Chowder
Eggs Florentine
Portuguese Collard Soup
Potage Vert
Summer Garden Italian Soup with Pesto
Tomato-Bean Chowder
Tri-Color Bean Soup

Dinner
Almond Chicken
Baked Zucchini Omelet
Beef and Vegetable Stew
Breast of Chicken Florentine
Broccoli Frittata
Bulgur Wheat, Tofu and Sweet Peppers
Chinese Pork and Vegetables
Cracked Wheat and Basil Pilaf
Cracked Wheat with Peas and Onions
Creamy Pasta with Broccoli, Cauliflower and
   Mushrooms
Deep-Dish Vegetable Pizza
Navarin of Lamb
Sole Florentine
Tex-Mex Chili
Tomatoes Florentine
Tuscan White Kidney Bean and Tomato
   Casserole

* Also suitable for dinner

Dishes Containing an Excellent Source of Fiber

Salads *
Bermuda Bean Salad
Broccoli Buffet Salad
Chick-Pea Salad with Red Onion and
    Tomato
Mediterranean Lentil Salad
Melon and Bean Salad
Spinach Supper Salad
White Kidney Bean Salad

* Also suitable for dinner

Desserts
Banana-Apricot Bran Muffins
Blackberries with Orange Cream Sauce
Coconut-Oatmeal Cookies (3)
Lemon and Fresh Blueberry Tart
Peach Blueberry Crisp
Peaches with Raspberry-Yogurt Sauce
Raspberry Coulis (sauce)
Raspberry Meringue Torte
Raspberry Sorbet
Strawberries with Raspberry-Rhubarb Sauce

Guidelines for Rating the Recipes as Sources of Nutrients

To assess the nutrient rating of a single portion of food, we followed the guidelines of Canada's Food and Drug Regulations (D.01.005 and D.02.004). These guidelines state that each serving of food must provide the following amount of each nutrient to qualify as either a good or an excellent source. Fiber rating guidelines were supplied by the Canadian Cancer Society.

Nutrient	Good Source	Excellent Source
Vitamin A (IU)	600	1200
Thiamine (mg)	0.25	0.45
Riboflavin (mg)	0.40	0.75
Niacin (mg)	2.50	4.50
Vitamin C (mg)	7.5	15.0
Calcium (mg)	150	300
Phosphorus (mg)	150	300
Iron (mg)	2.0	4.0
Dietary fiber (g)	2.0–3.9	4.0 +

All recipes in this book were tested and analyzed using 2% milk, low-fat yogurt and 2% cottage cheese.

REFERENCES

Burkitt, Dennis P. "Etiology and prevention of colorectal cancer." *Hospital Practice*, February 1984, pp. 67–77.

Canada's Food Guide Handbook (Revised). Health and Welfare Canada. Health Promotion Directorate, 1982.

Canadian Nutrient File. Bureau of Nutritional Sciences, Food Directorate, Health Protection Branch, Health and Welfare, Ottawa.

"Cancer and Diet." Draft report. Toronto: Canadian Cancer Society, 1985.

"Cancer Prevention Research: Summary—Nutrition." Mimeographed. National Cancer Institute, 1984.

CANDAT System for Nutrient Analysis, University of Toronto.

Cummings, John H., and Stephen, Alison M. "The role of dietary fibre in the human colon." *CMA Journal* 123: 1109–14.

Dietary Standard for Canada. 3rd ed. Canada Bureau of Nutritional Sciences, Department of National Health and Welfare, Ottawa, 1975.

Eastwood, M. A., and Passmore, R. "Nutrition: The changing scene." *The Lancet*, 23 July 1983, pp. 202–6.

"Does fiber-rich food containing animal lignan precursors protect against both colon and breast cancer? An extension of the 'fibre hypothesis.' " Editorial. *Gastroenterology* 86: 761–4.

Goldsmith, G. A.; Miller, O. N.; and Unglaub, W. G. "Efficiency of tryptophan as a niacin precursor in man." *Journal of Nutrition* 73: 173–6, 1961.

Gori, Gio Batta. "Dietary and nutritional implications in the multifactorial etiology of certain prevalent human cancers." *Cancer* 43 (1979): 2151–61.

Handler, Semour. "Dietary fibre: Can it prevent certain colonic diseases?" *Postgraduate Medicine* 73 (1983): 301–7.

Kritchevsky, David. "Fibre, steroids, and cancer." *Cancer Research* 43: 2491S–5S.

Meyskens, Frank. "Vitamin A and Its Derivatives (Retinoids) in the Prevention and Treatment of Cancer." Mimeographed.

Miller, A. B. "Diet, Nutrition and Cancer." Mimeographed.

National Research Council. *Executive Summary: Diet, Nutrition, and Cancer*. Washington, D.C.: National Academy Press, 1982.

Nutrient Value of Some Common Foods. Health and Welfare Canada, Health Services and Promotion Branch and Health Protection Branch, 1979.

Nutrition and Cancer: Cause and Prevention. American Cancer Society, 1984.

Procedures for Calculating the Nutritive Values of Home Prepared Foods. Agriculture Research Service, U.S. Department of Agriculture, 1966.

Recommended Nutrient Intakes for Canadians. Bureau of Nutritional Sciences, Health Protection Branch. Health and Welfare, Ottawa, 1983.

Rietz, P. Wisso, and Weber, F. "Metabolism of vitamin A and the determination of vitamin A states." *Vitamins and Hormones* 32:237–49, 1974.

Rozen, Paul, et al. "The low incidence of colorectal cancer in a 'high-risk' population: Its correlation with dietary habits." *Cancer* 48 (1981): 2692–5.

U.S. Department of Health and Human Services. *Diet, Nutrition & Cancer Prevention: A Guide to Food Choices*. Washington, D.C.: U.S. Government Printing Office, 1985.

Willett, Walter C., and MacMahon, Brian. "Diet and cancer: An overview. Part I." *The New England Journal of Medicine* 310 (8 March 1984): 633–8.

———. "Diet and cancer: An overview. Part II." *The New England Journal of Medicine* 310 (15 March 1984): 697–703.

Williams, R. R., et al. "Cancer incidence by levels of cholesterol." *Journal of the American Medical Association* 245: 247–52.

INDEX

244